ARGENTINA
CHILE
PARAGUAY URUGUAY

ARGENTINA
CHILE
PARAGUAY URUGUAY

Series editor
Michael Shichor

I NBAL
Travel Information Ltd.

Inbal Travel Information Ltd.
P.O.Box 39090 Tel Aviv Israel 61390

© 1993 edition
All rights reserved

Intl. ISBN 965-288-083-3

Distributed in the United Kingdom by:
Kuperard (London) Ltd.
9, Hampstead West
224 Iverson Road
West Hampstead
London NW6 2HL

U.K. ISBN 1-85733-030-7

CONTENTS

TABLE OF MAPS

Preface

Writing this guide, we have aimed at coming out with a comprehensive, in-depth companion for the tourist who wants to get to know the South American continent in a direct and personal way.

The modern traveler is interested in a significant, relevant, first-hand experience when touring foreign lands. He wants to get to know new and different worlds and is well aware of the effort involved. This book is written for this traveler — curious, intense, experienced and open-minded — the tourist who really and truly wishes to meet South America, face-to-face.

While writing this guide with special emphasis on enlarging upon and clarifying general areas, it was not done so at the expense of the plethora of practical details which are of vital import, if you are to fully succeed in your venture and truly enjoy the experiences awaiting you. An attempt has been made to create an information pool, which would combine material relevant to understanding the **what**, while contributing to the practicalities of the **how**.

Aware of the responsibility involved in being guide and companion to all who choose to see South America "through our looking glass," we have tried to compile as many facts and details as possible. From this pool of information, let each person take what fits best, what is most appropriate.

In the course of this work, we have labored to separate the wheat from the chaff and have tried to be as precise as possible. Naturally, many of the impressions and recommendations included in the guide are subjective. However, the guide do contain those elements which will fulfill the expectations of the kind of tourist mentioned, and will guide and assist you in making the most of your trip, in as enjoyable, comprehensive and pleasant a way as possible.

Michael Shichor

Using this guide

In order to reap maximum benefit from the information concentrated in this guide, it is advisable to read the following material carefully and act upon it.

Before setting out, it is important to read the Introduction in its entirety. The information contained there will supply you with details which will help you in making early decisions about your trip. Once you arrive at your destination you will already feel familiar and comfortable there, more so than would otherwise be the case.

In the chapters dealing with the individual countries you will find a broadly-based Introduction, whose first section deals with general topics, while the second part includes practical information about the country, its customs and ways.

The country's capital is the next section in the chapters. The information here — suggestions, recommendations and advice about the city — will guide and assist you from the time you arrive and until you leave.

From here on, the chapters are organized geographically: the different regions are presented in logical sequence, with each region surveyed along major touring routes. Following main sites noted, you will find suggestions for touring the areas around them — using the site as both your point of departure and return. In each of these touring sub-sections too, the sites are noted according to their geographical order rather than their importance, so as to make it easier to follow along the way.

As you read through, you will notice that similar information is mentioned in more than one place. This is meant to assist tourists who decide to start their tour from a particular place along the way, but have not arrived at this point via the route described or suggested in the guide, and with no prior knowledge. This allows for greater flexibility in planning your tour, without being tied to the geographical divisions or considerations of this guide.

For travelers crossing borders by land, you will find in each border town discussed a section on the procedures required for continuing into the neighboring country. Treat this as you would treat a plan to go from one site to another: read the material dealing with both places — the place from which you are coming and the one to which you are heading.

At the end of this guide we included a short vocabulary, and an alphabethic index of sites and places.

When mentioning information about transportation, accommodation, food, etc., we have tended to simplify and have preferred to give general guidelines, placing more emphasis on existing possibilities than on variable specifics. It is always disappointing to find that what you have counted on seeing or doing is not available once you finally get to the location. We have therefore tried to avoid giving specific details about subjects given to frequent change, preferring rather to advise you of those places where relevant, here-and-now information can be obtained once you are actually on the spot.

Therefore, an important rule of thumb should be to consult the local Tourist Office in each place you visit. Their addresses are mentioned in the text. They can advise you of the latest updated information for the specific time of your visit.

As for updating — this kind of guide to this part of the world cannot afford to march in place. A technical update from year to year is not enough, either. A finger on the continent's pulse is ever necessary. Up to the day this guide went to press, we attempted to confirm its relevance and up-to-dateness. However, it is only natural that due to frequent changes which occur, travelers will find certain time-related facts somewhat less than precise when they arrive at their destinations, and for this we apologize in advance.

To this end, cooperation and assistance from you who have enjoyed the information contained in this guide, is necessary and vital. It ensures, first and foremost, that those who travel in your wake will also enjoy and succeed in their ventures, as much as you have. For this purpose, we have included a short questionnaire at the end of the guide and we will be most grateful and appreciative to those of you who will take the time to complete it and send it to us.

Have a pleasant and exciting trip!

*I*NTRODUCTION

A Special Place for Tourists

South America's exciting, exotic charm combines forces with the veteran tourist's natural curiosity. When these are reinforced by a significant drop in the costs of touring and by a constantly developing tourist infrastructure, it's no wonder that South America has become a new and captivating destination for travelers. Here is a continent that offers innumerable experiences, sights and impressions. On the one hand, it has incredible untamed scenery — canyons, deserts, mountains, jungles, rivers, and glaciers; on the other hand there's an astonishing and varied "human landscape" — a blend of cultures and races woven into a fragile and enchanting social fabric. Anyone seeking an encounter with rare worlds — a fascinating harmony of nature and scenery, man and animal, progress and antiquity — will find it here.

A trip to South America, whether for business or for pleasure, is wholly different from a trip anywhere else. Before we set out we must prepare, investigate, interpret, comprehend. As we travel, too, we engage in a process of learning, becoming acquainted and adjusting. Our ordinary ways of life and thought, attitudes to time, people, and things are simply not the same as those found in South America. Its languages, foods, clothing and customs are all quite remote from those we know. As we head for South America, we must disabuse ourselves of many biases; we must open ourselves up, both emotionally and intellectually, to wholly different messages and impressions. Though it's certainly true that the transitions are not so sharp between New York and Caracas or between Paris and Buenos Aires, the contradictions remain in full force. They accompany the tourist every step of the way, and place him in daily confrontation with his own values, opinions, and habits. The greatest return one can expect from a trip through South America is the knowledge of the existence of another world, one which lives, thinks and behaves differently, a world no better and no worse — merely different.

South America invites the tourist to share numerous experiences and ordeals — cosmopolitan cities, ancient villages that have not changed in centuries, untamed scenery of mighty grandeur, massive power projects, and all the rest. Here you'll find a fantastically wealthy elite beside shameful poverty, incomparably primitive scenes alongside technological wonders. Wonderful outings on foresaken trails will take you to Indian tribes who still go about naked, fish with harpoons, and hunt with bows and arrows. Other journeys will lead you to some of the world's best-known and most important archaeological sites.

South America has it all — for the family on their annual vacation, for the youth out to wander with a backpack, or for the retired couple on their second honeymoon. Each will find what he is seeking here. There's enough here for everyone, on every topic and in every field. On every itinerary, every form of travel, visitors are sure to find what they want — and more.

It is important to mention again that the substantial difference between "North" and "South", which accounts for Latin America's exotic splendor, requires fundamental and thorough preparation. The sharp transition obliges you to be open and tolerant, and to reinforce those qualities with advance study and suitable intellectual and emotional preparation. These guarantee a successful tour, out of which you'll get the most enjoyment; in their absence you're liable to encounter many difficulties which may well spoil your pleasure. Under all conditons and in any event it's worthwhile to behave with great patience and to accept South America for what it is — beautiful, wild, fascinating. This, after all, is the purpose of our visit, one unequalled anywhere on Earth.

*I*NTRODUCTION

Part One — Our First Steps

Before we set out we must consider a number of important points: deciding upon our route, destinations, and the like. The paragraphs that follow will guide you in these matters.

Making the decision to go

Who's going

Anyone can visit South America. Due to the great variety of sites, plentitude of things to see, and abundance of areas of interest on the way, there's almost no one who won't find what he's seeking. A great many **young tourists** spend several months exploring South America from one end to the other, wandering along the roads with backpacks and a few coins in their pockets. It's a nice "timeout" from the rat race, in addition to being an enjoyable and fascinating experience. These backpackers, known in local parlance as *mochileros*, come to know the continent perhaps better than most natives, and enjoy unrestricted mobility on all of South America's highways and byways.

More and more **middle aged** tourists have been frequenting South America in recent years, generally after having come to know both the United States and Europe. Now, in search of new and interesting places to visit, they've packed their bags and wandered to the faraway southern continent. Faraway? Not really. For the tourist, South America is closer today than it's ever been. It's no longer a backward continent, but rather a bustling and popular place, connected to the rest of the world by excellent air service.

There is no longer anything to fear about going to South America, as far as you arrange your immunizations before arrival and avoid focuses of disease. Sanitary conditions and the public services offered tourists are constantly improving, and today are not significantly inferior, in the large cities, to those we're used to in the West. Transportation services, hotels and restaurants have also conformed to a great degree to the new tourist's demands and, though difficulties still occur, the experienced tourist has no reason to refrain from visiting. Vacation and resort sites, too, are flourishing, and many people combine rest and recreation with their visit.

INTRODUCTION

As trade between Latin America and the rest of the world expands, a great many **business people** have been combining business and pleasure, enjoying the experience of getting to know different economic systems. The Latin American business world is lively and effervescent, and has adopted Western work patterns and behavior in the large cosmopolitan cities. Grand hotels, superb restaurants, and office, guide and rent-a-car services are available for the businessman and tourist of means. The South American ambience, the "flexibility" of the clock, and tendency to do things lightheartedly and at leisure leave their impact here, too, though when you get down to it, business is conducted strictly and thoroughly.

Bringing the children along requires special preparation. In many places — mainly in Andean countries such as Bolivia, Peru, Ecuador, and Colombia — it is difficult, for example, to obtain milk products. Sanitary conditions are not the best, and are liable to cause problems for adults as well. At the same time, do not hesitate to take children from the age of 7-8 years old to the large cities or the famous tourist sites. These are served by convenient access roads beside which you'll find visitors' facilities. There is no problem in touring with children in Argentina and Chile — quite the contrary.

How to go
The most comfortable way to go is, of course, with **organized group tours**. Many companies specialize in providing this kind of service — generally rather expensive — in a number of Latin American countries. Here you'll be assured that your trip will involve a minimum of difficulties and breakdowns, though you'll be deprived of personal contact with the natives, the ability to set your own timetable and itinerary, and more. It's nevertheless important to remember that there are few English speakers in South America, and visitors who don't speak Spanish or Portuguese are liable to find themselves in tight spots, especially when meandering in remote locations outside the cities.

South American group tours are varied and diverse, so that it is hard to relate to them as a single unit. Every visitor should draw up a list with a number of destinations and objectives, carefully examining the means by which he'll reach them with the greatest success and least expense.

Another way of going, of course, is the private, individual trip, where you're free to choose your own dates, destination, pace, budget, etc. Indeed, there's no greater freedom than that of a long, extended tour, where one has no obligation to preset an itinerary and timetable, but can suit these to the needs and desires of the moment.

*I*NTRODUCTION

Backpack tourism is especially popular among the young, and the young in spirit. Many spend several months in South America, making their way through the continent from country to country and site to site. It's a fascinating and pleasant way to travel. Most such visitors pick up some Spanish or Portuguese en route, get to know the natives, and get to interesting places that few visitors reach.

Backpack tourism is cheap, pleasant, and easy. The visitor should not expect many difficulties, and excluding a few countries where the police pick on tourists — such as Peru, Colombia and, to a certain extent, Argentina — it's highly improbable that you'll encounter any problems that will mar the pleasure of your trip.

Mochileros, with their packs on their backs, are usually received cordially. Tourists of all nationalities tend to meet anywhere on the continent and continue together.

Women, too, have nothing to fear in South America. Apart from several places which I wouldn't advise young women to enter alone, and apart from the fact that they shouldn't go about in dangerous urban areas late at night, I find no reason to be deterred. Traveling in pairs or small groups helps a great deal to solve these problems.

By traveling in this manner, you won't have to carry a lot of money; a few ten dollar bills per week will enable you to get along fine and in relative comfort. At the same time, bear in mind that such a journey does involve difficulties: the means of transportation you'll use aren't very good, the hotels will offer no more than the bare essentials, and so on. Hence, you'll need extra time, more strength, and lots of patience, openness, and good humor.

Well-off tourists, and those whose time is limited and who want to get in a lot of sites comfortably without wasting precious time on the road, can get the most out of their visit by careful advance planning and by making reservations. One should carefully select the sites you consider most important to visit, and draw up a timetable for your trip.

Reservations are not always essential, a fact which allows for greater flexibility en route. In this guide we've noted the places, routes, and dates that attract crowds. If you've placed these on your itinerary, be sure that you have a reliable travel agent make reservations before you set out. Make sure he obtains written confirmation since overbooking is a common phenomenon in South America and is liable to cause you great unpleasantness.

Business people would do well to arrange all matters

*I*NTRODUCTION

beforehand. The big cities frequently experience unexpected pressure on hotels, flights, and car-rental firms; though ordinary vacationers would hardly notice these problems, they are apt to cause delays and annoyance to a businessman on a tight schedule.

Where to go
In our opening paragraphs we noted that South America is rich in all kinds of places to visit. Therefore it is important to determine and locate the types of places that attract you in particular.

Mochileros setting out on an extended visit can expect to discover many of the beautiful continent's hidden secrets on the way, and will meet and enjoy its abundant treasures. Others, especially those whose time is limited, will prefer to designate one or several countries, and do them throughly. Both sorts of tourists might give preference to subjects in which they are particularly interested, and plan their trips so as to achieve the maximum in these spheres. We will survey below a number of categories in which we'll try to sketch out various directions of interest. Individual tourists will choose the categories that attract them, and draw up a plan that includes one or several.

The first possibility involves those **natural and scenic attractions** which are found throughout South America. They are divided into several types:

Glaciers and lakes are located chiefly in the continent's southern section, in southern Argentina and Chile. Here you'll find some of the world's most beautiful tour routes, enchanting scenery, friendly people. Many Andean peaks in the region feature well-developed ski areas, in top condition, because here the seasons are reversed. In Europe, holiday-makers are tanning themeselves on the beaches. North of Lima, Peru, in the vicinity of Huaraz, you'll find lovely hiking trails that demand good physical condition, the ability to adapt to unusual climatic conditions and a willingness to live primitively. All these routes require first-class camping gear.

For a pleasant stay on the **seashore** there's nothing like Brazil. Resort towns with pristine beaches abound along the Atlantic coast, especially between Vitoria and Puerto Alegre and in the Nordeste (North East). These are especially popular among Brazil's wealthy, and tourists frequent them primarily at Carnival time in February and March. Their great advantage — like that of the ski areas — is in the reversed season. Here you can swim and sunbathe from January to March, while most of Europe is buried in snow. The few coastal sites in Argentina and Chile serve mainly the local population. Peru and Ecuador have lovely beaches, though these lack a developed service infrastructure. There are developed beaches in Colombia and Venezuela, with the popular ones located along the Caribbean. Hotel occupancy and prices are high during the summer months (June-August), and it's important to make advance reservations.

A long strip of exclusive resort clubs has sprouted along the Caribbean coast, where you can spend a seaside vacation under ideal conditions, renting gear for fishing, sailing, diving, and more. Some of the beaches, especially those in the Caracas area, are rather neglected; their level of upkeep has deteriorated perceptibly.

About one-third of South America is covered with thick **jungle**. On the exceedingly popular jungle excursions tourists can encounter out-of-the-way cultures and get a first-hand impression of ancient ways of life that are rapidly disappearing. It's important to remember that jungle trips require special effort, organization, and experience. You can take such trips in Brazil, Bolivia, Peru, Ecuador, Colombia and Venezuela. Each of these countries has extensive jungle regions.

The jungle's harsh and unpleasant climate — an oppressive combination of high temperatures, high humidity, and frequent rainfall — explains to a large extent why the area has not been settled, though it also deserves credit for the lush wild vegetation. This flora, watered by giant rivers such as the Amazon, the Orinoco, and their tributaries, is of decisive importance in reducing air pollution and maintaining the natural environmental equilibrium in all of South America. An outing to the jungles must be planned carefully and with great caution. Though most of the jungle is free of malaria, it is recommended taking medication against that disease, along with water purification tablets and mosquito repellent.

Travelers visit the jungle cities of Peru and Brazil in great numbers, either on organized tours or on their own. Though the former are very expensive, it's worth remembering that the "unattached" visitor, too, will find a visit to these areas far from cheap. Prices in and around the jungle towns are far higher than elsewhere as goods must be imported from far away. Be prepared for this, and bring along a sufficient amount of the local currency.

The jungles in Ecuador's eastern region are home to a number of Indian tribes, and are accessible as a relatively "short hop" from the capital. The jungles in Ecuador offer a maximum return of enjoyment and interesting experiences while demanding minimum investment of time, effort, and expense.

INTRODUCTION

Wildlife: Though the jungle might appear to be **the** place for observing wildlife in its natural habitat, this is in fact not the case. It is true that jungle tours can give you a glimpse of thousands of strange and varied species of birds, insects, butterflies, and even reptiles, monkeys, and wild boars, but you can't assume so. You must penetrate deep into the jungle, and there's no guarantee that you'll find what you've come for there, either.

By contrast, the Galapagos Islands off Ecuador are famous for their abundant wildlife, most of it unique. It is rather expensive to visit, and it's best to make reservations for a flight to the islands, and on the ships and boats that sail among them. The lovely nature reserve on the Paracas Islands off central Peru has thousands of birds and sea lions, and is far less expensive and more convenient to visit. Bolivia and Chile, too, have nature reserves with a multitude of wild animals, primarily of the llama family.

In Brazil, in the area of the Bolivian border, there are vast stretches of marshes known as the Pantanal, inhabited by an abundance of birds, alligators and other animals. The best time to visit here is during the dry season, between May and September, when one can really appreciate the variety and profusion of wildlife.

The Valdéz Peninsula in southern Argentina is another fascinating reserve, with penguins, whales, sea lions, and more. The best time for visiting it is October or November, when the animal population reaches its annual peak.

Another planning strategy places the emphasis on South America's **complex social structure**, concentrating on sites from **the continent's past**, as well as those which accent its special present.

Archaeology: The glory of pre-Columbian settlement in the southern half of the Americas is, of course, the Inca Empire and its center, the city of Cuzco, Peru. From these, the Inca (emperor) and his men dominated the tribes from Ecuador in the north as far as central Chile in the south. Few pre-Incan remains have survived in South America. Remains of what is thought to be the oldest settlement in all the Americas have been discovered at Puerto Varas (Southern Chile), and are being studied thoroughly. Pre-Incan civilizations existed primarily in Tihuanacu, Bolivia, around the village of San Agustin in southern Colombia, and in various locations in Peru. While the tourist will certainly want to visit San Agustin and Tihuanacu, the pinnacle of his archaeological experience will undoubtedly be a visit to the Inca sites, with the lost Inca city of Machu Picchu as the highpoint.

INTRODUCTION

Folklore and folk culture: Age-old Indian traditions have blended with the Spanish influence to produce a unique and extraordinary compendium of folklore and culture. All of South America, and the Andean countries in particular, excel in uncommonly beautiful handicrafts of unique character and style. Visiting these countries is like an extended shopping trip. This activity centers on the marketplaces — in large cities, country towns, and remote villages. In some, the barter system is still practiced. The markets of South America are colorful, effervescent, lively, and enchantingly beautiful. Most commerce is carried on by women, and they are most skillful at it. As you meander through the markets choose carefully, check quality, compare prices, and bargain, **always** bargain.

Most South American countries have a rich and varied folklore. Folk music varies from country to country: while quiet cowboy songs typify Argentina and Venezuela, Brazillian music is usually stormy and rhythmic. Music and dance in the Andean countries draw on Indian sources; typical musical instruments are the *charango*, the drum, and the reed flute. Music and dance dominate Latin American life. Numerous holidays and festivals are celebrated on the continent every year, and there's hardly a month when some part of the continent isn't gearing up for a festival. National festivities reach their peak with folk festivals, most in February or March. The largest and most famous is the Brazillian Carnival, unequalled anywhere in the world for beauty and joy. The most important festivals in Peru and Bolivia are held in February-March and June-July.

When to visit and how long to stay
Getting to know South America inside and out is a matter of month after month of intensive touring. The first condition for success is command — albeit of the most rudimentary nature — of Spanish (or, for Brazil, Portuguese). *Mochilero* touring of this sort usually lasts from three months up to more than a year, and allows you to visit most countries on the continent, exploring them exhaustively and comprehensively. Eight to ten months seems the optimal length for such a trip, broken down more or less as follows: two to three months in Argentina and Chile, three to five months in the Andean countries (Bolivia, Peru, Ecuador, and Colombia); two to four months in Brazil; and one more month for the remaining countries.

The tourist with this much time available can fix his original port of entry at whatever point is cheapest to reach, and move around in accordance with weather conditions and the various special events that take place throughout the year.

Argentina and Chile

The period from September to March is best; plan to visit the southernmost regions close to the middle of that period, when the weather there is best. Before September and after March the continent's southern reaches suffer harsh and unpleasant wintery weather, when touring is almost impossible. These countries' central and northern areas can be visited the year around.

Brazil and Venezuela

The period from October to June, the hot season, is recommended. Then you can go most places with ease, tan on the beach, roam the jungles, visit the cities, and so on. The desire to participate in the Carnival, celebrated annually in February or March determines for most tourists when they go to Brazil, and this is how it should be. Participating in the Carnival is undoubtedly an experience not to be missed; what's more, it's held at the best time of the year for a visit. Yet, this is the peak of the tourist season, and you better make reservations well in advance for hotel and other tourist services.

The Andean countries

These may be visited the year round, though the summer months (November-February) are the wettest, with showers liable to mar your enjoyment. During those months excursions to the mountains and jungle are difficult, so it's a good idea to make the effort to come during the winter (May-September), when although it's a bit cooler, the skies are clear and the weather excellent.

On the Galapagos Islands (Ecuador), as in the countries along the equator (Ecuador, Venezuela, and parts of Brazil, Colombia, and Peru), the weather is stable the year round, with no extreme differences among the seasons.

These climatic details describe somewhat generally the course of the season according to a rough division of the continent, and are meant for those traveling for extended periods. Those making shorter visits will find a more precise description of the climate in the chapters on each country; furthermore, a section dealing with local weather is included for each of the large cities.

Tourists who want to know as much as possible of South America within a limited time period, may opt for a number of different possibilities, according to their special interests. In all events, it seems that any visit to South America, even if you wish to focus on a certain region and a simple field, requires at least three to four weeks. It's most desirable that it be planned with enough flexibility to allow for possible changes in your intinerary.

None of this applies, for example, to those coming for a week-long organized tour of Brazil to attend the Carnival, or for ten days of sailing among the Galapagos Islands. But apart from such limited frameworks you should allow a longer period. The great distances, extreme variation from place to place, range of sites, and tour and holiday possibilities make this much time necessary. One must always bear in mind the chance of delays on the way, so that a packed and precise timetable — reminiscent of one's last visit to Switzerland — would be wholly inappropriate here.

How much does it cost?

Since the mid eighties, fierce competition among the various airlines has led to tremendous cuts in airfares to destinations in South America. Today they are not much higher than for flights of similar length to other destinations and we are the fortunate beneficiaries.

Another factor which played a role was the depreciation of the local currencies. The difficult economic situation of the Latin American countries finds expression in inflation and frequent devaluations of their currency against the dollar, which has gained greatly in strength in recent years even in comparison to stable European currencies — and all the more so in comparison to the South American currencies, which generally serve as legal tender in rickety economic systems that have been in a distressed state for some time.

From the tourist's point of view, of course, there's a distinct plus to this situation. Domestic price rises do not always keep up with the rate of devaluation, and sometimes people with dollars or a stable European currency to spend will find prices for meals, lodging and shopping which may appear ridiculous when judged by Western standards. However, local people, earning local incomes, can not always afford even minimal needs.

South America is, therefore, a better tourist bargain then ever before. On the one hand, airfare is cheaper than in the past; on the other, expenditures for transportation, accommodation, food, shopping and so forth are far lower than they used to be. The cost of living is not uniform everywhere, and prices, of course, vary from country to country. The cheapest countries to visit are the Andean ones, while the most expensive are Venezuela, Uruguay, and Paraguay. Even the last three, however, which in the not-too-distant past were expensive even by European and American standards, have become significantly cheaper, and a visit there today is no more expensive than an intermediate-priced tour in Europe or North America. Countries once considered prohibitive, such as Argentina, Chile, and Brazil, have become much less expensive, and the devalutation of their currencies gives you the chance to enjoy a tour of reasonable standards.

When dealing with luxury tourism, there's almost no gap with the West. The best hotels in Bogotá, Caracas, Lima, Rio, São Paulo, Buenos Aires and the like are rather expensive, especially at peak tourist season or at holiday or Carnival time. Car rental rates resemble those the world over, but first-class restaurants tend to be less expensive than their counterparts in the Western world.

In conclusion, it can be said that the range is broad; each of us must choose a path in accordance with our means. On every budget, though, tourists will find South America open, ready to meet them, and easy on the wallet.

First Steps

Once you've decided how, when and where to go, all that's left is to make practical preparations for the journey. The next section deals with these matters, spelling out everything that must be done before leaving home, in order to make the trip as successful, easy, comfortable and inexpensive as possible.

Documents and papers

Anyone going to South America requires a valid passport, except for citizens of certain South American countries who may cross into neighboring states with nothing more than an identity card. Some of the Latin American states require that your passport be valid for at least six months beyond your date of entry. It's best to get your passport some time prior to your trip, for some of these countries require you to obtain an entry visa in advance, and issuing this visa generally takes several days.

In our chapters on each country, we've spelled out the relevant regulations and documents you'll need; study them before you go. We should again mention that immigration regulations in the South American countries are in a constant state of flux; you **must** consult the embassy, consulate or tourist bureau of the country you intend to visit, shortly before your trip, in order to obtain up-to-date and reliable information.

Countries that require an entry visa have fixed procedures for issuing them. You'll need to present a passport, an entry and departure ticket, a photograph, and relevant travel documents (reservations, a letter from your place of work, etc.) The visa takes from one to three days to be issued, and usually involves no difficulties. All visa matters should be seen to in your own country, but if necessary, they can be obtained en route, in each of the countries you visit on the way.

A tourist card issued by airlines or distributed at frontier posts to those arriving by land has replaced visas in many cases. This card, which is free, must be filled out before you land or at the border station, and handed to the immigration officials along with your passport. A stamped copy will be attached to your passport, and returned when leaving the country.

We must stress that, as a rule, government clerks, police and military personnel check documents punctiliously, so keep them on you at all times, properly stamped and arranged. Many tourists have found that letters of reference (for example, a letter confirming that you were sent on business by your employer), various certificates (preferably with your photograph), and documents that have an official look to them are frequently of help in getting pesky clerks or policemen to leave you alone.

Due to frequent changes, find out before arrival which immunizations are required at your destination country, and how long before departing you need the vaccinations. This is specially true for cholera.

A tourist's national driver's license is accepted in most South American countries, on condition that a Spanish translation has been attached. Even so, we recommend that you obtain an International Driver's License and make sure that one of its languages is Spanish.

A Student Card is good for certain discounts and benefits. In Argentina and Chile students are granted discounts on public transportation, though foreign students may have to engage in lengthy bargaining to receive them. In Peru, significant discounts are given to students on tickets for museums, archaeological sites, and more. Venezuela discounts certain domestic flights. The essential condition for using your Student Card is that it be valid and bear your photograph.

One should not go to South America without an **insurance policy** covering health and baggage. Theft is a common occurrence throughout the continent, and the uninsured tourist is liable to suffer great financial damage. The matter of health insurance, however, is even more serious. Because disease is rife, and medical care and drugs are expensive, under no circumstances should one leave a matter as important as health insurance to chance or luck; no knowledgeable tourist would ever set out without being properly insured.

Though it can hardly be described as a document, you'll find in your travels that an MCO card is as important as if it were one. An MCO is a flight voucher issued by airlines that are members of IATA, and is honored by all other IATA members. At many border points where you'll be asked to show a departure card, and when you apply for a visa, an MCO will satisfy the requirement in most cases. It's important to check that its value is specified in dollars and in no other currency, for the voucher is calculated according to the value in the currency in which it was paid. At the end of your trip you can apply your MCO to pay for the flight ticket you want, or you can redeem it where it was issued or at the airline office.

Health

Most serious diseases have been totally eradicated in South America, and linger on only in the most remote jungles. Malaria no longer strikes in the cities and towns, though those wishing to penetrate deep into the jungles should bring malaria pills as a preventive measure.

Intestinal diseases are very widespread in South America, due to the poor sanitary conditions and inappropriate food storage methods. Be prepared for the near certainty that at some stage you'll come down with intestinal trouble. It's worth your while to bring along any medication you're used to taking. Don't hesitate to consult a doctor in serious cases, for common diseases such as hepatitis are liable to cause you great distress if not discovered in time. Bear in mind that in 1991 the colera attacked many countries in South America, especially in the Andean countries, where the epidemic killed thousands of people.

Avoid fresh vegetables (eat only boiled ones) and fruits. Drink bottled water only, and make sure that it wasn't opened before. Despite the fact that in most large cities the water undergoes filtration and purification, it's still contains pollutants and bacteria, which not infrequently cause stomach aches and more serious ailments. Carbonated drinks and bottled water will help you overcome the problem (we're not referring to mineral water but to ordinary water that has been boiled and purified). When you're in the country or in places where bottled drinks are unavailable, boil your drinking water and purify it with chlorine tablets.

Mosquitoes and other flying pests are especially common in tropical areas, and are a real menace. **Don't go there** without large quantities of mosquito repellent and — no less important

INTRODUCTION

— ointment to spread on the bite when the repellent fails to work. A visit to Asuncion, Paraguay, or the jungles of eastern Ecuador cannot but end with dozens or hundreds of painful bites.

Every tourist must bring along a small kit with first-aid supplies and medicines. Many kinds of medication are hard to find in South America, and those which are available are expensive and not always usable due to their age or storage conditions. Before you set out, see your doctor in order to obtain an adequate stock of essential medications. A short list of essential drugs and medical items follows:

Medication for intestinal diseases.
Painkillers.
Fever pills.
Anti-malaria pills.
Chlorine tablets for water purification.
Antibiotic ointment.
Antiseptics.
Gauze pads, bandages and adhesive tape.
Medication for chronic illnesses.

The chronically ill, and heart and asthma patients, should consult their doctors concerning the treatment they may require in the climatic conditions and altitude of the lands they're going to visit. Asthmatics should be doubly cautious when going to high elevations, where even healthy people find it hard to adjust to the thin atmosphere.

Women should bring tampons and birth-control pills in sufficient quantity since these items are difficult to obtain in Latin America, except in some of the large cities.

Before setting out, it's best to have a thorough checkup to ascertain that your health permits you to take the trip. Medical care in South America is generally not of the highest quality, and it's best to try not to need it. See your dentist for preventive treatment to forestall problems that might arise during your tour. South American dental care is definitely not recommended, except in truly urgent cases.

For the trip itself, I'd recommend bringing an extra pair of eye glasses and the lense prescription. Contact lenses, though generally convenient to use, are liable to cause problems and discomfort in dry areas and at high elevation.

Thus far we've been speaking of the continent in general. It's obvious that in certain places — mainly cosmopolitan capital cities — the sanitary conditions are good and medical services advanced. Nevertheless, do yourself a favor and set out well-equipped and prepared for most eventualities.

INTRODUCTION

Finances

The most popular and convenient currency to use and exchange in South America is the U.S. dollar, recognized and sought after everywhere; converting it presents no problem in the large cities. The Pound Sterling, Deutsch Mark, and Swiss Franc are also recognized, but exchanging them can involve problems, especially on the black market.

Currency laws vary from country to country. How much money to take and in what form depends to a great extent on the regulations in effect in the countries you decide to visit.

In most South American countries a black market in foreign currency is active. For cash dollars, moneychangers will give you local currency at higher rates than the banks offer. When visiting these countries, it's worthwhile to carry more cash and fewer travelers' checks. Credit card transactions and bank transfers involve the official exchange rate, since charge slips are calculated according to that rate and the transfers are paid in it — in local currency. Given that the difference between the official and "black" rates may reach 50% and more, it's only wise to avoid using these financial means.

The theft epidemic that has spread through some of the South American countries — especially Colombia, Peru, Brazil, and Venezuela — has led many banks to refuse to cash travelers' checks out of fear that they may be stolen, and, at times, tourists are put through an exhausting bureaucratic procedure. A letter of credit is not efficient either; getting it honored is a slow and complicated affair and here, too, and payment is made at the official rate.

Those traveling for short periods can make it easier on themselves by carrying cash, whereas long-term travelers would do well to divide their resources into a number of baskets, to minimize risk.

In certain countries — Uruguay, Venezuela, and at times Bolivia and Ecuador — travelers' checks can sometimes be converted into cash dollars for a fee, but the regulations in these matters are always changing and cannot be relied upon. This point is particularly important for tourists who want to stock up on cash en route to countries with black markets.

It's worth your while to bring a credit card. Their use is widespread throughout South America, and can be used to purchase goods, services, and for cash withdrawals. It's important to note that cash withdrawals involve a 4%-5% commission; you should consider whether this service is worth the price. In any case, using your credit card is worthwhile only in countries where there is no black market, so that your account will be debited at the same rate as that at which you would change money on the spot.

The alternative to carrying cash or using a credit card is travelers' checks. We recommend using small denominations — nothing over $50; hundred-dollar travelers' checks are harder to cash. In small towns, it is difficult to exchange travelers' checks in any case; not only is the exchange rate low, but there is a high commission as well. It's best to stick to travlers' checks issued by *Bank of America*, *Thomas Cook*, and *American Express*.

Always keep your money, credit cards, and documents **well-hidden** in your clothing. Guarding against theft here requires precautionary measures that we're not accustomed to in Europe and North America; nevertheless they are essential, and mustn't be scorned.

What to take

As a general rule, the less you take the better. The advantages of traveling light far outweigh the satisfaction of a few extra clothes — after all, you're going on a trip, not a fashion show. When all is said and done, a large portion of what you take never gets used in any case, and you quickly learn that most of what you took along was quite unnecessary.

Remember, whatever you need — you'll manage to find during the trip — perhaps not of the same type, model, or quality you are used to, but I have yet to meet a traveler wandering around the world. During the trip you'll be picking up many souvenirs and presents, so you should really take along the bare necessities — but plenty of resourcefulness.

Clothing depends on your destination and the season. Businessmen must be smartly dressed, although a jacket and tie are not usually necessary. In the large cities, appropriate evening dress is customary for both men and women, and sportswear for young people and children. *Mochileros* will feel most comfortable in jeans and casual wear, although they should also take along more festive wear for events that require this.

Lightweight and simple clothes are always appreciated, and are easy to wash and carry. Avoid taking elegant evening attire that requires careful transport and special care. It just isn't worth the effort.

I wouldn't suggest taking along more than one backpack or suitcase. These too should be at the most average in size. Baggage weighing more than 15 kg can be a real burden, and more than 20 kg can be even expensive. Many airlines are strict about the baggage limit, and travelers with overweight have to pay for it.

Comfortable walking shoes are perhaps the most important item. These are appropriate for any type of trip or travel. It is not an exaggeration to say that a bad pair of shoes can utterly ruin a trip. So make a point of getting good walking shoes and don't skimp.

Camping Gear

Those embarking on an extended tour and intending to explore the entire continent should put everything in a backpack, including camping gear. When buying camping gear, be sure that its quality is appropriate for your needs. Remember that it must serve you for long months, and that cheap equipment, saving you money at the time of purchase, is liable to prove a painful impediment when you're on the road.

A list of essential items follows:

A lightweight **backpack** with **internal** metal frame, lots of pockets, and laces to which a sleeping bag, mattress, and other gear can be tied.

A **sleeping bag:** Chose one appropriate for the season and the area to which you are headed. For a lengthy trip through a number of climatic zones you should get a warm sleeping bag (-5 or -20 degrees Centigrade) made of down. It must be of excellent quality, well sewn, and with a reliable zipper. Sleeping bags come in various sizes and shapes; be sure that yours matches your dimensions. The "mummy" style, wide at the shoulders and narrow around the legs, is the best of all. It holds body heat well and is easy to carry. Synthetic-filled sleeping bags are much cheaper, but are much larger, bulkier, and heavier. Remember that you'll have to carry it on your back — week after week and month after month — and the inconvenience will outweigh your savings. On the other hand, bear in mind that the down bag has one great disadvantage: when it gets wet, it loses its efficiency and special qualities; sleeping in it then is downright unpleasant.

A **mattress:** To soften the bed of rocks on which you'll spend many a night, we recommend — highly, if you've got a down sleeping bag — an easy-to-carry mattress. There are two common types: foam-rubber and inflatable (especially made for capming). The latter costs more, but provides comfort and ensures a good night's sleep, essential after a full day of walking.

A **tent:** We recommend a two-man, two-layer model with a floor. A one-man tent isn't enough, for you're unlikely to find yourself alone on outings into the country. A two-layer tent provides better protection against rain, retains heat, and repels moisture.

A **cooking stove:** This is essential on hikes through the countryside, and economical in town. Since gas for camping stoves is almost unavailable in South America and comes at great cost when it is at hand, we think it best to use a kerosene stove. The most popular models are made by Colman and the Optimus company of Sweden. They are reliable, safe, and easy to carry. Remember to exercise great caution when using them. Flammable materials may cause disaster if you don't treat them with the caution they deserve.

Utensils: Bring the minimum, but choose good ones. Metal or aluminium is best. Food should be kept in plastic or cloth bags, since cans take up more space in your pack.

Miscellaneous: Pocketknife, flashlight, rope, etc.

Buying equipment represents one of the largest expenditures of your trip. It's therefore worthwhile to do some comparison shopping and not buy hastily. At the same time, I must again stress that economy must not be at the expense of quality, for the "saving" is liable to cost you dearly on the road. It's also worth noting that camping equipment is in great demand in South America, so that at the end of your trip your gear can be sold for a reasonable price; not much lower than what you paid for it.

The traditional centers for buying camping gear are London and New York, where you'll find the widest selection and the most attractive prices. Though London has many stores that handle camping gear, the best, in my view, is the Youth Hostel Association store at 14 Southampton Street (Tel. 836-8541). This is a gigantic store where you'll find it all — from shoelaces to emergency dehydrated rations. A tourist could enter this store stark naked and come out a few hours later with everything needed for a trip around the world. YHA members receive a 10% discount on all purchases.

In New York you can pick up your gear at any of hundreds of camping and sporting goods stores. The largest, Paragon, offers a seemingly inexhaustible selection of merchandise, at prices suitable for all budgets.

Photography
One of the most enjoyable aspects of a trip is taking photographs. It is worth making your photographic preparations in advance, acquiring appropriate equipment, and learning at least the basics of how to use your camera.

Many tourists wander through South America with sophisticated and complicated photographic equipment. South America is

*I*NTRODUCTION

a photographer's paradise, fertile ground for expression and creativity. Those who are familiar with the secrets of the art will come equipped with several cameras, lenses, and a range of film.

If, however, you wish to commemorate your trip without lugging a mobile studio around with you, it is recommended to take one camera with three lenses: a standard lens (50mm), a wide-angle lens, and a telephoto lens. A good lens that combines all three functions is the 35-210 zoom. Buy good and reliable equipment, and remember to wrap it well and to insure it. Avoid taking fancy and expensive equipment, since it is likely to get knocked about on the way. Such equipment can also attract thieves. Film is expensive in most South American countries, so take along plenty of film, since you can always sell what you don't use. As a general rule, use ASA 64 film, which is suitable for almost every type of light and weather conditions you'll encounter in South America. ASA 400 film is also worth taking, since it is hard to find, and particularly expensive when available. If you have to buy photographic supplies in South America itself, do so only in the large cities, since elsewhere, not only is film hard to come by and exorbitantly priced, most of it is also likely to have long since past its expiration date.

In South America film is developed in various sorts of laboratories, and it's not always worth taking the risk. As a rule, it's better to develop films in the United States or Europe. In some locations, such as Buenos Aires, São Paulo or La Paz, you can have your film developed with relative safety in Kodak laboratories. Slide film whose purchase price includes developing should be sent directly to the company laboratory, which will return it directly to your home address.

For those carrying video cameras, keep in mind that in some countries Betamax is more popular than VHS, and Video 8 is not always available, nor are the accessories (filters, batteries, etc.). Bring with you all the necessary equipment. When using rechargeable batteries, remember that some countries use 220V and others 110V. Bring along an adaptor with the proper amperage. Those who buy pre-recorded video-cassettes, pay attention to the fact that some countries use the NTSC (American) standard, while others use the more widespread PAL (German). Check the labels before you pay!

Language
You won't have any language problems in South America's large cities. Most people dealing principally with tourists have sufficient command of English to help you get what you want, and it can be assumed that shortly after your arrival you'll

pick up enough of the local conversational "code" to express basic needs. The problems begin when you venture outside the professional tourism framework, and even on its fringes — taxis and restaurants. Few taxi drivers or waiters speak English. Communication is in Spanish only, as are most restaurant menus.

It's even worse in outlying areas. English-speakers are few and far between in the towns, and in villages — nonexistent. On the roads, too, and even in tourist bureaus, airline offices, and banks, it's hard to find someone fluent in the language of Shakespeare, Keats and Milton, or even with enough English to understand a request for a glass of water.

Nor will a command of Spanish or Portuguese solve the problem altogether. In many places — Paraguay, northern Bolivia and the mountain towns of Peru, for example — ancient Indian languages are used. Although most locals speak Spanish at one level or another, it's hard to maintain verbal communication with them in the accepted sense of the term.

Those who've set their hearts on a long, thorough exploration of the secrets of the South American continent absolutely must acquire the basic linguistic skills before setting out. It's true that one picks up a language during a trip, and that within a month or two one is able to carry on a basic conversation with the locals, but advance preparation will make things much easier and increase your enjoyment. No less important is the fact that advance study will establish a correct grammatical foundation, to which a large vocabulary will be added as you go. On-the-road study, though easier, is built atop a shaky foundation, which will demand great efforts to repair afterwards.

How to get there

By air: Most European airlines maintain service between their respective capitals and various destinations in South America, as do the national airlines of the South American countries. The latter also fly to various destinations in the United States, as does *Eastern*.

A number of ticket options are available to and from South America; their terms and fares vary from airline to airline and from country to country. Excursion tickets, limited in time, are generally the cheapest, followed by youth and student tickets. The most expensive are ordinary tickets sold at IATA prices. A combined ticket, by which different sections of the route are flown on different airlines, is usually more expensive than flying all sections with the same airline.

*I*NTRODUCTION

Planning your flights requires thorough preparation and comprehensive market research. Careful investigation and resourcefulness can save lots of money and cut the price of your trip. The open market and fierce competition have led to a situation in which passengers aboard the same plane on the very same flight may well have paid completely different fares.

As a rule a round-trip ticket is worthwhile, unless you're making an extended trip and don't want to commit yourself about where and when it's going to end. Airline tickets bought in South America are subject to excise taxes at rates that vary from country to country; this makes them significantly more expensive. A round-trip ticket purchased outside the country from which you're returning is exempt from tax.

Those who want a one-way ticket should check which routes and combinations may make the trip cheaper. Such routes, for example, go via the Carribbean islands, Central America, and so on. Certain destinations are traditionally more expensive than others. Flights to São Paulo, Buenos Aires, Santiago, La Paz, and elsewhere are far more expensive than those to Lima, Rio de Janeiro, and Bogotá. Relatively low-cost flights reach the latter group of cities from London, Paris, and Miami. It's a good idea to inquire at travel agencies which specialize in these destinations about the cheapest and best way to get there.

Ordinary tickets are more expensive one-way than round-trip. Their great advantage lies in the fact that they are calculated on a mileage basis. Holders can change dates and arrange for stopovers on the way, so long as these remain within the permitted mileage. Thus, for example, a New York-Buenos Aires ticket gives one the right to stop over in Miami, Caracas, Belem, Rio, and São Paulo at no extra cost.

London and Miami are known as preferred ports of departure for Latin America; here you can usually find the cheapest tickets. A significant portion of these tickets are sold over-the-counter only, and travel agents in other countries are not permitted to sell them. A stopover in one of those cities and a visit to some of these agencies may be worth your while, even though you must remember that two days in London cost money too, as does a separate ticket to London. At times it may be cheaper to buy a slightly higher-priced ticket where you live, with the margin offset by the savings in time, stopover expense, and the effort involved in getting around a foreign city.

The national airlines of Venezuela (*Viasa*), Colombia (*Avianca*) and Peru (*Aero Peru*) are known for being less expensive than the other South American flag carriers. They fly to numerous destinations, but you must change planes in their respective capitals. European airlines such as *Air France*, *Iberia*, and the Portuguese *TAP* also offer seasonal packages worth taking advantage of. Never buy until you've checked and compared prices!

When buying discounted tickets, be very careful about their validity and reliability. Remember that any change involves additional payment, and it's best to know how much is in question in advance. Avail yourself of the services of reliable travel agents — there are charlatans in this field too. Best of all are travel agencies that specialize in tourism to South America, and have package deals with various airlines.

By land: An overland trip from North America via Central America is a unique experience. It can be done by car, bus, or train, and you'll need to do the Panama-Colombia stretch by sea or air. The highway there still isn't suitable for traffic, and is impassible several months out of the year. Due to political tensions in Central America, you should check exactly when and how to cross various countries, and, even more so, when and how not to. If you're driving, bring along plenty of spare parts, and have someone along with mechanical knowledge. Your car papers must be in good order, since they'll be inspected every time you turn a corner.

INTRODUCTION

Part Two — Easing the Shock: Where Have We Landed?

Previous sections of this introduction have dealt with the preparations and arrangements necessary before the trip begins. Now we shall survey some relevant details concerning the trip itself, to make the experience of landing in this alien world a bit easier. The material we're about to present is meant first of all to facilitate your adjustment to South America, but reading it before you go may be of great importance in determining the form and nature of your tour. Here you'll find much **useful information** about all spheres of your trip which will help you overcome quickly, comfortably, and efficiently the range of problems liable to arise at the very beginning of your trip.

The paragraphs that follow offer some general advice, and in the chapters on each respective country, you'll find more specific information on those countries and their sites.

Accommodation

South America offers a wide variety of accommodation possibilities. All the large cities have luxury hotels, some of which belong to the world's great hotel chains; standards here equal those in the Western countries, with prices set accordingly. In the large cities you'll also find locally owned luxury hotels, whose prices are lower although the level of service is in no way inferior.

Intermediate-class and inexpensive hotels abound. Almost all hotels outside the cities charge intermediate or low rates, and many are very inexpensive. Lodging is significantly cheaper in the Andean countries than in the lowland countries (Brazil and Venezuela), but conditions there, too, are far worse.

Be careful when choosing a hotel that is not first-class. In many places these are not regulated in any way. At the same time we must note that the Ministries of Tourism in most South American countries are making an effort to enforce hotel regulations. In the large cities and major tourist centers you'll find that most hotels are clean, reliable, and altogether satisfactory.

Away from the big tourist centers and along the roads, there

*I*NTRODUCTION

are always places to stay. Almost every village has a house that serves as a hotel, but don't expect much here — at best a creaky bed and rickety chair. Sanitation and cleanliness, too, are not the best.

Youth hostels aren't popular in South America, though you will find them in some places. On the other hand, it's customary to put up young travelers in churches, schools, youth clubs, and even fire stations — for no charge.

Camping grounds are rather rare. In some countries — mainly Argentina, Chile, and Brazil — they do exist and can serve the tourist public. They aren't organized along North American lines, and the tourist must provide his own tent and sleeping equipment. On many routes tourists spend their nights under the stars in improvised campgrounds and an informal atmosphere.

Food and drink

In the culinary field, too, we've landed in a very strange place. We've all heard the legends about Argentinian steaks and Brazilian coconuts, but we should also be ready for what comes along with them — guinea-pig (*cuy*) in Peru, eel in Chile, and similar terrors elsewhere.

The South American cuisine, like everything else on the continent, combines Indian tradition with Spanish influence, and its national character is determined by what's grown where. A lot of meat is eaten in Argentina, Uruguay, Paraguay and Venezuela; lots of fish and seafood in Chile and Peru; and tropical fruit in Brazil. Potatoes and rice are standard side-dishes in every restaurant; so is soup, a very popular item throughout the continent and many varieties are served.

Milk products are hard to get in the Andean countries, in contrast to Argentina, Chile, and Brazil where they are plentiful — and excellent. *Empanadas* (stuffed pastry), *mate* (South American tea), and many other delicacies are only some of the contents in the bursting menu of excellent food and drink enjoyed by the local populace. We'll cover them in detail and at length in our Introduction to each country.

South American restaurants are innumerable. Every second house serves as one, and every streetcorner has two more. In the cities, a variety of food is served at all levels of quality, while in towns and villages native and peasant cooking is the most common fare. Hygienic conditions aren't the best, but that's something you get used to as time and upset stomachs pass... Western manners and dress are customary in the better restaurants, while the more popular ones favor a free and informal atmosphere. Eating at streetside stands, kiosks, and market stalls is a common practice. It's a quick and cheap way to get a meal, and how most of the locals get their nourishment. Try it, but remember to check how clean, or perhaps how "undirty" the place is. Mealtimes vary from country to country, according to the climate.

Fruit and vegetable lovers will have problems in the Andean countries, where most produce may be tainted with various diseases. Even if they appear healthy to the eye, their insides are liable to be infested. You must therefore adopt an ironclad rule about fruit and vegetables: peel them, cook them, or throw them out. If you can't peel or cook it, **don't try it!**

Vegetarians will manage quite well. Although vegetarian restaurnts aren't very common, the major foods on which a vegetarian diet is based are available in abundance, and can be prepared yourself.

Domestic transportation

Airlines link the South American countries with one another. International flights are frequent and convenient, and prices resemble those of short international flights in the West. Domestic flights are another story. Here the range is broad, complications are rife, and confusion reigns.

In Brazil, Argentina, Peru, and Colombia the airlines offer an open ticket for unlimited flights during a predetermined time period. In these countries, where covering distances overland requires many days, this is an offer certainly worthy of consideration. To go from Rio de Janeiro to Manaus or from Buenos Aires to Bariloche takes days or weeks by land, and the cost of an individual flight is high. In addition, *Aerolineas Argentinas* has reduced-price night flights, which cost about the equivalent trips by bus. You must therefore weigh the alternatives well and decide accordingly. An unlimited-flight ticket may be bought only **outside** the country in which you intend to fly.

The armed forces of the South American countries also operate flights that carry civilian passengers. These are cheaper than their civilian counterparts, but take off at irregular intervals and generally involve antiquated aircraft.

Another typical problem of domestic flights is overbooking. Airlines are not reliable when issuing tickets, and frequently sell more tickets than the number of seats at their disposal. You must therefore get to the airport early; otherwise the flight is liable to fill up and leave you waiting for another. Cancellations, delays, and changes of routes are also common occurrences, for which the tourist must be prepared.

Be very sure to mark your gear, although even this doesn't guarantee that it will reach its destination. The care of passengers' luggage, especially in Peru, is negligent and contemptuous. Try to carry as much as possible, and relegate to the baggage compartment only the necessary minimum, **after** you've packed and marked it properly.

Driving a private or rented car is widespread in all South American countries. More and more tourists choose this way to get around, and avail themselves of the large international car-rental companies or local firms.

If you want to bring your own car, you should stock up on spare parts and make sure your documents are in order. Bureaucratic difficulties are especially frequent at border crossings, and garage services are rare in the hinterlands. Consult Auto Club experts in the United States or Europe before you set out for up-to-date material, including maps and the addresses of local Auto Clubs (which we've provided in the chapters pertaining to each country). Auto Clubs in South America are very active, and their personnel provide assistance and guidance to members of similar clubs abroad.

Your car must be in top mechanical condition before you set out. In the Andean countries many roads reach thousands of meters above sea level, where engines must be specially tuned. Note that the road networks of Colombia, Venezuela, Brazil, and Bolivia are undeveloped (apart from main highways) and difficult to drive on. It's better to avoid driving there, and find another way of getting around. When traveling off the main roads, be sure to have enough fuel for the return trip, plus spare parts — service stations are almost nowhere to be found. A breakdown here is both unpleasant and expensive.

Car-rental rates vary from country to country, but usually they are around an international average for mid-sized cars in the large agencies. Local agencies can sometimes be cheaper, but do not offer the same level of service. The minimum age for renting a car is 22 (25 in some countries), and the customer must leave a sizeable deposit or a credit card. It's important to insure the car when you rent it.

River boats are a common means of transportation in a number of areas, especially the eastern portions of the Andean countries and northwest Brazil (the jungles). Here you'll find that the only way to get from one settlement to another is by boat or ship along the river, and not infrequently you'll have to rent your own to reach your destination. Rental fees are high, but energetic bargaining will drive them down to something almost reasonable.

The major means of **public transportation** include trains, buses, trucks, and taxis. **Trains** operate only in some of the countries, and most are old, slow, and uncomfortable. They are not as common a way of getting around as they are in Europe, so don't plan a tour based on the railways. **Buses**, by contrast, are the most popular form of transportation, and connect all places of settlement. In several countries — Brazil, Chile, Colombia and Argentina, for example — the buses are modern and comfortable; in others they're motorized crates. Differences in quality and service are extreme, precluding a uniform and precise description. On some routes, you'll find smiling stewardesses; elsewhere you'll find terrible overcrowding and rampant theft. In any case, the bus remains the cheapest and most efficient way of getting around on land. **Shared taxis and minibuses** run on many intercity routes. Their fares are higher than the buses, but their advantage lies in far greater speed, comfort and safety. **Trucks** (*camiones*) carry passengers mainly in the poorer countries, where they ply remote dirt roads with their loads of shoulder-to-shoulder animals and people, the latter seated on piles of freight and clinging to their baggage lest it tumble off. It's a unique experience by all accounts — a cheap way (sometimes the only way) of reaching many remote places.

Hitchhiking is common in Chile and Argentina, chiefly in their southern regions. Hitchhikers there — especially women — get lifts easily, and vast distances can be covered quickly and cheaply. In the Andean countries, an accepted practice is to demand payment from a passenger, even if he thought he was getting a free ride. In Brazil and Colombia tourists have been attacked and their gear stolen: avoid hitchhiking in these countries by no means!

Urban transportation is efficient in most large cities. Bus lines, subways, taxis, and *colectivos* (shared taxi service) contribute to mobility in densely-populated urban areas and are usually rapid and reliable. In many countries, particularly the Andean ones, taxis have no meters and the fare must be agreed upon with the driver — **before starting out.**

Personal security
One of the most severe problems that visitors to South America are liable to encounter is protecting themselves and their

belongings. A combination of social and political ferment, plus the desperate poverty, makes violent outbursts all too common. Sometimes these are directed at the authorities, in the form of hostile underground activity, and sometimes aimed at the tourist, whose valuable baggage attracts thieves. The problems are especially serious in Colombia, Peru, Brazil, and Venezuela — in that order. In the Introduction to each of those countries, we have included guidelines on appropriate behavior and preventive measures. Argentina, Uruguay, Paraguay, Chile, Bolivia, and Ecuador are considered to be tranquil and relaxed; have no fears about touring there.

Local currencies

The various South American currencies are noted for their worrisome instability. In recent years they've been considerably devalued against the dollar; for the tourists, this has lowered the cost of a stay there significantly. If on an extended visit, you'll find that for every dollar you change on your last day you'll receive more local currency than you got when you arrived. Accordingly, it's worthwhile to change money only to cover your immediate needs since within a few days you are likely to get more for your dollars.

Banks and moneychangers (*Casa de Cambio*) change currency; the latter usually offer a slightly higher rate and far less bureaucratic red-tape than the former. Though several countries do not allow private dealing in foreign currency, and restrict activity to the major banks, black-market moneychangers will always find a way to offer you a more attractive rate. Be extremely careful about dealing with them — verify their reliability and be sure to count what they give you.

Most airports also have some arrangements for converting foreign currency. If you've arrived on a weekend or holiday, change enough to cover your needs until the next business day. In the city itself you probably won't find a bank open, and may be forced to change money at a poor rate. Cash dollars are always preferred, but it's best to hold onto these for countries where a black market operates, and use travelers' checks elsewhere.

When entering a new country by land, don't change more money at the border checkpost than you'll need to reach the nearest large city, where you can expect to get a better rate. In any event, check and compare rates carefully with a number of moneychangers before you decide; differences among them are by no means small. Count the money you're given very carefully, making sure you get what you paid for.

INTRODUCTION

Many moneychangers will try to exploit your innocence by holding back a few bills from the stack they hand you.

When leaving a country, get rid of any remaining local currency; it's worth considerably less in other countries, even those right across the border, and sometimes in the country itself, if you are back the next day.

Tourist services

A well-arranged and efficient system of services awaits the tourist in most South American countries. As tourism increases, governments become more aware of its tremendous economic impact. They have begun investing in expanding and improving the infrastructure and services which will help tourists get oriented and acclimated. This infrastructure includes not only hotels and restaurants, but also information centers, transportation services, guides, various publications, and more. Major airports will greet you the moment you touch down with counters to provide information, hotel reservations, car rental, and baggage checking. The bus and taxi fares from the airport into town are usually fixed by the government.

Almost every city has a tourist information bureau which offers guidance, maps, and other material. One of the noticeable drawbacks of these bureaus is the lamentable fact that their personnel often speak only Spanish, so that a tourist who cannot get along in that language will find it hard to avail himself of their services.

In addition to the tourist bureaus, several other organizations offer tourists information and assistance. The most important are the various Auto Clubs (*Automóvil Club*), which will keep you updated in matters of transportation and tour routes. There are also the military geographical institutes (*Instituto Geográfico Militar*), where you can obtain maps for hiking tours, the nature reserve authorities, etc.

Medical and health services

The most common health problems that a tourist to South America is liable to suffer are intestinal problems and difficulties in adjusting to the thin air at high altitudes. In both cases you'll probably need nothing more than short and routine treatment, which can be obtained at any regional clinic.

For more serious problems you'll have to go to a hospital. In national capitals and other large cities there are British or American hospitals, to which tourists should turn in case of need. In other cases, it's best to turn to English-speaking private physicians to whom you can describe your ailments, though you must be cautious about accepting treatment which seems inappropriate to you.

First-aid services in South America aren't the best, and still can't treat many health problems. You must therefore be doubly careful, and seek out qualified medical help in any case of suspected illness.

Dental treatment that can be put off should be put off. When that is impossible, visit a qualified dentist who has modern equipment.

Altitude — how to cope with thin air

The high elevation of South America's mountains requires one to take appropriate measures. Remember that the atmosphere is thin at these altitudes. The amount of oxygen is less than at sea level, upsetting the body's equilibrium. If you breathe at your normal rate you'll simply take in less oxygen, and consequently suffer from asthma-like sensations of choking and weakness. A certain amount of attention or caution may alleviate the problem and lessen its impact. Common side-effects are dizziness, nausea, headaches, and at times fainting. To avoid these reactions — which involve a certain discomfort even if they are not dangerous — you must take a number of precautionary measures.

First, it's best to reach the mountains by an overland route, in order to moderate the rate of ascent and give your body a longer period of time to acclimatize. If you arrive by air, there will be a sharp transition which results in a quicker and stronger impact. In any event, be sure to set aside the first twenty-four hours for rest, relaxation, and reduced food intake. This will grant your body a suitable interval to adapt to the lower percentage of oxygen in the atmosphere.

At high elevations you should refrain from physical effort, including that considered insignificant under normal conditions. Walk slowly, do not run or carry heavy loads, slow down even more when walking uphill or climbing stairs, and take frequent rest stops. Keep physical activity to a minimum: don't smoke, and avoid large, heavy meals. If necessary, you can buy special medication in drugstores which expand the blood vessels, thus increasing the amount of oxygen supplied to the body. Asthmatics, heart patients, and pregnant women tend to suffer more at high altitudes and it's recommended that they stay away from these areas as much as possible.

In most cases, as we have said, rest will help but sometimes this may have to be augmented by medical care and short periods of oxygen treatment. Hospitals, clinics, and even ordinary institutions recognize the problem, are experienced at treating it, and will be glad to help. As time passes, the body grows accustomed to the new situation and can resume normal activity — if more slowly and cautiously, and less strenuously.

Discounts for students and young travelers

In South America students are eligible for discounts on public transportation and admission to various sites. The discounts are not offered on all occasions, and certainly not automatically. For details, consult the section on documents, and the text, where you will find these discounts mentioned wherever they are offered.

In regard to accommodation, few places offer reduced youth rates and those which do, are mentioned in the relevant chapters.

Behavior and manners

The rules of manners accepted in the West apply here as well. The "dress code" is similar, though less formal. Both men and women wear sporty evening wear for official events, concerts or dinner in an elegant restaurant. In the daytime, light and airy clothing is wholly acceptable. For men, shorts are out of place except on the beach. In certain places, such as Caracas, the police can fine anyone who's improperly dressed in public. In Brazil, seashore dress is acceptable, but only in town and not on an intercity bus, for example. Women should dress modestly and avoid revealing garments. At holy places, those improperly attired are not allowed to enter.

Behavior toward women is somewhat archaic here, a matter which carries with it a certain grace and charm. Among descendants of the Indians as well, whose women bear the brunt of the physical burden, women are accorded respect and are treated with great consideration.

Latin Americans are friendly and hospitable. Many tourists are warmly welcomed into local homes, where they are made to feel at ease.

Among the European communities in Argentina and other countries it is customary to greet guests with a friendly kiss on the cheek. It's a gesture of friendship, and expresses no intimacy of any kind. The South American way of life is conservative and restrained; conspicuous permissiveness is nonexistent here.

In Spanish it is accepted practice to address people with the formal *usted* rather than the familiar *tu*. This serves to express respect and esteem rather than distance and estrangement.

It's customary to tip restaurant waiters (10%-15% of the bill) and service personnel (a small amount). Taxi drivers with whom you've negotiated a fare at the beginning of your trip do not expect a tip.

Keeping in touch

Postal and telephone services in Latin America are far from efficient. They are slow and clumsy, unreliable, and some are even expensive. An airmail letter sent to South America is liable to spend an extended period (up to several weeks) en route, perhaps not arriving at all.

Poste Restante (General Delivery) service is available in national capitals, but one shouldn't rely on it too much. Mail which arrives for you at the post office will only be kept for one month. *American Express* offices accept mail for their customers, and we recommend this method: have your correspondents send letters to an *American Express* office, where they will be kept for you until you get there.

Sending postal items from South America also requires attention. Mail letters only at post offices; use airmail, preferably registered. Film and important items should be sent registered, and only from main post offices. Avoid stamps in favor of a post-office cachet, since stamps not infrequently catch the eye of the sorter, who appropriates them for himself; more seriously, he destroys the contents. Letters encounter prolonged delays on the way, and if your tour lasts for two or three weeks your letters are likely to reach friends and family when you're already back at home, planning your next vacation.

Sending parcels involves much effort, time, and trouble. Parcels must be of fixed weight, and need to be boxed and wrapped. Those weighing more than one kilogram require inspection by a customs clerk, who sits — of course — somewhere other than the post office. The parcel has to be left open for inspection; only then can you seal it. Parcels may be sent by air or surface mail. The former is fast and sure, but is immeasurably more expensive than surface mail. Though surface is cheaper, it is far slower, and your parcel may spend many months in transit. It also happens that surface-mail parcels "get lost" and do not arrive at all. Surface mail is considered reliable from Argentina,

Chile, Ecuador, and the Brazilian coastal cities, but not from Peru, Colombia, or Bolivia.

South America has telephone links to the rest of the world. International phone service is slow and expensive, but the connections are usually of satisfactory quality. Placing an international call from your hotel is liable to involve a wait of several hours. It's therefore wise to make most such calls from the telephone exchange found downtown in the large cities. These have several booths to which callers are summoned, each in his turn. The minimum length for such a call is three minutes. Collect calls are not always possible; it depends on where you are and to where you're calling. (This is not the case in Brazil, where the International phone service is quick and efficient, and one can make collect calls from any public phone.)

Shopping and souvenirs

Any tour of South America will add many kilograms of souvenirs and purchases to your luggage. Whether it's a Dior suit from Buenos Aires, a poncho from La Paz or jewelry from Brazil. Every traveler, even the most frugal, will end up buying at least a few of the innumerable souvenirs encountered on the way. And this acquisitiveness is perfectly justified.

In South America you'll find an amazing concentration of crafts and other artifacts, called *artesanía*, most hand-made — the glory of local craftsmen and artists. Their beauty and the special character of these items will have you digging into your wallets time and again.

Those touring only one or two countries will find information on the characteristic wares of each country in the relevant chapters, and will soon discover the wealth of possibilities. Keep in mind a number of important rules so as to avoid later problems with budget and weight (or rather excess weight).

Firstly, remember that all of South America resembles one gigantic market. It's hard to find a product exclusive to a single place, though there are, of course, differences in quality, types, and the like. Accordingly you'll be able to compare styles, prices, and quality, to ponder the various options... and to bargain! Bargaining is essential here; if you accept the stated price, not only will you pay more than you should but you'll also hurt the vendors' feelings, for they look forward to this give-and-take with their customers.

Each of the South American countries has its own characteristic forms of *artesanía*. These give artistic expression to the economic condition of the country in question and the sources of its treasures. Thus Chile abounds in metalcrafts, Argentina in clothing, Brazil in precious stones, and the Andean countries in woollen fabrics and woodcrafts.

Andean *artesanía* is noted for its strong Indian influence. In this region you'll find lovely woollen products, musical instruments, pottery, and astonishingly beautiful woodcarvings. Wall hangings, various garments, and antique fabrics are only some of the local treasures, and it's only natural that we'll cram them into our suitcases in considerable quantities. If you are travelling many months, it's best to send these home by mail (see above), for otherwise they're liable to interfere with the rest of your trip, getting in your way and causing problems.

In the cities you'll find tourist shops that offer top-quality merchandise at prices to match. As you travel you're bound to find these where they're made, closer to their natural environment and at their natural prices.

Overland border crossings

To explore South America properly, we must cross borders rather frequently. Whether during a combined tour of Argentina and Chile, a journey from Colombia to Ecuador, or on any other route, we'll encounter a number of traits common to all these inspection points.

All frontier stations are staffed by immigration officers in charge of the gates to their respective countries. They allow traffic to pass only during certain hours, which vary from station to station. In most cases border crossings are open from morning to nightfall, sometimes closing for an afternoon *siesta*. Some stations are open for only half a day on weekends. Check out the situation thoroughly before you reach the border, so as not to lose a full day's touring.

The main crossing points have separate lines for tourists and local citizens; crossing procedures here are simpler and quicker. In most countries you'll have to fill out a tourist card, stamped by the immigration clerk, which indicates how long you are permitted to stay. Always be sure to request the maximum time allowed — generally 90 days. Though getting an extension once you're in the country is possible, it can be very time-consuming.

Moneychangers congregate near crossing points. When changing money with them beware of being misled as to the exchange rates or in counting the bills.

Border posts can be reached by taxi or local bus. Direct bus routes from one border town to its counterpart on the other side are more expensive. It's therefore best to get to the border, cross on foot, and continue by vehicle on the other side after having taken care of the formalities.

Taxes and custom duties

Tourists must pay duty only on valuable items brought in as gifts, cigarettes and alcohol in excessive quantities, or commercial samples. These excluded, tourists can bring in personal belongings, including all required gear.

Among the many taxes imposed in South America, tourists are obliged to pay two: a port tax when leaving the country, and in some countries an excise tax on air tickets purchased there. Port taxes vary from country to country, as do the rates of the air ticket tax. When planning your return trip, it's therefore convenient to find out where to end it according to the tax you will have to pay. Sometimes these taxes can add more than 10% to the price of the ticket.

Working hours

The afternoon *siesta* is almost the Latin American trademark. In every country, businesses, shops, and offices close for two or three hours in the afternoon; during that time it's hard to find a seat in a restaurant, and even the streets seem more crowded.

Most businesses open early in the morning and stay open until evening. Office reception hours are usually only before noon. On weekends most businesses and offices are closed. Shops are open half-day on Saturdays, and are closed Sundays. Many museums are closed on Mondays.

Holidays and festivals

South America's holiday season, on a continent-wide basis, lasts the entire year, though most special occasions tend to be concentrated in February-March, June-July, and December, when you can celebrate the carnivals in Rio and elsewhere, *Inti Raimi* (the Sun Festival) in Cuzeo, Peru, and Christmas everywhere. During those seasons, much of the local population are themselves on vacation, and the general ambience isn't conducive to business. On national holidays, most services and many institutions are closed. When planning your tour, be sure to keep the dates of holidays in mind, and arrange matters so that your visit won't suffer on their account.

*I*NTRODUCTION

Weights and measures, temperatures, electricity, time

The metric system is used throughout South America, with the meter (slightly more than a yard) as the unit of distance, and the kilogram (-2.2 pounds) for weight. Temperature is measured and reported in degrees Celsius. The voltage varies from country to country, and sometimes even between different parts of one country. The most common is 220 V, but 110 V is used in many places.

South American clocks lag behind Greenwich: GMT is three to five hours ahead of South American time, depending on location. The following table gives the time difference between South America and New York and London:

12 Noon	New York time	(GMT) London time
Asunción	11:00	16:00
Buenos Aires	11:00	16:00
Bogotá	12:00	17:00
Caracas	11:00	16:00
La Paz	11:00	16:00
Lima	12:00	17:00
Montevideo	10:00	15:00
Quito	12:00	17:00
Rio de Janeiro	10:00	15:00
Santiago de Chile	10:00	15:00

SOUTH AMERICA

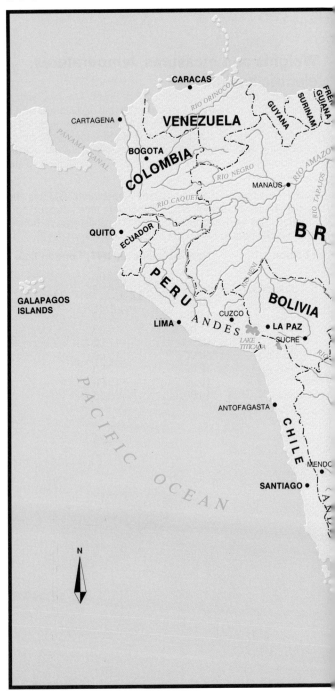

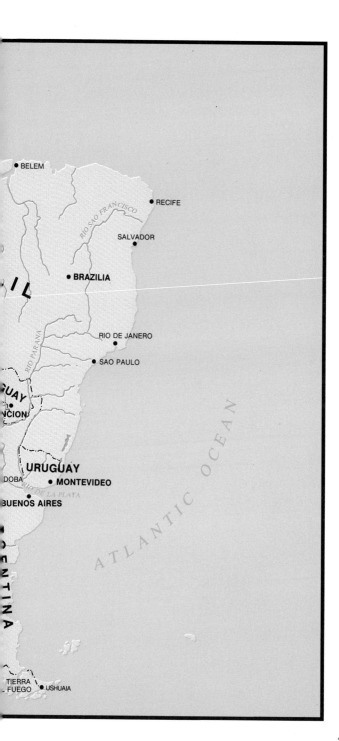

BELEM

RECIFE

RIO SAO FRANCISCO

SALVADOR

BRAZIL

BRAZILIA

RIO DE JANERO

RIO PARANA

SAO PAULO

URUGUAY

NCION

URUGUAY

DOBA MONTEVIDEO

RIO DE LA PLATA

BUENOS AIRES

ARGENTINA

ATLANTIC OCEAN

TIERRA FUEGO USHUAIA

A RGENTINA

The Republic of Argentina, the eighth largest country in the world and the second largest in both area and population in South America, is an important tourist center. Tourists to these parts will find a wide range of places to visit and topics to capture their imagination: they can explore the exquisite countryside with its spectacular scenery, and experience a wide variety of cultural and social life and local folklore — not to mention enjoying this gourmet's paradise, with its cuisine based on meat, meat, and more meat.

Argentina is undoubtedly one of the most interesting countries in South America. It is a land of contrasts, with a strife-torn history of intermittent foreign and civil conflicts. A country that only a few decades ago was among the richest in the world is today, due to incompetent administration, in critical economic straits, with massive unemployment, and foreign debts totalling tens of billions of dollars. But the roots of the problem strike much deeper.

During your stay in this country, a vast range of sights will greet you: from the tropical forests in the north to glaciers in the south, from the Atlantic beaches in the east to the peaks of the Andes in the west. You will encounter giant rivers, lakes, glaciers, and other natural phenomena, as well as huge cities, small villages, and isolated farms. Along with intellectuals and cultural and artistic giants, you will find gauchos (cowboys) and colorful Indians.

Argentina combines European traditions and mores with a Latin American way of life — with all its advantages and disadvantages. You will notice the mixture of colonial architecture, restaurants specializing in Italian or French cuisine, western apparel and mannerisms, and native music and dress, all representing a glamourous social and national mixture.

Argentina will swiftly capture the heart of the newly arrived tourist. You will find a warm welcome, and will be quickly embraced into the fold. You cannot fail to notice the essential difference between this country and those around it, especially when you reach Buenos Aires — one of the largest and most beautiful cities in South America. The Argentinians themselves are well aware of their superiority vis-a-vis their neighbors, and act accordingly. In South America, the joke goes that if you buy an Argentinian at the price he is **worth** and then sell him at the price **he thinks he's worth** you will have made the deal of a lifetime... There is something to that.

In any case, whether you come for a short visit to Buenos Aires — and there is no doubt that such a trip is worthwhile — or whether you intend to explore in depth the mysteries of this vast country, which only a few even of its own inhabitants are fortunate enough to know intimately, you can count on having a rich and varied experience. Argentina, more than any other South American country, is equipped to handle tourists. The sophisticated network of public services makes it easy for visitors to find their way around, thus transforming your trip into a pleasant and exciting experience for the entire family.

History

The dominant motif in the history of this country, from the day the Spaniard Juan de Solís first set foot on its shores in 1516, is the continual domestic strife. Throughout the nearly five centuries since Argentina, with an indigenous population estimated to have been approximately 300,000 people, was discovered by the Old World, the country has not enjoyed many years of military, political, or economic tranquility.

Juan de Solis was killed by the Indians as soon as he landed on the shores of La Plata. It was only in 1536 that the first Spanish force of any significance arrived. Numbering several ships and hundreds of men, led by Pedro de Mendoza, it laid the foundations of Buenos Aires. However, the settlers, weakened by continuous attacks of the local Indians, soon left the area. Under the leadership of Domingo Irela they moved to Asunción, conquering large areas of Paraguay on the way. Pedro de Mendoza's expedition brought horses with them, and cattle which thrived on the fertile pastureland, and became the basis for Argentina's prosperous meat industry.

At the same time as Buenos Aires was abandoned, and the Río de La Plata left to the Portuguese (who had already conquered Brazil), groups of Spaniards began infiltrating Argentina from the north (arriving from Peru, which was already in the hands of Pizarro) and the west (Chile). These pioneers founded several towns, the most important of which are Tucuman, Salta, Jujuy and Córdoba in the north, and Mendoza and San Rafael in the west. It was only in 1580 that Buenos Aires was again resettled, this time by Juan de Garay. The inhabitants gained their livelihood, until 1594 (when the Spanish government enforced trade restrictions), from the harbor through which gold and silver from the Peruvian mines were exported. In 1617 a local semi-autonomous administration was set up, headed by Arias de Saavedra as Governor, with its capital in Buenos Aires.

The trade restrictions, which remained in force for nearly two hundred years, naturally gave rise to a small-scale smuggling industry. However this did not contribute to the town's economic or population development. At the same time, serious battles were being waged against the Portuguese from Brazil, who held a strong military outpost in Colonia, on the Uruguayan side of the gulf, and attempted to stem the development of this important port. In 1776, when it finally became clear that the area could not be dominated from Peru, which is some 4,000 km away, Buenos Aires was declared an autonomous viceroyalty including within its borders Uruguay, Paraguay, and Bolivia. Two years later, all trade restrictions were rescinded and Buenos Aires once again became a free port — a change that paved the way for its development and prosperity. The population of the town soon doubled and its inhabitants, the large majority of whom were Creoles (Spaniards born in South America), grew in power, so that from posts of limited influence in the Cabildo (town council) they soon achieved positions of real importance.

The year 1806 marked the begining of the conflict between Argentina and Great Britain when the British, in pursuit of Napoleon's allies, captured Buenos Aires. However, the British were soon ousted, thanks to the stalwart resistance of the Creoles. A further attack in 1807 was also repulsed. The memory of these attacks, as well as the subsequent British domination over the Falkland Islands, has remained a thorn in the side of the Argentinians.

Their success in repulsing the invaders strengthened the self-confidence of the inhabitants. Therefore when the French conquered Spain in 1808, exiling King Ferdinand VII and attempting to impose their authority on Spain's American colonies, the Cabildo of Buenos Aires convened and on the 25th of May, 1810, decreed the establishment of a "Council for Self-Rule". They deposed the viceroy, entrusting the administration to a *junta*, which included Manuel Belgrano, the designer of the Argentinian flag and one of the country's great national heros. To this day, Argentinians celebrate the 25th of May — the day on which Spanish rule was abolished — as their National Day. They also celebrate the 9th of July, since it was on this day in 1816 that the National congress assembled in Tucumán, declared Argentinian independence.

During the Napoleonic wars, instability reigned in the European colonies in South America. The Spanish viceroy exiled to Peru, attempted to conquer the rebellious Argentina, but the small armies of Generals Belgrano and San Martín overcame him, and the danger of renewed Spanish domination receded. However, this victory was accompanied by radical changes in the structure of Argentina: Paraguay broke away and declared itself an independent republic (1811) and Bolivia was re-annexed by the viceroy in Peru. The most severe problem was the internal polarization within Argentina itself. The split between the inhabitants of Buenos Aires — mainly cultured Europeans, merchants and professionals — and the provincial landowners and rich cattle breeders, who could call out armies composed of the gauchos employed on their ranches, continued to widen. The city-dwellers aspired to set up a united state with a central government in the capital, whereas the landowners sought a confederation that would formally unite the various provinces while religiously preserving their rights to administer their own ecomomic and internal affairs.

The harsh struggle between city and province, between centralized state and confederation, continued throughout most of the 19th century, and was accompanied by political disputes and military uprisings, years of oppressive despotism, and repeated rebellions.

At the same time the capital continued to develop and grow. Bernardino Rivadavia, who in addition to being Argentina's first president was also mayor of Buenos Aires in the 1820's, enacted far-reaching reforms that contributed to the social and cultural development and prosperity of the town. The most important of these reforms were those encouraging immigration from Europe, and the institution of freedom of religion and freedom of the press. Rivadavia, whose term in office contributed greatly to growth and stability in this stormy century, was forced to resign and leave Argentina in 1827, when his army did poorly in a war against Brazil. Although the Brazilian army was repulsed by the Argentinians in the Uruguayan lowlands, the Brazilian navel blockade of the Río de la Plata had a catastrophic effect on Argentinian trade, and Rivadavia had to pay the price. After a short period of anarchy, Manuel Rosas was elected governor; by harsh and oppressive measures he managed to restore order in Argentina. Rosas, a federalist, was brutal towards his opponents, while entrusting wide powers to his supporters in the provinces.

At the same time, Rosas waged war against Bolivia's territorial annexations and involved himself in Uruguayan domestic struggles. His policies led to a confrontation with France and Great Britain, and in 1838 these countries sent warships to blockade the Plata, causing serious damage to Argentina's economy and fostering unrest and rebellion among the Argentinian population. Urquiza, governor of Entre Rios Province, who had signed a pact with Brazil and Uruguay, raised an army of over 20,000 men and overthrew Rosas.

Urquiza, like his predecessors, was unable to bring peace or stability to Argentina. Under his influence, the establishment of a federation on the lines of the United States was approved and treaties were signed with France, England and the United States. Some of the agreements granted these powers free movement along Argentina's rivers. This proved detrimental to Buenos Aires' economy, which was based on customs revenues and port services. As a result, the city rebelled and seceded from the federation; only in 1859 was Buenos Aires re-annexed into the federation, by Urquiza. But not for long! Bartolome Mitre, who was mayor of Buenos Aires, led another rebellion and defeated President Derqui, Urquiza's successor. Subsequently in 1862 Mitre was elected president of Argentina.

The next twenty years laid the foundations for Argentina as we know it today. The five-year long "War of the Triple Alliance", between Paraguay on the one hand and Argentina, Uruguay and Brazil, on the other, broke out in 1865. The war ended without a decisive victory for either side, despite the unprecedented losses in men and property on both sides.

Following the war, the internal situation improved, in spite of the continuing strife between the various provinces. At the end of the 70's, when the skirmishes with the Indians of the south intensified, General Julio Roca expelled them with great brutality, killing thousands. This opened the way for new settlements in the south, in faraway Patagonia and Tierra del Fuego. The people of Buenos Aires, who opposed Roca's policy on the division of the new territories, rebelled, but the revolt was swiftly quashed by the General's army. The status of the city was changed; formally both the national capital and capital of the province, it now became an autonomous district (like Washington D.C.) and the capital of the federal republic. The town of La Plata was designated capital of the province. This change finally stabilized the relationship between Buenos Aires and the rest of Argentina. Roca, who was considered a national hero, was elected president of the country. His moderate policy, which favored peace and economic growth, was welcomed by most of the power groups in the country. The ensuing boom served to widen his support and increase his power and influence in subsequent years.

Roca devoted the ten years of his rule to strengthening Argentina's economy and furthering its technological and industrial development. The mass immigration from Europe, especially from Italy and Spain, brought with it a progressive element. This immigration was further supported by foreign investors, especially the British. It was during these years that the basic export economy was established. Meat refrigeration methods were implemented and a rail network was built to facilitate the transport of goods from the north and center of the country to Buenos Aires. From there they were sent to Europe, particularly to England. The fruits of these huge investments and the concomitant boom in agricultural development, together with a hundredfold expansion in the area of cultivated land and increased sophistication of meat processing and storage methods, all contributed to Argentina's becoming one of the most important and richest grain and meat exporters in the world by the begining of the twentieth century.

These processes were accompanied by territorial stabilization. The fencing-in of ranches and pasturelands curbed the greed of the landowners; their legions of workers gave up their nomadic existence on the boundless pampas for the organized discipline of the restricted *estancia* (ranch), large though these were. At the same time, there was a new trend towards greater political participation by the general public, in particular that of the middle class, which essentially consisted of the recent immigrants from Europe. They organized as a bloc, clamoring against the ruling landowners for free universal suffrage. They did not hesitate to use violence in order to achieve their aim; the results shook the regime, which was forced to gradually yield to their demands. But the pace of reform was too slow for the public's liking.

Only in 1916, did the birthpangs of democracy end when the first general elections were held in Argentina. Irigoyen, a leading activist for democratic reform, was elected as president. His term of office, during the First World War, was characterized by far-reaching social changes. In the process, the landowners and industrialists lost some of their traditional power. Irigoyen was careful to adopt a neutral stance in Argentina's foreign policy, and refused to suport the United States against Germany.

During the war, the country enjoyed an economic spurt, since the countries of Western Europe and the United States bought huge quantities of meat and grain. In fact, until the crash of 1929, when the West stopped buying, the Argentinians continued to enjoy prosperity. By the outbreak of the Second World War the economy had recovered, and except for occasional radical agitation that was quickly suppressed, Argentina continued the process of internal consolidation while restricting her involvement in the affairs of the continent or the West.

When war broke out in 1939 a new polarization was evident, between the opponents of fascism and Nazism, led by the Socialist and Radical parties, and the more conservative government, which aligned itself with Germany and Italy, and adopted a policy of isolationism. With the entry of the United States into the war, this polarization intensified, leading, in 1943, to a military coup. This coup paved the way to power for Argentina's best-known modern leader, Juan Domingo Perón.

On the 4th of June 1943, a group of officers forced President Castillo to resign, appointing in his stead General Arturo Rawson, who was himself replaced, after only two days in office by General Ramírez. Less than a year later he was also forced to resign, accused of being a puppet in the hands of the allies. Throughout this period Perón, then a young colonel, was head of the War Office in the *Junta*. At the same time, he was gathering popular support, especially among the trade unions, with which he was involved in his additional capacity as Minister of Labor, dealing with Social Welfare. Perón saw to the well-being of the workers, and won for them huge salary increases, social and retirement benefits, and the like. When Ramírez was deposed and replaced by General Farrell, Perón was appointed Defense Minister (May 1944) and, a few months later, Vice-President. Perón equipped the army and expanded its ranks, at the same time continuing to improve the lot of the workers. The economic situation of the country, which supplied the United States and Britain with vast quantities of food throughout the war years, steadily improved, and her economic independence enabled Argentina to adopt a nonaligned position in the war. Nevertheless, when it became obvious that Germany was about to be defeated on the battlefield, Argentina swiftly declared war on her, at the end of March 1945, thus appeasing her critics and ensuring her entry into the United Nations.

Within the country itself agitation against Perón, particularly on the part of the industrialists, landowners and radicals, intensified. On the other hand, Perón enjoyed the unqualified support of the President, the loyalty of the army, the police and the affection of the people. Perón, aware of the significance of this agitation and its latent threats, moderated to some extent his harshness towards his opponents, granted the universities a certain amount of autonomy, sanctioned political organizations and freed hundreds of political prisoners. This liberalization encouraged his opponents to take action. In September 1945, they staged a huge demonstration in the streets of Buenos Aires, in which 300,000 people participated, demanding a curtailment of Perón's powers. The government reacted harshly by arresting hundreds of people, among them some of Argentina's leading personalities. When the wave of arrests reached the top echelons of the army, opposition to Perón intensified. On the 9th of October, he was arrested by presidential decree and imprisoned, but as a result of strikes organized by his supporters in the trade unions he was released after a week. Perón's arrest gained him a permanent place in the national pantheon as the hero of the workers, championing their cause and preventing their exploitation by the rich, and also as the man who gave their country an independent foreign policy.

In February 1946, Perón was elected president by democratic vote and immediately began implementing his national aims. His main ambition was to strengthen the economy in order to enhance Argentina's international standing. He used the vast sums that had accumulated from export profits during the war years to purchase industrial equipment, to improve the railway system, to set up power plants, and to further industrialization. Aided by his wife, Eva Duarte Perón (known by the affectionate diminutive "Evita"), a film actress whom he married in 1945, he continued his openhanded social policy, distributing company profits to the workers and lavishly honoring his public commitments. Eva Perón, who as head of the "Eva Perón Fund for Social Aid" distributed vast sums of money to the needy, enjoyed considerable political influence. Her death, in July 1952, traumatized the country, and considerably influenced her husband's political outlook.

Perón continued his policy of giving industrial and urban development priorities over agriculture. He nationalized the banks and public utilities and increased the government's involvement in the economy. In 1949, he had the Constitution amended, abolishing the clause prohibiting re-election of a president; in 1952 he was elected for a second six-year term. Argentina began to experience economic difficulties, mainly in the form of a galloping inflation and financing difficulties. Perón turned to foreign financiers for help, while stubbornly pursuing his spendthrift policies. The economic collapse, the opposition of students on the one hand and industrialists on the other, and his attempts to stifle the church's criticism of him, all contributed to his downfall in 1955.

Perón's opponents, who understood the problems inherent in his economic policy, concentrated on obtaining foreign credit and capital and on encouraging export, at the same time limiting and even reducing wages. In spite of the efforts of the interim president, Lonardi, to forge an understanding with Perón's supporters and the Church in order to reinstate liberal constitutional government, the military managed to seize power again and establish a military dictatorship. The new rulers adopted a violently anti-Peronist stand, disbanded the remnants of the Peronist party and swiftly suppressed a military uprising by the supporters of the ousted president. Over succeeding years,

Perón's supporters limited themselves to restricted participation in the new regime. Successive presidents pursued a moderate economic policy, devaluing the local currency to attract foreign capital and encourage export. The war against inflation, which involved limited credit and imposing various restrictions and prohibitions, created a political and economic situation that was new to a nation that had been accustomed to wild extravagance. Strong pressures were exerted on the government, which was increasingly forced to rely on the army to preserve its authority. The anarchy led to a quick succession of governments and presidents, each of whom had to contend with the problems left by his predecessor. Lack of public support meant that they were unable to implement any significant changes. The question of how to deal with the Peronists also contributed to the national chaos. The military's intermittent seizures of power helped control tempers for short periods, until 1966 when a strong military government was once again established.

This government held power until 1973. During its existence, the economic, social and political fabric of the country was destroyed, leading to major riots in May, 1969. The swift decline of the economy, civil unrest and fear of the future led the military government to allow the return of Perón from his exile in Spain. He arrived in Argentina in November 1972, staying only a month. Under his influence his candidate Hector Campora was elected president in the elections that were held a few months later. Two months after taking office he resigned, thus opening the way for Perón's return from exile and his subsequent election as President in October 1973.

President Perón died on July 1, 1974. His widow, Maria Estela Perón known to the crowds as Isabelita, who was her husband's vice-president, assumed the reins of power assisted by some of his advisers. Her rule was characterized by internal anarchy, harsh violence, mass arrests, and the liquidation of political opponents.

This state of affairs led to another military coup. At the begining of 1976, Maria Estela Perón was overthrown, and replaced by a military *Junta*. The *Junta* dissolved the Congress, and abolished all democratic institutions. Throughout the military regime, thousands of people were killed, tens of thousands arrested, many of them were never seen again; to this day their fate remains a mystery. Entire families of Peronists or of suspected anti-Government activists were arrested, and many young people were jailed for long periods. International organizations and political pressure were unable to penetrate the conspiracy of silence regarding the fate of those who had vanished, the *"desaparecidos"*. Even though occasional reports filtered through, regarding the existence of anonymous graveyards containing hundreds of corpses, the Argentinian government continued to turn a blind eye. It was only in April 1983 that the government's spokesman in Buenos Aires declared that the missing people should be considered "as if no longer alive". His announcement led to a furor in the West.

The rule of the military *Junta* brought with it a relative silence, calm on the surface although accompanied by internal tension and a harsh and brutal regime. By 1982, when the failure to run the country's economy was obvious, and the corruption too widespread to be hidden, a wave of internal unrest menaced the regime, and the government leaded by General Galtieri attempted to divert public attention from internal and economic problems to foreign affairs. In April 1982, Argentinian forces invaded the Falkland Islands, or, as they are known to the Argentinians, the Malvinas, in an attempt to capture them from the British, who had controlled them for over one hundred and fifty years. A desperate war was waged for these small islands, inhabited by some 2,000 English-speaking subjects of British extraction. The British Army, obliged to defend the islands against the Argentinian invasion, fought under harsh conditions, far from their home base and in stormy and treacherous weather conditions. The war lasted for several months, during which time both sides suffered heavy losses. In the end, Her Majesty's Army routed the Argentinians, who were suffering from shortage of food, arms and vital equipment.

As a result of this heavy defeat on the battle field, General Galtieri was forced to resign. His successor scheduled free elections. The unity and fervor that had characterized the months of war vanished, as Argentina embarked on yet another economic crisis.

The election campaign was dominated by the *Junta's* political and military failures and the issue of the *desaparecidos*. On October 30, 1983, the Radical candidate Raul Alfonsin defeated the Peronist Italo Luder. This was the first defeat suffered by the Peronist party ever, a fact which had far-reaching political and social implications.

Alfonsín's administration knew ups and downs, having to face attempts to be overthrown by extreme right-wing military forces, opposed to his policy of democratizing the national institutions, including the Armed Forces. Shortly after his successor in office was elected, he had to resign because of the social upheaval and food riots in the main towns. In the Argentine political system, coming close to the end of office is an achievement in itself, and Alfonsín was the first since Perón's first term to reach it.

ARGENTINA

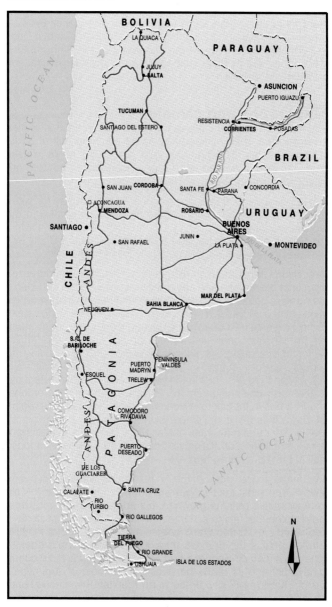

Carlos Menem, the picturesque head of state since May 1989, leaded the Peronist party, but his policies are very pragmatic and even opposed to the Peronist tradition, both in the internal front as in the foreign arena (e.g., backing the U.S. in the Gulf war in 1991, instead of pleading the Argentinean neutrality also called Drago doctrine). At the last years of the 20th century, the country seems to be on the right track towards political and economical stability.

Geography and climate

Argentina is the eighth largest country in the world. It stretches over an area of 2.77 million km² in the southern half of South America. It is 3,500 km long and 1.400 km at its widest. The Republic is divided into 22 provinces whose borders are historically, rather than geographically, determined.

On the east, Argentina borders on the Atlantic Ocean for some 2,500 km; its western border more or less runs parallel to the continental divide in the Andes. In the north, Argentina borders on Bolivia and Paraguay, and in the north-east, on Brazil and Uruguay. These boundaries generally follow large rivers.

Argentina's topography is extremely varied. It is characterized by climatic extremes and marked differences in flora and fauna. Its western border is flanked by the Andes range, which reaches a height of 3,000-4,000 meters above sea level (the highest peak is approximately 7,000 m). The eastern slopes are not as steep as the western ones, and form a broad mountainous region which at its widest point extends for some 500 km, including the inner range of mountains. To the east of these mountains are the lowland regions: the Chaco (which continues into Paraguay) in the north, extending from the Paraguayan border to Córdoba; the Pampas in the center extending from Córdoba to the region of Bahía Blanca; and Patagonia in the south, extending from Bahía Blanca to the Straits of Magellan. The lowland plains are fertile, consisting of alluvial soil deposited by rivers, and loess soil in the more rainy areas.

In contrast to the aridity of the Andes slopes, with their canyons and nature sites, the Pampas are known for their fertility. Most of Argentina's grain is grown in this area. It is the agricultural development of this region that has made Argentina into one of the world's most important food suppliers. The Andes foothills stretch across the Pampas through the center of the country (the provinces of Mendoza and San Juan). This area is rich in vineyards, and its grape harvests supply most of Argentina's wine. The *Gran Chaco* in the north (capital: Resistencia) with its temperate climate, is covered with forests, and serves the lumber industry and as pastureland. Argentina's "Mesopotamia", which includes the provinces of Misiones, Corrientes and Entre Rios, sandwiched between the Parana and Uruguay rivers, is also extremly fertile. In fact, the only non-arable area is the rocky dunelands of Patagonia, and this is mainly due to its cold, harsh climate and the strong winds that hinder the growth of any kind of plants.

Argentina is sliced by a network of giant rivers, which also serve as important transportation arteries. The enormous amount of water that flows through these rivers, together with a relatively high precipitation rate (the rainy season is the summer, from November to March) make Argentina especially blessed with ground water, particularly in the plains.

Argentina's climate varies extremely from one part of the country to another. The northern region has a sub-tropical climate, the Pampas (including the province of Buenos Aires) have a temperate climate, while sub-arctic conditions prevail in Tierra del Fuego. More details concerning the climate are given below.

Population, Education and Culture

Argentina has about 32 million inhabitants, mostly of European descent. Unlike her neighbors in Latin America, only a few of the indigenous inhabitants remain, while the Creoles (Argentinian-born Spaniards) have generally assimilated into the waves of mass immigration from Europe. Some of them married Indians, and these are the forebears of the legendary *gauchos* (cowboys), who live mainly in the northern provinces. Successive Argentinian governments opened their doors to "anyone in the world who wishes to settle on Argentinian soil" (as stated in the Constitution). In particular, they encouraged the immigration of whites from Italy and Spain. Over the last 100 years, the country's population has increased twenty-five-fold(!), and the immigrants, who settled mainly in the towns, have contributed in no small measure to urban growth and development.

Approximately 40% of the immigrants came from Italy, and another 30% from Spain. Together, these groups fashioned the image and character of the country. There was also an influx of immigrants from England, France, Poland, Russia, and Germany, but these have, on the whole, assimilated into other demographic groups.

Most of the Europeans settled in the large towns, where they created a cultural, social, and commercial life along European lines. School and university education, social welfare, artistic and cultural life, fashion, as well as forms of polite behavior are also borrowed from European norms. This is especially apparent in the capital, Buenos Aires. More than a third of Argentina's population is concentrated in what is known as "greater Buenos Aires", the huge metropolis that is home to 12 million people. An additional 40% of the population live in towns with more than 25,000 inhabitants. A mere 20% of the population live in agricultural settlements spread over the huge expanses of the Argentinian country-side.

The European immigration had a decisive influence on the social structure of the country. The illiteracy rate is relatively low (about 15%, although some people prefer to stick to the "historically best" of 7%) in comparison to other countries in South America, and the education network has expanded in an attempt to contract it even further. Both primary and secondary education are free and many students go on to university.

Social security is yet another proof of the preponderance of Western values in Argentina. The national insurance system has created an economic security which in turn has led to a socio-economic stability unparalleled in Latin America.

Freedom of worship allows members of all religions to practice their beliefs as they see fit. In fact, 95% of the population are professing Catholics and Christianity is the official religion.

The official language is Spanish, spoken with different accents in various parts of the land. In certain areas, especially in the north, Indian dialects are spoken, but these tend to be mixed with Spanish. European languages, in particular Italian, English and German, can be heard in the large towns.

Economy

In her economy, Argentina also stands apart from her neighbors. In spite of an extremely shaky economy, the Argentinians have one of the highest standards of living on the continent. Although Argentina is traditionally thought of as a meat and grain producer, and is still one of the world's main storehouses of grain, a trend towards increased industrialization has made itself evident during the past few decades. Although the strength of this trend has fluctuated according to the policies of successive governments, there is nevertheless a clear tendency to expand the country's industrial infrastructure, especially in terms of the production of export goods and import substitutes.

The main economic bastion remains, as always, agriculture. Around 12% of the land is cultivated, and of this, 60% is devoted to cereal crops, especially corn and wheat. About 80%

of the corn and wheat crops are exported. As far as livestock is concerned, the poultry industry has evolved considerably over the last few years, alongside a corresponding increase in the number of cattle and sheep. At present Argentina boasts some 50 million head of cattle and some 30 million head of sheep, which are used for meat and for the flourishing dairy products industry. The quality of the meat is world renowned, and a huge industry has evolved for processing, freezing and exporting meat.

Industry is advancing by great strides, and this has been accompanied by the construction of an increasing number of power plants to lay the groundwork for the establishment of a large-scale industrial network in many varied fields. Argentina's main industrial production is still based on processing agricultural products, although recently efforts have been devoted to developing high-technology fields such as electronics, machinery and petrochemicals. Quarries, mines and oil wells have become a pivot of the economy, and much effort and capital have been devoted to their development in the last few years. Today 36% of the gross national product is derived from industry, which employs 25% of the national workforce. Approximately 80% of Argentina's exports are agriculture-based, and her imports are, on the whole, restricted to raw materials, spare parts, arms, machinary, etc. Argentina's trade balance has been in the red for many years now, and she has accumulated enormous debts over the years, amounting to over 50 billion dollars.

General Information

How to get there
By air: The easiest way to get to Argentina from Europe or the United States is by plane. *Aerolíneas Argentinas* runs scheduled flights daily from New York and Miami (The flight from New York takes less than 11 hours). Some of the flights have intermediate stops at Rio de Janeiro and São Paulo. Most South American carriers also have scheduled flights between the United States and Buenos Aires, but they take a longer route with stopovers and changes of plane. If you are not taking a direct flight, you should book with the Brazilian airline, *Varig*, whose flights stop at Rio or São Paulo, since they offer extremely pleasant flights and excellent service.

The major European airlines fly to Buenos Aires, usually with intermediate stops. *Aerolíneas Argentinas* and *British Caledonian* offer two direct flights a week from London to Buenos

Aires, and *Varig* offers three. It is well to bear in mind that such flights are quite expensive, but they are based on mileage, which means you can have stopovers at no extra charge (see "Setting Out").

There are daily flights from most South American countries, either on the respective national airlines or *Aerolíneas*. Anyone starting from a nearby country with the intention of touring Argentina, should consider buying a "Visit Argentina" air ticket (for more details, see "Domestic Transportation").

Airports: Buenos Aires is served by two airports. Flights from other South American countries land in several of the other large cities as well (see the section on the cities for further details).

By land: Argentina has many crossing points along her borders. There are frequent bus services from frontier towns to their Argentinian counterparts, but they are fairly expensive. Further details are given in the sections on the individual cities themselves.

There are rail connections between Argentina, Bolivia and Paraguay. The rail service to Chile no longer operates due to lack of passengers. Train trips are long and tedious, and the trains old and slow. If you intend to travel by rail through South America, consider buying an unlimited travel pass for a period of 20, 30, 60, or 90 days in the Pullman carriage (reclining seats), which is the most comfortable and, indeed, essential if you are traveling long distances. The pass is valid in Argentina, Uruguay, Chile, Bolivia, Paraguay, and Brazil, and will make traveling considerably cheaper. You can buy the pass at the Rail Office, Calle Florida 729, Buenos Aires (open all day till 8pm, half-day Saturdays, closed Sundays). You should, however, bear in mind that bus travel is much quicker and no less comfortable than by train (except in Bolivia).

You can also enter Argentina by car, provided you have international documents and a customs form from the Automobile Club. It is a simple procedure if your car has a license plate from a neighboring country. The driver must be in possession of a valid international driving license.

By ship: It is also possible to cross the Río de la Plata from Uruguay by passenger boat. Daily service is available, with the boat leaving Montevideo each evening and arriving at Buenos Aires in the morning. The journey is convenient, pleasant and cheap. There is another ferry from Colonia. For further details, see the chapter on Uruguay.

Documents

Argentinian immigration procedures tend to change frequently and it is advisable to check with Argentinian authorities shortly before departing. North Americans need visas. So do business visitors from all countries. Western European tourists do not require a visa.

Tourist visas are provided by Argentinian Consulates worldwide, after applicants fill out forms and submit a passport photo, a letter of recommendation and a round trip ticket. The visa is valid for one year and grants you three months stay in the country with unlimited exit and entry. If you intend to travel overland through South America and have difficulties obtaining a visa for Argentina, you would be well advised to obtain a visa in one of the other Latin American countries, since the Argentinian Consulates there are less particular about formalities (in particular, the possession of a round trip ticket).

You **must** carry your papers with you wherever you go, as you will often be asked to show them. If you are unable to produce them upon request you may find yourself in a very unpleasant situation.

Traveling overland, entering the country from Chile, some tourists have been asked to give a detailed account of their planned itinerary in Argentina. This is then listed on a special form attached to one's passport. Should this occur, you will have to have the form stamped at the police station within 12 hours of your arrival at each town. You should be careful to follow this procedure, to avoid unpleasant repercussions.

When to come; national holidays

Given the size of the country and the variety of climate, this question loses some of its relevance. The best time to travel is between September and March. Touring is more difficult between April and August (winter), especially as one goes further south. The weather is very stormy in Patagonia and Tierra del Fuego and you should avoid visiting these areas during the winter. The weather in Buenos Aires is pleasant throughout most of the year. You would be well-advised to visit Peninsula Valdez during October-November.

The national holidays are as follows: January 1, Good Friday (Holy Week), May 1, May 25 (Creation of the First Argentine government), June 20 (day of the Flag), July 9 (Independence Day), August 17 (Death of San Martín), October 12 (Columbus' Day), and December 25.

Where to stay

Argentina offers a large selection of **hotels** of varying quality, classed by stars, as in most Western countries. In addition, there are many small, inexpensive pensions, which are usually clean and situated near a railway or bus station and near the town center. Breakfast is not usually included in the price. Star-graded hotels have a fixed maximum rate determined by the Ministry of Tourism, but a service tax (about 15%) and value added tax are added, and you should bear this in mind. You can avoid the service tax by paying for services within the hotel (meals, laundry, etc.) separately each time you use them.

Argentina has a well-developed network of **camp sites** which provide all amenities. The camp sites are spread all over the country, in parks and on the outskirts of cities. Although they are far from the city centers, they are cheap, clean, and safe, and it is well-worth putting up with this slight inconvenience. Recommended.

There are only a few **youth hostels** scattered round the country. In the smaller towns, though, young people can usually find free sleeping accommodations in schools, fire stations, youth clubs, etc. Another money-saving possibility is sleeping in gas stations. For further details, see below "Hitchhiking".

Wining and dining

Argentina is without doubt a gourmet's paradise. We have already sung the praises of its meat dishes. Suffice it to add that a steak at an average restaurant weighs several times more than a "large" steak in other countries.

The most common offerings are *asado* (grilled meat), *churrasco* (a thick juicy steak), and *parrillada* (mixed grill including roast beef and sausages — recommended). The *empanadas*, pastries filled with meat and vegetables, are very popular in South America, as are *chorizos*, which are spicy sausages. The *milanesa* schnitzels are excellent, and so is the popular dish *arroz con pollo*, which consists of rice with pieces of chicken and vegetables in sauce.

Pizzas, and Italian dishes in general (especially the cheese dishes), are definitely recommended. There is a wide variety of pizzas: especially recommended are those with a thin crust and lots of extras. There is also an excellent selection of cakes, ice cream, chocolate, and candy. The *confitería* (a cross between a café and a snack bar) offers light meals plus a wide choice of cakes that taste excellent! Chocolate lovers would be extremely foolish to forego the pleasure of tasting the chocolates of Bariloche, especially if you are still under the delusion that Switzerland has a monopoly in this area. As for *dulce de leche* (milk simmered with sugar until very thick), this is the national delicacy.

Breakfast and lunch are eaten at the usual times, but it is rare for dinner to be served before 9pm. Most restaurants are still packed with diners much later than that. Most of them tack on a whopping service charge (up to 25%), so keep this in mind!

Evening meals are often accompanied by domestic wines. Connoisseurs will order Chilean wines, which are superior to the local vintage. With dessert one drinks *mate*, a kind of tea which is very popular in South America.

Domestic Transportation

There are many and varied ways to get around the country.

Hitchhiking: Hitchhiking has become increasingly popular, especially during the past few years when public transport has become more expensive. Many young tourists prefer to hitchhike, since it is a quick, comfortable and cheap way of traveling almost anywhere. Other advantages of this method are that you get to know the local population and improve your Spanish. The further you are from a city, the easier it is to get a lift. If you get picked up by a truck traveling on a main highway, you can cover vast distances in no time at all. If you are going to hitchhike, take a tent with you and ask to be put down at gas stations. If you should get stuck there for the night they will let you pitch your tent behind the station, which is equipped with showers and lavatories. Remember though, that there have been numerous cases of hitchhikers being assaulted or robbed.

Buses: There are several private companies providing bus services to all parts of the country. Most roads are paved, so you can reach almost any destination conveniently and quickly. Students are usually offered a discount, but foreign students may find that this does not apply to them.

Train: Argentina has an extensive rail network that links the northern, western, and southern parts of the country with the capital. The trains have Pullman cars (reclining seats), and first and second classes. The Pullman cars are served by a steward who attends to the passenger's comforts. The dining cars offer good food at reasonable prices. Train journeys are long and slow, and in the pampas (around Bahia Blanca) and the north (the Salta-La Quiaca route), it is extremely dusty. The southern terminus of the railroad is Bariloche. Trains are cheaper than buses, and those who plan extensive journeys can obtain a train pass for unlimited travel around the country (see "How to get there").

A RGENTINA

Car rental: There are many car rental companies throughout the country, especially in the large cities and tourist centers. This is a comfortable, albeit expensive, way of traveling, and is especially suited to groups of four. The large international companies accept reservations from abroad, so that a car will be waiting for you at the airport. Bear in mind that driving in Buenos Aires makes midtown Manhattan seem like a country lane: if you can avoid it, do!

Private car: This is a convenient means of travel, since most roads in Argentina are paved, and there is no shortage of gas stations and garages. The Argentinian Automobile Club (*Automóvil Club Argentino*) is located at Avenida Libertador 1850, Buenos Aires. The club has many branches all over the country, which provide maps, information, and guidance. It also owns hotels, motels, and hostels. If you are traveling by car, you should get in touch with the club; you will find them efficient and helpful, especially if you are a member of an automobile association.

Plane: *Aerolíneas Argentinas*, Austral, and the military airline *Lade* fly all over the country. Although the flights are quite expensive, bear in mind that an overland journey from Buenos Aires to Bariloche, for example, takes 36 hours each way! Flights from Buenos Aires to Bariloche, Río Gallegos, and the Iguaçu Falls are the most heavily booked, and you should try to make reservations ten to fourteen days ahead. *Aerolíneas* has night flights several times a week on the main routes, such as to Río Gallegos, and these are 50% cheaper than the day flights. There is a large demand for these flights, but they are worth the effort.

Aerolíneas also offers a *"Visit Argentina"* ticket, which can not be purchased in Argentina or in any neighboring country (Chile, Brazil, Uruguay, Paraguay or Bolivia), allowing you to visit 4 destinations (U$S 360), 6 destinations (U$S 410) or 8 destinations (U$S 460); you can visit any place once only. *Lade* also provides service south from Buenos Aires in old military planes. The flights are slow and make many stops, but they are far cheaper than *Aerolíneas'* flights. *Lade* flights operate in Tierra del Fuego and on some routes in Patagonia.These are not included in the pass, but they are not all that expensive either.

Currency
Since January 1992 the Argentinean currency is the *Peso*, and the rate is 1 Peso = US$ 1. There are coins of 5, 10, 25 and 50 cents, and notes with the 1, 2, 5, 10, 20, 50 and 100 designations.

The use of credit cards is widespread in Argentina. Bank

transfers of foreign currency to Argentinian banks are paid out only in local currency, at the official rate, and with high comissions involved.

Business hours
Most shops are open from 9am till 7pm, or even later in downtown areas. Restaurants and cafes generally stay open till the small hours of the morning, or even around the clock. Banks are usually open from 11am-2pm but each bank keeps its own hours. Government offices are open in the morning during the summer, and in the afternoon in the winter. Post offices are open from 8am-8pm, and on Saturdays until 2pm.

Measurements, electricity and time
Argentina uses the metric system. Clothes sizes follow the European system, and shoe sizes the American, although the shop keeper will understand if you tell him your European shoe size.

The voltage in Argentina is 220V. Argentinian time is GMT-3.

A suggested itinerary for touring Argentina (including Chile)
So as not to miss places of interest, you should begin your trip from Brazil in the northeast, travel to the far south, and then back along the western side to the northwest and Bolivia. This is a basic outline for a logical, comprehensive travel route that will save you both time and money. You can, of course, adapt it to your requirements and means. The suggested itinerary is as follows:

From the Iguaçu Falls to Buenos Aires.
From Buenos Aires south to Tierra del Fuego, via Mar del Plata, Península Valdés, and Patagonia.
From Tierra del Fuego to Chilean Patagonia.
From southern Chile to the lake district and Bariloche.
From the lake district to Mendoza.
From Mendoza to Córdoba, and then north to Bolivia via Tucumán, Salta, and Jujuy.

A RGENTINA

Buenos Aires

Buenos Aires is known as "the Paris of South America", and with good reason. Its avenues are broad with a constant flow of noisy traffic day and night. Its buildings are imposing, from skyscrapers to single-story houses, the architecture a mixture of European styles with a strong Spanish influence. The people wear the latest fashions, dance to the latest music, and dine out on the best of international cuisine.

Buenos Aires is a bustling, multi-faceted city, full of opportunities for pleasure and entertainment, a city whose streets are never silent. Argentina's capital honors the principle of "living around the clock" more than any other European or American city. The cafés and discotheques in the Recoleta district are as full at five in the morning as they are before midnight. Here you can drink to your heart's content in the popular cafés, gorge yourself on food unsurpassed in quality and quantity the world over, attend cultural and folklore events on an international level, and more.

Buenos Aires was founded in 1536, neglected and re-founded in 1580. Today its population, including the suburbs, is around 12 million. The city serves as the economic, cultural, and national hub of Argentina, and its central position in the life of the Argentinian people is evident in every sphere. The city is endowed with a large variety of cultural, artistic, scientific, and commercial institutions. While touring the city you can see the exclusive residential districts in the north, the bustling commercial zone in the center, and in the south, the picturesque quarters around the port area. Here in the south, in the neighborhoods of La Boca and San Telmo, you cannot fail to marvel at the gardens and public squares, the old harbor, and the nightclubs from which the strains of the tango issue forth, creating that unique atmosphere which makes Buenos Aires so special and so captivating.

How to get there
By air: Buenos Aires has two airports, with dozens of daily arrivals and departures. If you are coming from abroad you will land at the International Airport in Ezeiza, some 40 km from town (some flights from neighboring countries land in Aeroparque). Once you have finished with passport control and customs, which should not take long, turn left to where most of the airport

ARGENTINA

The Obelisk at Avenida 9 de Julio

facilities are situated, including public transport into town. By far the best way of getting to the city is the airport bus, which takes 40 minutes to reach downtown. You can buy tickets in the terminal itself. Ask the driver to let you off downtown, since the last stop is some distance beyond. The taxi fare downtown is fixed (not metered), and is approximately four times the price of a bus ticket. Agree on the price before you enter the taxi, and on no account pay before you reach your destination. If you wish to save, you can take bus 86 from the International Hotel near the airport. When leaving Argentina, you will have to pay an airport tax.

The other airport, Aeroparque, is in Palermo, near the river bank, only five minutes from downtown. It handles mainly domestic flights, some of them reaching destinations in neighboring countries. You can catch a taxi to take you downtown. The journey is quick and cheap, paid according to the meter.

By land: Buses link the city to other parts of Argentina and to neigboring countries. Most buses depart from and arrive at the downtown Retiro terminal, while others use the Once terminal, which is next to the subway (line A). Trains from the center, north, and west of the country terminate at Retiro station (which has three terminal buildings). Those from the south go to Constitución station, while those from the northeast go to Lacroze station. A few trains from the west go to Once station. There are buses to all parts of the city from every station.

By ship: Ships call at the port of Buenos Aires from Montevideo and Colonia. This is a cheap, pleasant and recommended way to travel. Passport control takes place on board the ship, and the customs check is simple and quick. When you leave the terminal on Paseo Colón, turn north to go downtown, which is within walking distance, or else take a taxi.

Where to stay

Buenos Aires has many hotels and pensions. Most hotels are located downtown, between Avenida de Mayo and Avenida Santa Fe, or between Avenida Nueve de Julio and Avenida Alem.

In general, the hotels and pensions are clean and safe, and there is no need to be unduly concerned in moderate-priced places.

Five Stars

Alvear: Av. Alvear 1891, Tel. 804-4031/45. A building with tradition, one of the best hotels in town. Very expensive.
Bauen: Av. Callao 360, Tel. 804-1600. It looks far from the touristic sites on the map, but it is perhaps the best located.
Claridge: Tucumán 535, Tel. 393-4301. With all the comfort an hotel of this category can offer.
Elevage: Maipú 960, Tel. 313-2082, fax 313-2182. Close to almost everywhere in town.
Hyatt Park: Cerrito 1433, Tel. 22-2541. Ultra-modern, and prices accordingly.
Libertador Kempinsky: Córdoba 698, Tel. 322-2095. Well located.
Plaza: Florida 1005, Tel. 312-6001, fax 313-2912. The favorite meeting place of local officials with foreign diplomats and correspondents, with one of the highest standars in town.
Sheraton: San Martín 1225, Tel. 311-6310. On a higher spot, facing the replica of the Big Ben in Plaza San Martín, the view from the upper stores is superb.

Four Stars
Dorá: Maipú 963, Tel. 313-7319, fax 313-8134. Excellent location.
De las Américas: Libertad 1020, Tel. 393-3432.
Sheltown: M.T. de Alvear 742, Tel. 312-5070.

Three Stars
Embajador: Carlos Pellegrini 1185, Tel. 393-9485.
Grand Buenos Aires: M.T. de Alvear 767.
Impala: Libertad 1215, Tel. 42-5190.
Romanelli: Reconquista 647, Tel. 312-6361.

Two Stars
Kings: Av. Corrientes 623, Tel. 322-8161.

What to eat, where and when
And so we come to the most pleasant part of this guide. Gourmets (and who isn't?) can look forward to a varied, rich, and boundless gastronomical experience during their stay in Buenos Aires. In addition to the 6000 (!) restaurants scattered throughout the city, there are tens of thousands of kiosks, cafes, and outdoor stands that sell food and candy; you can hardly walk 100 meters without passing one. As a multi-faceted metropolis, Buenos Aires caters to almost every taste. One thing, however, it will not tolerate: a diet! Anyone who has not eaten or at least tasted its cakes, pizzas, ice creams, chocolates, custards, cheeses, and choice meats cannot claim to have visited Buenos Aires. To be in Buenos Aires without enjoying its wonderful food is like being in Paris without visiting the Louvre, or being in New York without seeing the Statue of Liberty. Therefore, be brave, forget your figure and, bear in mind Oscar Wilde's sage remark ("I can resist anything but temptation"), allow yourself to be tempted, and enjoy it. Given this unlimited profusion of restaurants, it would be pretentious as well as superfluous to attempt to provide names and addresses of the most highly recommended. We will therefore restrict to giving general guidelines to help you choose which of the ten restaurants on the block you wish to try, and what food is worth ordering, although one choice is as good as another, so you can't go wrong no matter what you order.

Let's start with the simpler options. A galaxy of candy and ice cream will lure you at every step. Ice cream is sold in a special shop known as an *heladería* which offers a wide variety of flavors. Select the size you want, but remember that the ice cream will tower twice the height of the cup. The various chocolate flavors are highly recommended (Bariloche chocolate, white chocolate,

BUENOS AIRES

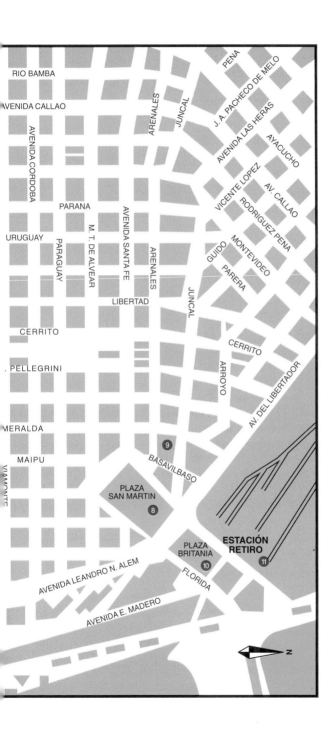

RIO BAMBA
AVENIDA CALLAO
AVENIDA CORDOBA
PARANA
URUGUAY
PARAGUAY
M. T. DE ALVEAR
AVENIDA SANTA FE
LIBERTAD
CERRITO
. PELLEGRINI
MERALDA
MAIPU
VIAMONTE
ARENALES
ARENALES
JUNCAL
JUNCAL
PENA
J. A. PACHECO DE MELO
AVENIDA LAS HERAS
AYACUCHO
VICENTE LOPEZ
AV. CALLAO
RODRIGUEZ PENA
GUIDO
MONTEVIDEO
PARERA
CERRITO
ARROYO
AV. DEL LIBERTADOR

⑨
BASAVILBASO

PLAZA
SAN MARTIN
⑧

PLAZA
BRITANIA
⑩

FLORIDA

ESTACIÓN
RETIRO
⑪

AVENIDA LEANDRO N. ALEM

AVENIDA E. MADERO

N

79

*A**RGENTINA*

chocolate with nuts, etc.), as are the custard flavors. You should concentrate on these rather than on the fruit flavors. The ice cream is usually made from high-fat milk, and the fruit flavors, which have a sour-milk base, just aren't as good. The others, as we have said, are a real delicacy.

Most of the chocolate you will find in the kiosks is Swiss type, and you are no doubt familiar with its taste. So make a point of buying from the shops specializing in the home-made product (*caseros*), which offer a vast assortment of chocolates sold by the kilo. You can find many such shops along Florida or in the galleria where Florida and Plaza San Martín meet. The Bariloche chocolate is the best of all, but almost impossible to obtain in the capital. Shops that claim to sell Bariloche chocolate usually sell chocolate based on a similar recipe, but manufactured in Buenos Aires.

There is an almost unlimited choice of superb cakes in cafés and pastry shops (*confiterías*). Cream cakes are generously filled with a brown cream, which is not always chocolate but often the local delicacy known as *dulce de leche*. In the confiterias you can order light meals, sandwiches, meat (*carne*) and cheese (*queso*) *empanadas*, as well as simple main dishes, all of them cheap and tasty!

Highly recommended are the pizzerias and Italian restaurants. The influx of Italian immigrants has left its mark on Argentinian cuisine, and pizza is considered an indigenous national dish.

Apart from the many extras that you can order on a pizza, there are two main types: those with a thin crust and those with a thick one. Although the thick crust is more filling, you should order the thin crust variety if you want to savor the other components.

The meat restaurants present of course the crowning glory of

Argentinian cuisine. In these restaurants, spread all over the city, the portions are huge! There is a never ending assortment of meat dishes, accompanied by salads, rice, and fried potatoes. (For a more detailed description of the meat dishes, see "wining and dining"). You will find dozens of such restaurants along Corrientes and Lavalle streets in the downtown area. If you want to enjoy an excellent meal, in a pleasant spot and at an exceptionally reasonable price, visit the **Los Carritos district**, which is situated along the river near the Aeroparque Airport. Here dozens of superior restaurants can be found, open day and night, serving the choicest Argentinian dishes in a relaxed and informal atmosphere. The wide road (Costanera Norte) leading to Los Carritos is lit up with neon signs all along the way, so you can't miss the place. You can also hire a taxi or travel by bus from Retiro station in a few minutes. The restaurants offer superb food, and although large (some seat hundreds of people), they are always full, day and night. An excellent meat restaurant in Costanera is *Los Años Locos* (on Avda. Obligado). Refer to the list of recommended dishes in the "wining and dining" section — and start practicing what we preach...

American style fast-food restaurants, whose "specialty" is usually hamburgers, can be found all along Calle Florida. On Carlos Pelegrini street, in the Colón theatre areas are a number of cafés and restaurants, some of which have tables outdoors. The Sheraton has an excellent restaurant on its roof, with a fantastic view. The Recoleta district also has an abundance of cafes and restaurants, and so do the San Telmo and La Boca quarters. You owe yourself a supper in La Boca, in one of the huge restaurants seating hundreds of diners, and accompanied by boisterous orchestras for your pleasure.

Below is a list of a few of the most popular and outstanding restaurants in town:

Regional cuisine
La Cabaña: Avda. Entre Ríos 436.
La Raya: Pavón 3062.
Las Nazarenas: Reconquista 1132.
La Payanca: Suipacha 1015.
La Rueda: Cochabamba 1021.
El Ceibal: Avda. Las Heras 2265.
La Carcel: Bulnes 1901.

Popular "Porteño"
Arturito: Corrientes 1124.

Chiquín: J. D. Perón 920.
Pepito: Montevideo 383.

Pizza
Los Inmortales: Lavalle 746.
Las Cuartetas: Corrientes 838.

Vegetarian
Giardino: Lavalle 835.
Yin-Yang: Paraguay 858.

Transportation
The streets of Buenos Aires are laid out in a grid pattern, and with the help of a map (given out free in hotels and tourist offices), you should have no problem in getting around.

Buses are frequent and fast, serving all parts of the city. The route number and destination are clearly marked on the front of the bus, and every bus stop has a list of the streets followed by that route. Many essential bus routes — essential especially for the tourist — begin or end at **Retiro station**, alongside Plaza San Martín.

The subway has five lines, which cover the busiest arteries. The C line goes between the Retiro and Constitución stations, intersecting the other four lines en route. Subway stations are indicated by a sign post with *SUBTE* written on it, and the letter identifying the line.

Black and yellow **taxis** are plentiful and easy to flag down, even during rush hour. Taxis are metered, and a ride in the center of town is fairly inexpensive.

The most convenient means of inter-city transport is train or bus. For longer distances, it is better to fly (see details in "Domestic Transportation").

Detailed timetables can be obtained at the Railway Information Center, Florida 729 (Tel. 311-6411/4), and at the Tourist Information Center. Most inter-city buses leave from the Retiro bus station.

Car rental is another possibility and cars can be rented from *Hertz*, *Avis* (at the Sheraton Hotel), and local companies. You can reserve a car via the international agencies or the doorman at your hotel. The minimum age for renting a car is 22; and you need to have an international credit card.

Tourist services
As already stated, Argentina in general and Buenos Aires in

particular have good tourist information services, which supply both verbal and written assistance and guidance. Avenida Florida has two **information booths** and the staff will be happy to help you in matters of transportation, tourist sites, entertainment, and so on. They can provide you with pamphlets, maps, and computerized information on a variety of topics. The blue booths are centrally located. The first is at the Florida-Paraguay intersection, and the second is at the other end of Florida, near the Plaza de Mayo. The main office is on Avenida Santa Fe 883, (Tel. 325-550), but the Florida branches are perfectly satisfactory.

The **tourist offices** of the provinces are also within walking distance of Calle Florida. These will provide you with lots of maps and detailed information about the provinces, tourist sites, parks, nature reserves and the like. Their material is usually available only in Spanish. The addresses of these tourist offices can be obtained from the tourist information booths on Florida.

The National Parks Authority also runs an information office that can supply interesting and useful material about nature sites throughout the country. Their office is at Avenida Santa Fe 680 (Plaza San Martín).

The **airline** offices are concentrated near Calle Florida and on Avenida Santa Fe (near Plaza San Martín). The main office of *Aerolíneas Argentinas* is at Calle Perú 2 (continuation of Calle Florida, Tel. 30-8551/9). *Aerolíneas* also has a large branch office on Avenida Santa Fe, near Plaza San Martín. The offices of the following companies are also situated along Santa Fe: *Eastern*, *Aero-Perú* (840), *Alitalia* (887), *Avianca* (865), *Ecuatoriana*, *Sabena* (816), and *Swissair* (846). On Florida are the offices of *Air France* (890), *KLM* (989) and *SAS* (902).

Austral (internal flights) has an office on Corrientes 485 (Tel. 49-9011), and *Lade* (army airlines) has one at Calle Perú 710 (Tel. 34-7071/3).

Tourist sites

Downtown
Like Chicago's Loop, sharply demarcated by railroad lines, downtown Buenos Aires can be defined fairly precisely as the area bounded by Ave. de Mayo in the south and Ave. Santa Fe in the north, and by Ave. Alem in the east and Ave. 9 de Julio in the west. This is the nerve center of the capital, and contains most of the government offices, commercial and financial institutions and exclusive stores. The popular pedestrian mall of Calle Florida, which bisects this area from

east to west, is one of the most familiar arteries to tourists, and serves as a focal point for the whole city.

We will start strolling from the **Casa Rosada**, the seat of the government, at the intersection of Av. Alem and Plaza de Mayo. This majestic building serves as the office of the president of the Republic, and holds an impressive library and a museum in its right wing (entrance trough Hipólito Yrigoyen 219, Tel. 46-9841; open Wed. and Thur., 9am-2pm, and Sundays, 2-6pm). The pink walls of its impressive facade derive from a decree issued by Sarmiento as president (in the 1870's), which tried to avoid the winning party at each election (the Red or the White party) to paint the building with its representative colour. The square in front of it, **Plaza de Mayo**, is considered by many to be the heart of the whole country. This square has witnessed huge demonstrations proclaiming both joyful events and times of sorrow. A white pyramid in the center of the square symbolizes peace and liberty. During the black years of the military regime, the square was the meeting point for hundreds of mothers who would gather there each Thursday, petitioning the government for information regarding dear ones who had disappeared during the civil war of 1976-1977.

Around the square are some of the city's most important buildings, such as the **Cathedral**, where General José de San Martín is buried. San Martín died in exile in France, but his body was brought back for reburial in Argentina. Soldiers wearing the uniform of San Martín's army stand guard over his tomb. Nearby is the **Cabildo** or town council, which houses a museum dedicated to the revolt against Spain in 1810 (Bolívar 65, Tel. 30-1782; open Tues.-Fri. and Sun., 3-7pm and during the summer from 4-7pm). Six blocks west along Ave. de Mayo, you will arrive at Ave. 9 de Julio, which the people of Buenos Aires swear is the widest in the world. Another 800 yards down Ave. de Mayo, is **Plaza del Congreso**, which is the largest public square in the city. In the center are fascinating statues, and, at the western end, the **Congress Building**. This majestic building, whose facade includes a monument to the Independence Congress of 1816, serves as the seat of the National Legislature. In 1976, when the Congress ceased functioning, the building was sealed off, until it was reopened at the end of 1983 with the restoration of democracy. One can take a guided tour of the splendid halls of the Congress Building, and sometimes the tour includes a visit to the office of a member of Congress (Av. Rivadavia 1860; Mon.-Fri., 4-8pm; closed January and February).

Turning north into Ave. 9 de Julio will bring us to cafés, restaurants, stores, and offices. The mighty **Obelisk** will be the first to catch our attention. Situated in **Plaza de la República**, the Obelisk, which is some 70 m tall, was erected in 1936 to mark the quarter centenary of the city and serves as a central landmark. Two blocks further on, on the west side of the street, looms the magnificent **Teatro Colón** (Tucumán 1161, Tel. 35-1430; open Mon.-Fri., 10am-4pm, and Sat. 10am-1pm; closed during the summer); built in 1908 from materials specially imported from all over the world. The most outstanding of its palatial halls is the Salón Dorado (golden hall) which is reserved for gala occasions. Its roof is covered with gold, and the hall itself is furnished with splendid crystal chandeliers and wall decorations. The auditorium is unusually impressive, with seats for 2500 people, and standing room for another 1000. The accoustics are superb, making amplifiers unnecessary. The audience occupies an elegant seating area and seven tiers of boxes upholstered in red velvet. The stage is huge — twice the size of the seating area. It is partitioned by a special metal screen, which is both fireproof and soundproof, so that while an orchestra is rehearsing on the front part of the stage, a dance troupe can practice behind the screen, without disturbing each other. Operating the stage is a difficult and complex procedure. The scenery can be suspended from the rafters, or stood on the revolving stage. The cellars of the theater are no less impressive. The three floors below ground level are used by 1000 employees for preparing costumes, wigs, shoes (the shoe department has thousands of pairs of shoes!), jewelry, laundry, and more. The Teatro Colón is without doubt the largest and most impressive artistic institution in the whole of Latin America. You should definitely take a guided tour of the building, which must be booked in advance. And if you are a lover of culture, attendance at one of the performances of the theatre is *de rigueur* (for details, see "Entertainment and cultural events").

You can take Calle Lavalle from the Teatro Colón, bringing you back to **Florida**. This pedestrian mall, full of stores, is the tourist's favorite shopping area, and yet, in spite of this, is not much more expensive than other parts of the city. There is an abundance and variety of goods, all according to the latest fashion (see "Shopping", below). Calle Lavalle and Avenida Corrientes, are the nightlife and entertainment centers, with many movie theaters, restaurants, and nightclubs (see "Entertaiment and cultural events"). A few steps to the left (north) on Florida, is the main shopping area. Many of the entrances actually lead to the *galerías*, or huge enclosed shopping malls, containing dozens of stores and colorful stands. It will cost you some effort not to spend money here.

At the end of Calle Florida is Buenos Aires' most important

Plaza de Mayo — Casa Rosada

and well-kept square, the **Plaza San Martín**, with its equestrian statue of the *Libertador*. To the right is **Plaza Britania** with its copy of London's famous Big Ben, and the **Retiro** train and bus terminal. (Incidentally, after the Falklands War, Plaza Britania was renamed Airforce Square.) The **Defence Ministry** and alongside it a **Military Museum** (Av. Santa Fe 750, Tel. 312-9774, open Wed. to Fri., 3-7pm; closed from mid-December to mid-March) are also situated in Plaza San Martín. Continuing westward, you can stroll along the impressive **Ave. Santa Fe** with its exclusive shops.

The northwest
Now that you are familiar with the downtown, you will want to visit other areas, which are no less interesting than the center itself. We will start with the northwestern sector of the city, the **Recoleta** district. Although the Recoleta is famous mainly for its nightlife (see "Entertainment and cultural events"), it is well worth a visit by day. Among its site is the **National Cemetery**, with the tombs of many of the city's outstanding personalities amid well tended lawns and shrubbery. A stone's throw away is the **National Museum of Fine Arts** (Av. del Libertador 1473; Tel. 803-8817; open Tues.-Sun., 9am-12.45pm, and 3pm-6.45pm, closed during January and the first half of February). This museum, which houses the works of Argentinian artists as well

A street in La Boca

as an European collection, is the most important in the city. A little further on is the imposing neo-classical building of the **Law Faculty**, which is situated near the **Italpark** — a huge amusement park, also recommended for adults.

Continuing in the same direction, you will come across another park — **Parque Palermo** (on maps it is designated by its official name: *Parque 3 de Febrero*). This huge park, which extends from the Aeroparque to Ave. Santa Fe, contains enchanting botanical gardens, a large zoo, sports fields, a luxurious racetrack, a bicycle track, a large planetarium, and much more. If you are a sports fan, the park offers a wide variety of equipment for rent, especially on weekends.

Olivos and Tigre
To the northwest is the prestigious suburb of Olivos, home to diplomats, government officials, and the president himself. The neighboring suburb of Tigre is where the Nazi criminal Adolf Eichmann was captured. Both suburbs nestle on the edge of the river. Olivos boasts a large marina as well as a picturesque arts-and-crafts fair every Sunday (see "Shopping"). Tigre, which borders the river delta, has many sports and recreation clubs as well as a landing stage for small boats.

La Boca

South of the center is the port district of **La Boca**, where Pedro de Mendoza laid the foundations for modern Buenos Aires. The area is full of industrial buildings. La Boca's population is mainly of Italian extraction. Bus 33 from Paseo Colón (behind the Casa Rosada) will take you to this picturesque quarter in a matter of 15 minutes. Most of its houses are painted in bright colors and richly ornamented, often with curiosities brought back by sailors. Many of the houses are built of sheet metal, because it's cheap. In this quarter you can absorb some of the enchanting atmosphere of the Italian colony, see half-sunk ships that will never again venture on the open seas, stroll among the work of local artists and sculptors on **Calle Caminito**, and, if you are lucky, you will be able to catch performances of a street theater (the Tourist Information Center can provide you with details). Then towards evening, to round off your day, go into one of the many clubs dotting the area, for a meal and entertainment (see "Entertainment and cultural events").

San Telmo

Between La Boca and Plaza de Mayo nestles the small but no less interesting San Telmo quarter. With its colonial architecture, it has become an artists' and fun-seekers' paradise with an abundance of restaurants, clubs, antique stores, art galleries, etc. The heart of the quarter is Ave. Independencia, which is within walking distance of Ave. de Mayo (eight blocks south along Calle Perú — the continuation of Florida). You can also take bus 29 from La Boca. Stroll through the pleasant streets of San Telmo with their red-brick houses, and enjoy the special atmosphere of the neighborhood. On Sundays mornings, there is an impressive flea market in **Plaza Dorrego**, intersection of Bolívar and Humberto (see "Shopping"). During the evening you can hear the rhythmic strains of the tango emanating from the open windows of the nightclubs — an experience you should definitely not miss (see "Entertainment and cultural events").

Entertainment and cultural events

Buenos Aires has a rich and varied nightlife. Whatever you fancy, you will find it here — and plenty of it. Details on current films, folklore presentations, plays, concerts, ballets, opera and other events can be found conveniently in the "Stage and Screen" section of the English language *Buenos Aires Herald*. We will begin here with an exposition of the various options.

Amusement park: Italpark has its entrance on Ave. Libertador. It provides dozens of the latest rides. The young, and the young at heart, are assured of a good time.

Bars: These are found all over the city (some are called *whiskerías*). The bars in Calle Reconquista (parallel to Florida) are frequented mainly by students and young people. They are inexpensive and the atmosphere is casual. These bars represent an excellent opportunity for getting to know young Argentinians, many of whom speak English. Recoleta too has its liberal quota of bars and cafés, but these are more exclusive, more expensive, and have a less intimate atmosphere.

Cinema: Over 300 movie theaters are located in all parts of the city, open day and night. The most convenient (as far as location is concerned) are those situated on Corrientes and Lavalle streets, and their selection is more than adequate. The films are usually in the original language, with Spanish subtitles. Tickets for evening showings should be purchased several hours in advance. Reduced price tickets can be bought in the gallery **Paseo La Plaza**, local 19; Tel. 45-7117 (int. 219).

Nightclubs and discotheques: These can be classed according to the neighborhood. Recoleta has a large number of discotheques with the latest music. The admission charge is high, but usually includes the first drink. The discotheques are crammed with young well dressed Argentinians, especially on Friday and Saturday nights. Then the whole area radiates a warm and pleasant weekend spirit. You will find an altogether different style of dancing in the La Boca and San Telmo districts. This is the cradle of the legendary tango; here the tango still rules, and from here its fame has spread throughout the world.

The nightclubs offer shows that include popular singers, musicians, comedians, and the like. Some of them serve drinks, and even meals. Among the best is the *Michelangelo Club.*

Plays, concerts and opera: The more traditional forms of evening entertainment are also available. Thirty theaters offer a wide variety of plays; of course in this case a knowledge of Spanish is essential. On the other hand, no knowledge of Spanish is required to enjoy the many excellent concerts, operas, and ballets performed in the capital.

Certainly, the most rewarding experience is to attend such a performance in the **Teatro Colón**. The high quality of its chorus and orchestra attracts world famous conductors, musicians and singers, who have set uncompromising artistic standards for the institution as a whole. It is difficult to obtain a seat. The box office is open every day from 10am, but usually only standing room is available, and even these tickets have to be bought a day in advance (at the box office, you can book only for that day's performance or the next day's). The vitality of the performance and the unforgettable experience it represents justify both your efforts to obtain a ticket and the discomfort of standing. Conventional evening dress is the rule for such performances. Concerts and ballets are given on days when there is no opera. The season at the Teatro Colón begins in April and continues into November-December. Performances begin at 9pm.

Banks and currency exchange

If you exchange dollars in a bank or a froeign exchange office (*casa de cambio*) you will receive the official rate (1 peso = 1 dollar) minus the regular commission. There's no problem at all to change travelers' checks or collecting transfers from abroad. Nevertheless, some people will offer you a somewhat higher rate for cash (specially for American currency) in the area known as **Microcentro**, the financial *City* of Buenos Aires, and mainly in Calle San Martín, between Sarmiento and Córdoba. The changers will identify you with ease, but you should be very cautious. If you have local friends who are willing to exchange money for you — so much the better. When you buy in stores in Florida, you can usually pay in dollars. Ask for the price of goods in pesos and then offer to pay in dollars — most shopkeepers will agree.

Before leaving the capital for other parts of the country, change enough money to cover all your expenses. In small towns you will encounter considerable difficulty in exchanging foreign currency, especially travelers' checks. Before changing money, compare the rates of the various moneychangers: the rates can vary significantly, and this is valid mainly for European currencies.

Postal and telephone services

The central post office is in Ave. Alem, between Corrientes and Sarmiento; it is open from 8am-8pm, (Tel. 311-5031). It offers telex, telegram, and international telephone services. Generally speaking, service is prompt and efficient. Sending a parcel, however, is a complex procedure, since the rates are based on weight classes, which change every so often, and an extra ounce can cause the price to shoot up. While sending parcels by air is very expensive, sea-mail, although slower, is as safe and cheaper. Customs and post office clerks inspect parcels, and are likely to raise many objections, for example refusing to accept clothes unless you have a laundry ticket to prove they are clean, etc. You must prepare a detailed list of all items in the parcel and leave it open for inspection at the post office. Only after this inspection will you be allowed to seal the parcel and hand it over for delivery.

International phone calls can be made from the Telephone Company's offices at the intersection of Avenida Corrientes and Calle Maipú, and it is open 24 hours a day. Rates vary according to destination, but to most countries calls are much cheaper during the weekends.

Photographic supplies

You would be best advised to come equipped with photographic supplies; but if you haven't managed to do so, you will find Argentina far cheaper than her neighbors in this respect. *Kodak* has its central office near Teatro Colón, where you can receive advice and assistance, as well as buy supplies and have film developed.

Books and periodicals in English

The capital has 800 bookstores, which sell an impressive variety of books from all over the world. All the stores on Florida sell books in English. International magazines, such as *Time* and *Newsweek*, are sold in most kiosks, particularly along Calle Florida. The *Buenos Aires Herald* is the local English-language daily, with a broad coverage of international news.

Shopping

In this field too, as in all others, Buenos Aires is noted for the rich variety of its shopping malls and available goods. The Argentinians invested a lot of money and effort into making shopping a pleasant and agreeable experience, and simply walking around the stores and galerias is enjoyable in its own right. You will find an endless array of clothes and shoes, souvenirs, arts and crafts, to mention but a few. Your problem will be not what to buy, but rather what not to buy.

Let's begin with leather goods, which are the pride of the nation. Here you can find absolutely everything, from traditional leather goods such as shoes, belts, coats, and purses, to the latest fashion in leather shirts, slacks, suitcases, and even book-bindings. Argentina's leather goods are beautiful and contemporary, and cheaper than in Europe. On the other hand, their quality is moderate, more or less comparable to that of leather goods from the Far East.

Calle Florida has many stores that sell leather coats and other leather goods — the largest and most impressive being the *Ciudad del Cuero* (city of leather) at Florida 940 (Tel. 311-4721), corner of Paraguay. The various boutiques of this magnificent galeria offer an impressive variety of exclusive high quality and limited edition designs. Alongside women's suits, jackets, and coats, you will find all sorts of leather accessories, including shoes, gloves, belts, purses and suitcases. On the second floor to the right is an art gallery with a fair selection of paintings, and a pleasant café. Further down the street (Florida 738) is *Bigs* which specializes in good quality coats and jackets at more reasonable prices.

Further on, you will pass by the famous shoe store, *Botticelli*, which has branches all over the world. Here you can purchase an excellent pair of shoes of superb design, workmanship, and material, at a price lower than at the New York, Paris, or Rome outlets (though still very expensive).

And finally the prestigious store, *Pullman*, which carries leather goods of superb quality at very high prices.

You can buy clothes in almost any store. Pierre Cardin and Yves Saint Laurent are prominent, and so are their prices, but they are still far less expensive than in other countries and they specialize in the very latest fashions. If you are a clothes-conscious male, you will find a good selection of top quality shirts, jackets, and trousers at *MacTailor's* — but again prices are high. At the giant branch of the British chain store, *Harrod's*, you will find absolutely everything somewhere among the four floors of tastefully displayed merchandise, and at reasonable prices.

Contemporary design quality leather goods can be had more cheaply than on Florida at *Campanera dalla Fontana* on Reconquista 735 (Tel. 311-1229). The store offers a wide selection of styles in different kinds of leather. Recommended!

The larger woman will find superb quality wear, of the best and latest design at *Medigrand*, in the store on Paraguay 665 just off Florida, or in one of the branch stores located throughout the city.

"Professional shoppers" whose appetite has merely been whetted in Calle Florida, can indulge themselves on Ave. Santa Fe, with its thousands of stores displaying an endless variety of goods. It is a good idea to make a tour of the stores first in order to compare prices (which are in any case expensive!). Bargaining is not proper here, but you need not feel ashamed of asking for a discount (*descuento*). If you are looking for arts and crafts or gifts, this is the place for you. But bear in mind that the nearer you get to the center and Calle Florida, the higher the prices. Nevertheless, this is the most convenient place to find such goods.

In addition to the prestigious stores downtown, the tourist will have an excellent opportunity to savor the special atmosphere of the various markets held here every Sunday. One of the most enjoyable and interesting is the antique market in Plaza Dorrego in San Telmo (see "Tourist sites"). The market opens in the morning and closes in the early afternoon. Here you can find a wide selection of antiques, ranging from furniture, telephones, coins, jewelry, and household items, to a variety of original souvenirs. You should, while in the area, also take a look at the various shops and pawnbrokers in the neighborhood. A marvelous arts and crafts fair is open every Sunday afternoon in the suburb of Olivos — excellent for handicrafts and souvenirs at reasonable prices. There are a number of markets in Buenos Aires itself which sell goods ranging from pets, books, coins and antique bank notes to second-hand clothes and just plain junk.

In the last years the big malls are in fashion. Some of them sell also bulky articles. Among the most popular, the elegant *Patio Bullrich* in Calle Posadas 1245, and the *Spinetto Shopping Center* on the block of the Calles Alsina, Moreno, Matheu and Pichincha, close to the National Congress; *Alto Palermo Shopping*, on Avenida Santa Fe and Coronel Díaz, and the *Salguero Shopping*, on Salguero and Avenida del Libertador, close to the new National Library.

Important phone numbers and addresses
U.S. Embassy: Colombia 430, Palermo (Tel. 774-7611).
Tourist Office (*Subsecretaría de Turismo*): Ave. Santa Fe 883 (Tel. 325-550/2232).
Emergencies: 107.
Ambulance: Tel. 344-4001; 923-1051/9.

Police: Tel. 101.
Official time: 113.
Radio Taxi: Tel. 93-4991/9; 552-2939; 953-4206; 953-7335; 47-2806; 47-2466; 47-3538.

Airlines
Aerolíneas Argentinas: Perú 2, 393-5122.
Austral Líneas Aéreas: Av. Corrientes 485, Tel. 49-9011

The Iguazú Falls

When you see the torrents of water thundering down on all sides, you cannot help being stirred by that feeling of awe one experiences when in the presence of Nature in all her sublimity. The Iguazú Falls, among the largest and most impressive in the world, are an enthralling experience, an amazing sight of overwhelming height, which gives the abstract words "natural wonder" a real and unforgettable meaning.

Of all the natural wonders and landscapes that South America has to offer the tourist, these gigantic falls, located on the border of Brazil and Argentina, near the common border with Paraguay, are of the most impressive. It is not surprising that they draw more than two million visitors annually. Every second, nearly 450,000 gallons of water come crashing down over a distance of 4 km, in hundreds of subsidiary waterfalls that are 60 to 80 meters high. This magnificent sight, together with the clouds of spray that envelop the area and the incessant roar of the cascading waters, recreates primeval nature in all her glory. And as if to complete the legendary quality of the place, the whole area is covered by a luxuriant tangle of tropical growth, a study in bright green, a feast for the eye.

How to get there
From Brazil: There is daily bus service to Foz do Iguaçu (the town on the Brazilian side of the falls) from Rio de Janeiro (travel time: 24 hours), São Paulo (17 hours), and Curitiba (12 hours). The buses are luxurious and the roads are good. The buses leave from the central bus station at all hours of the day and night. You must buy your ticket **at least** one day in advance!

Cruzeiro do Sul and *Varig* fly daily from Rio via São Paulo to Foz, and back.

From Argentina: The falls are 300 km from Posadas, and many buses run from the Posadas train station to Puerto Iguazú (the town on the Argentinian side of the falls). A train leaves Buenos Aires daily for Posadas. The journey takes about 20 hours, and from there you must continue by bus to the falls. *Expreso Singer* has a direct bus several times a day from Retiro Station to Posadas (20 hours) and on to Puerto Iguazú (4 more hours).

Aerolíneas Argentinas runs regular and frequent flights from

ARGENTINA

IGUAZÚ FALLS

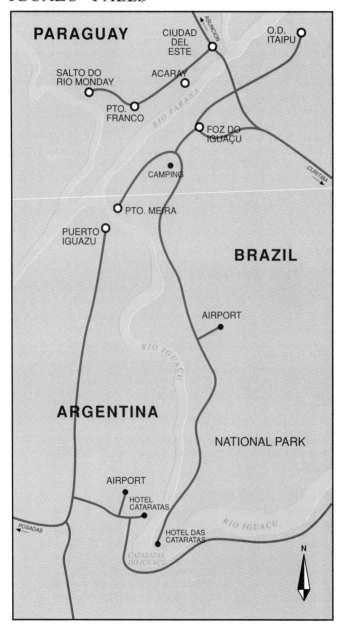

Buenos Aires to Posadas, from which buses leave frequently for Puerto Iguazú. Direct flights to Iguazú, and especially return flights, are heavily booked.

From Paraguay: Buses from Asunción cover the distance to Foz in about seven hours, along Paraguay's only paved highway. The *Nuestra Señora*, *Rapido Iguazú*, and Pluma companies run several buses a day to the Brazilian side (Foz) and back. The buses are comfortable and the journey pleasant, usually with one intermediate stop.

Food and lodging
You have three options: to stay in Puerto Iguazú (Argentina), to stay in Foz do Iguaçu (Brazil), or to stay in Ciudad del Este (Paraguay). Your best bet is Brazil, since it offers the best tourist facilities. So, if you're coming from Brazil, stay there until you continue your journey. If you're coming from Argentina on the way to Brazil, cross the border and stay in Foz. And if you're coming from Asunción, the same advice holds: cross the bridge to the Brazilian side.

Foz do Iguaçu (Brazil)
This city of more than 200,000 people is geared entirely to cater to the local and foreign tourists who come to visit the famous falls. Its long avenues and adjacent streets are packed with dozens of hotels of varying quality.

Where to stay
Hotel das Cataratas: Rod. das Cataratas km 28; tel. 74-2666, fax 74-1688. Opposite the falls, superb view.
Diplomat: Av. Brasil 278; tel. 73-3155. A walking distance from downtown.
Foz do Iguaçu: Av. Brasil 97, tel. 74-4455, fax 74-1775. Cheaper.

Behind the bus station you will find the popular restaurants where you can sit outside and enjoy a good and inexpensive meal.

Puerto Iguazú (Argentina)
The town has many hostels and hotels of reasonable quality covering all ranges of prices.

Internacional Iguazú: Parque Nacional, tel. 20790. The most luxurious and expensive (about US$ 150 a double room with a view to the falls, slightly cheaper if it doesn't), with a swimming pool, casino and an excellent restaurant; situated along the falls.
Esturión: Av. Tres Fronteras 650, tel. 20020. Another five-star hotel, in town.

Cataratas: Ruta 12, km 4, tel. 21100. Four stars, very good service.
Alexander: Av. Córdoba 665, tel. 20633. Three stars.
Libertador, P. Moreno y Bonpland (near the bus station), tel. 20416. Three stars.
Paraná: Av. Brasil 367, tel. 20399. Very modest, and yet can be recommended.

Near the bus station you can find cheaper arrangements in hostels (*hospedajes* and *hosterías*).

There are also several camping sites nearby; the best is *Pindo*, 1/2 km outside town in the direction of the falls (buses from town to the falls pass by the entrance).

As far as food is concerned, you will not go hungry. All the large hotels have good restaurants — offering both Argentinian and Brazilian cuisine — and there is no shortage of restaurants in town. Behind the bus station you will find the popular restaurants where you can sit outside and enjoy a good and inexpensive meal.

Evening is a good time to visit Ciudad del Este, a city still referred by many as Puerto Stroessner, its former name, with its streets crammed with stores, restaurants, and casinos. Prices here vary according to the changing value of the dollar in the neighboring countries, so that sometimes you will find "bargains" and sometimes everything is outrageously expensive.

How to tour and what to see
The falls are on the border, but more than 80% of them are in Argentinian territory. The best vantage point, where you can see the entire falls in all their vast splendor, the rich foliage, and the surrounding area, is undoubtedly from the Brazilian side. Every hour, buses marked *Cataratas* or *Parque Nacional* leave the central bus station in Foz for the falls. The journey lasts about 30 minutes; after you have paid you will be let off in front of the luxurious *Hotel das Cataratas*. From here you follow a long, winding path through the dense undergrowth to the heart of the waterfall area, where you can look out over the whole region — a truly breathtaking sight. The most exciting part of the hike is crossing the narrow bridge that leads almost into the heart of the great **Floviano Falls** — and being soaked to the skin by the flying spray. At the bottom of the cliffs is a small elevator to take you back up to the top, from where you can return to the hotel (lunch at its excellent restaurant is highly recommended), and back to town (buses leave once every hour). Before returning to town you may wish to turn right,

The Iguazú Falls

into the beautiful park, and enjoy the thousands of magnificent butterflies. On the Brazilian side, a helicopter ride to the site is available (*Helisul*, tel. 74-2414.)

You will need more time to visit the Argentinian side of the falls, but don't spare this time. Buses leave for the falls from Puerto Iguazú (near the Tourist Office in the main street); the trip lasts about half-an-hour. Here, too, you have to pay the admission fee to the park before getting off the bus. Then you can start walking the miles of concrete paths alongside the torrential falls. Walking along these narrow paths is an extraordinary experience, with water thundering by on all sides soaking you with its spray, and the wondrous sight of the falling arc that splits apart at the bottom of the falls. You can walk for hours and not tire of the sublime views, the breathtaking beauty, the unbridled power, the vastness of it all. On this side, the paths lead in various directions, all clearly marked. The last bus back to town leaves at 6pm.

The Argentinian and Brazilian waterfalls are situated on either side of the Iguaçu River ("raging waters" in Guarani — the language of the Paraguayan Indians). In order to travel from one side to the other you must cross the border and the river. Crossing from Argentina to Brazil is a simple matter — all you have to do is walk to the river bank and take the ferry over. (Cars are also allowed on the ferry although not at all seasons). Once in Brazil your passport will be stamped, and then you can board any bus for Foz itself, and go on to the falls.

If you want to cross from Brazil to Argentina, take the bus marked *Porto Meira* from the central bus station to the river, and then the ferry over to Argentina. If you plan to return to your initial side of the border the same day, you don't have to have your passport stamped. Just tell the immigrations official what you're planning — if you're coming from Brazil, you can obtain a visa from the Argentinian consulate in Foz.

When you visit the falls wear comfortable walking shoes with skid-proof soles, and take along a plastic bag in which to put your camera and papers so they won't get wet.

Itaipú

Twenty kilometers upstream from Foz, at Itaipú, Brazil and Paraguay have erected on the Parana River a giant hydroelectric plant, one of the largest in the world, which since 1984 supplies some 12,000 megawatts of power. This bi-national venture was a heavy economic burden on both countries, being very criticised. The plant was originally intended primarily to meet

Brazil's power needs. Paraguay undertook to sell Brazil the surplus energy generated by the dam, and anticipates revenues of hundreds of millions of dollars a year from the sale.

Travel agents in Foz organize trips to the plant, which include slide shows and explanations of the construction of the huge dam. Although you will only be allowed to visit certain sections of the site, it is very interesting.

The construction of this immense dam caused the destruction of a wonderful nature spot — the Sete Quedas waterfalls, the volume of whose waters was double that of the Niagara Falls. The project caused the flooding of vast areas upstream, and no trace is left of the waterfalls, which are now buried under lago do Itaipú — the lake which was created when the dam was built.

Central Region

Mar del Plata

Mar del Plata (the Silver Sea) lies 410 km south of Buenos Aires. It is the Argentinians' favorite holiday resort. Spread along the shores of the Atlantic, with broad beaches and sunny weather, the city has become an important entertainment and tourist center, with hotels, casinos, restaurants and other attractions to delight the vacationer. Hundreds of thousands of people make the five-hour journey from Buenos Aires to Mar del Plata for a yearly holiday or short weekend break.

The peak season is in the summer, from October to April/May, when the city's population of 400,000 swells to include an additional 2.5 million vacationers! If you can possibly avoid visiting Mar del Plata during this season, do so. If not, book your hotel well in advance.

The main attraction is of course the sea (bathing in Buenos Aires' Río de la Plata is forbidden because of pollution). The beaches are equipped with deck chairs, cafés and other services. The **Playa Grande** (Large Beach) is the most prestigious, and has private beach clubs open to members only. Nearby are the most luxurious hotels and restaurants. **Bristol Beach** contains the city's largest and most famous casino. Near **Playa Perla** and around the bus station are the cheapest hotels and pensions. All the beaches rent a large variety of sporting equipment, such as scuba gear, boats, fishing tackle, water skis, etc.

Trains leave Constitución station in the capital for Mar del Plata almost hourly, and the trip takes less than five hours. The trains continue south to Bahia Blanca and Bariloche. There are many buses on the same route. *Aerolíneas* and *Austral* run daily flights to the capital (40 minutes). By car the trip takes about 5 hours on Route 2. The area around Mar del Plata has **lagoons** and **nature reserves** where you can camp and enjoy the quiet, tranquil and pleasant beaches.

Where to stay
Dorá: Buenos Aires 1841, Tel. 2-5002, fax 9-0772. Four stars, very good service.
Provincial: Blvd. Marítimo 2502, Tel. 2-4081. By the beach and next to the Casino building, four stars; very expensive.

Gran Hotel Casino: Boulevard Marítimo 2300, Tel. 2-4011. Three stars, in the twin building of the Provincial, a bit more moderate.
Argentino: Belgrano 2225, Tel. 3-0091. Three stars.
Catedral: Moreno 2327, Tel. 2-3770. Inexpensive.

Where to eat
There is no problem to find a suitable restaurant for every taste and every budget. In Mar del Plata we recommend the seafood:

La Forcheta: Almafuerte 247.
El Timón: in the port.
Taberna Baska: 12 de Octubre 3301.

Córdoba
Córdoba disputes with Rosario being the second largest town in Argentina, with its million inhabitants, and is an important commercial and economic center. The main tourist attractions are not in the city itself but in the province, especially for health tourism in the lakes and the hills. Córdoba was founded in 1573 as Córdoba de la Nueva Andalucía, and its university runs since 1614, being the oldest in the country. People in Argentina nickname this town *La Docta* ("the well educated") and its student population developed a tradition of upheaval; here started many of the crucial movements in the country's recent history.

The modern office towers that have sprung up over the last decades have almost entirely replaced the colonial buildings and the city's numerous churches, but a few still stand in the shadow of these giant new edifices. We can see the principal remnants of bygone days precisely downtown, around the **Plaza San Martín**, with the old **Cabildo** (colonial Town Council) which serves now as HQ of the provincial police force, and the old **Cathedral** consacrated in 1872, its main tower dating from 1752. Many figures of the country's history are buried here. Behind it are the **Santa Catalina Monastery** and the residence of the Bishop, where the Tourist Information Center operates (Rosario de Santa Fe 39, Tel. 35-041).

One block from here, is the house which belonged to the later Viceroy Rafael de Sobremonte, build in 1712. Perhaps the most beautiful colonial house in town, it is now the site of the **Provincial Historical Museum** (Rosario de Santa Fe 218, Tel. 44-837).

Where to stay
Córdoba is in the very center of Argentina, geographically and

economically. That's why tourism is so developed here, as one can see even in one of the best organized bus stations in Argentina, and one of the largest airports (international). The city offers many hotels of different standards.

César C. Carman: Av. Sabattini 439, Tel. 34-516. Four stars, next to Parque Sarmiento.

Crillón: Rivadavia 65, Tel. 46-093. Four stars, at the very center of the city; one of the favorites among businessmen, perhaps because of its fine French restaurant.

Dorá: Entre Ríos 70, Tel. 42-031, fax 24-0167. Well located, good service.

Mediterráneo: M.T. de Alvear 10, Tel. 24-0094. Four stars.

Nogaró: San Jerónimo 137, Tel. 22-4001. Four stars.

Felipe II: San Jerónimo 279, Tel. 44-752. Three stars, moderate.

Ritz: San Jerónimo 495, Tel. 45-031. Three stars, moderate.

Waldorf: Av. Olmos 531, Tel. 28-051. Three stars, close to the train station.

Royal: J.D. Perón 180, Tel. 45-000. Next to the central bus station, two stars.

In the area close to the train and the bus station, you can find many inexpensive hotels.

Where to eat

But first, a few words about what to eat; one of the typical dishes of Córdoba is the mackerel and other fish varieties from the many rivers and lagoons of the province. However, during the summer, fish can be spoiled very quickly. Avoid raw vegetables and fruits. In July, during the annual "Córdoba's sweet tradition" or whenever they visit the town, lovers of sweets must try the *alfajores* filled with fruit jam and the local *dulce de leche* (milk jam, very sweet). Córdoba's honey is also famous, produced in San Marcos Sierra.

La Alameda: Obispo Trejo 170. Regional cuisine
Hamster: P. Lugones 370. German
Emir: Blvd. Illia 71. One of the many Arab restaurants in town.
Granix: Nueve de Julio 32. Vegetarian.

From Córdoba you can reach almost every point of the country; buses link the town with Buenos Aires (10 hours), Tucumán (10 hours), Salta (14 hours) and Mendoza (10 hours). Buses also run several times a week to Posadas and the Iguazú Falls; the journey takes close to 24 hours. There is a train service from Córdoba to Buenos Aires in the south, and to Tucumán in the north.

Mendoza

This pleasant city, the Argentinian wine capital, is named after Pedro de Mendoza, who founded Buenos Aires in 1560. Mendoza was almost entirely destroyed by an earthquake in 1860 and was rebuilt — with low houses. Today, the city itself has a population of 200,000 and preserves an aura of quiet provinciality and friendliness. The province of Mendoza is richly endowed with natural reserves of petroleum, uranium, marble and lead, to mention but a few, all of which accelerated industrial development. The harvest of her many vineyards goes into her world famous wines. Mendoza has 1400 wineries, which have made Argentina into the fourth largest wine producer in the world.

How to get there

Mendoza lies on the highway linking Buenos Aires with Santiago de Chile. Route 7 from the capital will take you right to the Chilean border, 200 km west of the city. There are many buses from Buenos Aires to Mendoza's spacious central bus station (a 20-hour trip). There are also buses from Córdoba (10 hours), and from Santiago de Chile across the Andes. There are several buses a week to Bariloche (a day's journey) and Tucumán.

There are two trains each evening to and from Buenos Aires. The route is extremely pleasant, passing as it does through green fertile plains. *Aerolíneas* and *Austral* have flights to Mendoza from Buenos Aires, Santiago, Bariloche and Córdoba. Night flights are cheaper than day flights.

Where to stay

There is no shortage of hotels, and they cater to all tastes and budgets.

Plaza: Av. Chile 1124, Tel. + fax 23-3000. Four stars, luxurious and expensive.
Aconcagua: San Lorenzo 545, Tel. 24-2321, fax 31-1085. Four stars.
Mendoza: Av. España 1210, Tel. 25-2000. Three stars, well located.
Palace: Av. Las Heras 70, Tel. 23-4200. Two stars, moderate, close to the train station.
Budget-class hotels are concentrated around the train station. There are also camping sites near town. One of them is *Cámping Challao*, Av. Champagnat, El Challao, 6 km from town.

Where to eat

The main street, the Avenida San Martín, has plenty of

restaurants and cafés, and so is Avenida Las Heras. You can eat well and cheap at the Municipal Market.

We don't have to remind you to taste local wine. Ice cream parlours are very popular here.

Tourist services
The **Tourist Office** is housed in a large building half way along Ave. San Martín (Block 11). Its staff will gladly supply you with comprehensive information and referals to the wineries. You should definitely take advantage of their services.

During the winter, the surrounding villages and small towns turn into **ski resorts**. Ski buffs can hire equipment and indulge their passion.

What to see
The beautiful streets of Mendoza are shaded by numerous trees that spread a pleasant atmosphere through the city. To these must be added the large, handsome **Park** named after **General San Martín**, which serves as a rest and recreation center for resident and visitor alike. In this spacious park, which lies at the foot of the mountains on the western side of the city, are a large lake, a zoo, and other attractions. The huge amphitheatre is the scene of the traditional **Wine Festival** celebrated the first Saturday of March every year — one of the most impressive festivals in the whole of Argentina. The large entrance gates to the park were imported from London in 1908. The camping site is located not far from them.

The city takes great pride in the fact that Mendoza was the launching point for General José de San Martín's campaign against the Spaniards across the Andes. During this campaign he helped Chile and then Peru (to which he traveled by sea) to achieve their independence. San Martín delivered an impassioned speech to the inhabitants of Mendoza, requesting their help in the war effort, and they gave generously of their jewelry and money. This historical event has been commemorated in the huge **monument** that stands in the middle of the park. At the southern tip of the lake, the building with the shape of a ship houses the small **Natural History Museum** (Tel. 23-0971). Within a walking distance lies **Plaza Independencia**, in the center.

Avenida San Martín, the main avenue, accommodates most of the city's public buildings, important offices, large stores, cafés and restaurants. In the afternoons and evenings the street is crowded with people, and its multicolored lighting blends in well with the atmosphere.

A trek in the Mendoza region

Mendoza's **Civic Center** is very impressive. It contains the district government buildings, the law courts and the municipal offices, with intervening stretches of well tended lawns, squares and fountains. From the seventh floor of the Municipal Palace you can enjoy the **Terraza Mirador** (Watchtower Terrace), with an incredible landscape. Following through Virgen del Carmen

Mt. Aconcagua

de Cuyo street to Avenida Mitre, you will find the **Government House**, on its fourth floor is the **Flag Hall**, with the original embroidered by the Ladies of Mendoza for San Martín's Army campaign to Chile.

A visit to one of the many **wineries** is, of course, a must. They are in the outskirts (Godoy Cruz, Guaymallén), and guided tours are available, in the course of which you will be able to follow the wine manufacturing process — starting with the initial fermentation, and going on to aging in vats, bottling, keeping the wine at a stable temperature and finally corking. The blend of up-to-date technology and traditional manufacturing methods is especially impressive. Wine tasting is usually offered at the end of the tour.

Some addresses:
Arizu: San Martín 1515, Godoy Cruz, Tel. 24-9207.
Escorihuela: Alvear 41, Godoy Cruz, Tel. 22-0157.
Giol: Carril Ozamis 1040, Maipú, Tel. 97-2535.
Toso: Alberdi 808, San José, Guaymallén, Tel. 25-7855.

On to Chile
You can fly or drive from Mendoza to Chile. Trains no longer ply this route due to lack of passengers. *Aerolíneas* and *Lan*

Chile run several daily flights between Santiago and Buenos Aires, stopping en route at Mendoza.

Traveling overland is a worthwhile experience, since the route passes through a number of interesting sites. Several companies have daily bus service to Santiago; you should buy your ticket at least one day in advance at the central bus station. The *O'higgins* and *Pluma* companies have modern, fast buses (8 hours) and offer excellent service, with stewardesses to see to your comfort.

The journey across the Andes is breathtaking in its beauty, especially in clear weather. The steep summits piercing the deep blue sky, the many tunnels carved into the mountainside, the winding road, take us through one of the largest and most famous mountain ranges in the world. As we travel west along Route 7 we are, in fact, taking the same route as that followed by San Martín's men. We pass Uspallata, a winter holiday resort, before reaching Punta de Vacas, where we will be subjected to Argentinian border formalities which may involve several hours wait. It is prohibited to bring fruit, vegetables, or fresh food into Chile.

Resuming our journey, we pass by **Puente del Inca**, a sport resort, and the best base for trekking in the area of the great mountains surrounding, and for climbing the highest peak in the Americas — the **Aconcagua**, approximately 7000 m.

Puente del Inca is named after the **Inca Bridge** (Puente del Inca), which, in spite of its shape, is a natural formation. It measures 20 m high, 20 m long, and 26 m wide, and is extremely impressive.

After a stop in Las Cuevas, 4200 m above sea level, to complete Chilean immigration formalities, we can continue our trip. The road now twists and turns against a backdrop of a breathtakingly enchanting rocky landscape. The vegetation on this side of the mountains becomes increasingly thicker and greener because the western slopes enjoy abundant rain released by clouds that form over the Pacific Ocean. The rest of the journey takes you through holiday and ski resorts and farming villages along the approach to Santiago de Chile.

Northern Argentina

The parched, mountainous region in the northwest of the country has its own enchanting character. The canyons, the yellow sand and irritating dust, and the many varieties of cactus give the impression of a desert, although in fact the climate here is mild and pleasant.

The local population is mainly Indian and Creole, and the influence of Bolivia to the north is evident in every aspect of the cultural and social life of the area. The white colonial houses with their large windows stand out in contrast to the ancient Indian traditions and folklore, which are apparent in the atmosphere, handicrafts and local songs.

How to get there

Regular rail and bus service connects the large cities in Argentina to Tucumán, Salta, and Jujuy — the main northern cities — as well as these three to one another. On weekdays, three trains a day leave Buenos Aires for Tucumán; over the weekend, there is only one train a day. The fast train (called *Independencia*) takes 17 1/2 hours, otherwise the trip can last 20 hours or more. From the Tucumán train station there are direct bus connections to Salta and Jujuy. You can reserve a seat on one of these buses when buying your train ticket in Buenos Aires, although there is usually no shortage of seats. The Buenos Aires-La Paz train also passes through all three towns. Trains (which are slow) and buses (which are fast) run between the three towns at all hours of the day.

If you want to fly, *Aerolíneas* and *Austral* both have several flights daily between Buenos Aires and Tucumán. Some international flights, mainly from Bolivia and northern Chile, have intermediate stops in Salta or Tucumán. Night flights to Buenos Aires are half-price, but they are very heavily booked and you must reserve a place well in advance.

From Bolivia (the border town is Villazón) you can catch many buses to Jujuy. There is only one passenger train a day, and it is slow, dusty and crowded. If you are traveling at night, bear in mind that it is very cold then, and dress accordingly.

NORTHERN ARGENTINA

Tucumán
San Miguel de Tucumán, which is 1300 km north of Buenos Aires, is the capital of Argentina's smallest province, yet it is the largest and most modern city in the north. This area once marked the southern border of the Inca Empire in what is now Argentina. The people of this town, which was founded in 1565 by Spaniards coming from Bolivia and Peru, lived mainly

A RGENTINA

North Argentina's characteristic flora — the cactus

by trading with northern communities. Tucumán today boasts a population of some 500,000 people and serves as the urban center of the entire northern part of the country.

The architectural remnants of the colonial period are swallowed up by the modern buildings and bustling commercial district. The streets are laid out in a grid pattern, with **Plaza Independencia** (Independence Square) and its statue of liberty at the center. Around the square are the government buildings, the **Church of San Francisco** (which you can visit during services), the **Tourist Office**, and the **Argentinian Automobile Club** (*Automóbil Club Argentino; ACA*).

Behind the square (on Calle 24 de Setiembre) is the **Museum of Folklore**, named after General Belgrano, who won undying fame in the town where his army overcame those loyal to the Spanish crown. The museum houses handicrafts and local works of art.

The most important site in the city is the **Casa Histórica** on Calle Congreso 151, corner of San Lorenzo. It was here that Argentina declared her independence from Spanish rule July 9, 1816. The original building was destroyed, but the actual room where independence was declared survived intact. Today the reconstructed building serves as a museum exhibiting various items from the declaration ceremony, portraits and the like (Tel. 22-0826). Every night you can see the light and sound show *"Tucumán cita a la Patria"* (Tucumán convokes the Fatherland), a revival of the historical events during the days when the representatives of the provinces gathered here, and subsequently decided to cut from the Spanish crown.

The **Miguel Lillo Institute** (*Instituto Miguel Lillo*, Miguel Killo 205, Tel. 23-9868) has an impressive collection of stuffed animals — well worth a visit. Tucumán's **University**, one of the first in Latin America, is at the corner of Ayacucho and General La Madrid streets.

Transportation
The town's **airport** is not far from downtown. The **central bus station** is in Ave. Peña, and the main railway station (General Mitre station) is at Catamarca 500. A centrally located, modern and comfortable **camping site** is situated at the edge of Parque 9 de Julio, near Ave. del Campo.

Tourist services
The **Tourist Office** is at Calle 24 de Setiembre 484 in Plaza Independencia (Tel. 18591). It is open until late evening.

Where to stay
Gran Hotel: Ave. de los Próceres 380, Tel. 22-2596. Near the 9 de Julio Park, an excellent five-star hotel.
Metropol: 24 de Septiembre 524, Tel. 31-1180. Four stars, centrally located.
Corona: on Plaza Independencia, Tel. 21-6219. Four stars, good and modern. One of the central points in town.

Presidente: Monteagudo 249, Tel. 31-1414. Three stars, good service. Swimming pool.

Where to eat
It is very hard for a visitor walking downtown, not to spot the many restaurants. As the range of prices can vary, ask to see the menu before you sit at a table, if it is not exhibited. A very popular *parrilla* (grill) among local people is *La Leñita*, in 25 de Mayo 377. Next to Plaza Urquiza you will find dozens of places to eat and drink. A good one is *La Fondue*.

Salta
The road to Salta — the most beautiful and interesting town in the north — winds through a wilderness of cacti, huge cliffs, wild green countryside, and along small rivers and canyons, under a fiercely blue sky.

Although more than 400 years have gone by since Don Hernando de Lerma founded the town on April 16, 1582, Salta has remained true to the spirit of its founder; the dazzling white houses are still built in the colonial style. The town now has a population of 270,000. The top of **San Bernardo hill** (1454 m above sea level, and 250 m above the city) affords a fine view of the straight avenues, the white houses and the red roofs, which typify Salta.

At the end of Ave. Güemes is the **statue of General Martín Miguel de Güemes**, the town's venerated hero who, together with the gauchos, routed the Spaniards in a frontal attack while General San Martín was attempting to outflank the Spaniards across the mountain range. This local battle, know as the Gaucho War (*Guerra Gaucha*), is celebrated each year by the local population during **Salta Week** (14-20 June), with a series of colorful events including firework displays, floats, popular songs and dances, and more.

Past the statue of the General and blending into the mountain is the **Archaeological Museum** (Ejército del Norte, in the corner with Polo Sud, Tel. 22-2960), with exhibits from various parts of the province.

The heart of the city, the attractive **Plaza 9 de Julio** with its arched buildings, is busy day and night. It houses the government buildings and the beautiful **Cathedral**, which was rebuilt in 1882. Its impressive interior and the **statues of Jesus and Mary**, around which many legends have grown, make it into an interesting and important historical site. The mortal remains of General Martín Miguel de Güemes lie here. You can visit it

Salta

during matins and vespers. On the other side of the square is the **Cabildo**, the Town Council, the oldest building in the city, and as old as Salta itself. Over the course of time the building has undergone many modifications, but the most notable and extensive renovation and expansion work, including the 14 arches and the high balconies, were carried out under Salta's first governor in 1780. The building houses two museums: the **Historical Museum** of the whole northern region, is particularly impressive. It is on the ground floor and open several afternoons a week. Upstairs is the **Regional Art Museum** (Caseros 549). Begining at this building is the modern pedestrian mall of **Calle Alberdi**, full of people day and night, shopping, idling, or in search of entertainment.

A block from the square, at the corner of Calle Caseros and Córdoba, is the magnificent **Church of San Francisco**, which also dates back to the origins of the town, but has been through many metamorphoses before attaining its present form with its conspicuous red and gold steeple. About 100 meters away, on the other side of Plaza 9 de Julio is a beautiful and well tended **square** named after **Manuel Belgrano**, dominated by his statue. The **San Martín park**, opposite the bus terminal, is popular with both children and adults in the afternoons, which is the best time to visit it.

Isolated villages along the "Tren a las Nubes"

On the outskirts of the city is an interesting but relatively expensive **crafts market** (*mercado artesanal*), mainly for tourists (buses 2 and 3 from the center will take you there). The shops opposite the main building are marginally cheaper.

Salta has a variegated folklore, influenced by the popular music and costumes of her northern neighbors (Bolivia). A folklore event is a must while you are here. Details can be obtained at hotels or the Tourist Office.

Around Salta
The Salta region is full of nature sites and if you have enough time you should definitely pay them a visit. The national park **El Rey** (The King), east from Salta on the border of Salta and Jujuy provinces, is considered to be one of the most beautiful nature reserves in the country. Getting there is difficult and complicated, but you will be well rewarded for your efforts.

The little town of **Cachi** is about 4 hours by bus from Salta (160 km). The road in some parts of it offers exceptionaly fine view especially at the impressive gorge of the Quebrada del Escoipe. The pastoral Indian town is a good place to get to know the local *artesanía*. You may wish to go on a round trip on the same day, or you can spend the night there. The town has a middle class hotel, and you can find there also very cheap accommodation.

A special and fascinating trip is the **Tren a las Nubes** (Train to the clouds), from Salta to **San Antonio de los Cobres** and to the Polvorillas viaduct, 63 meters high and 250 meters long. The round trip takes 14 hours, only once a week from May to November. You will enjoy great views and admire the engineering operation, with tunnels, zig-zags and viaducts.

Traveling by the *Tren a las Nubes* is very expensive. The inexpensive alternative is the cargo train that leaves Salta to San Antonio de las Cobres and on to **Socompa**, on the Chilean border. This train is very slow and such a trip will take a few days (take hot clothes and food).

Where to stay
Salta has a good variety of hotels, most of them in the downtown area. Around the bus station you can find several moderately priced. Inexpensive accommodation can be found around the train station.

Salta: Buenos Aires 1, Tel. 21-1011. Next to the square, the best (and most expensive) in town, with a good Italian restaurant.
Portezuelo: Ave. Turística 1, Tel. 21-6027. Somewhat far from

downtown, towards the San Bernardo Hill, four stars, very good service.

Victoria Plaza: Zuviría 16, Tel. 21-1222. Three stars, next to the square.

Residencial Astur. Rivadavia 752. One block from the Automobile Club (ACA), moderate prices and recommended.

Where to eat

The only problem you can find in Salta, is making your mind up what kind of food you would like to eat. For such a little town, the variety is amazing... Alongside the **Recova**, surrounding the 9 de Julio square, you will find many bars selling *empanadas* at lunch time. This is one of the typical dishes here, and it is delicious, we strongly recommend to try at least once, but refrain from the more piquant stuffs.

Guisería Picantería Elite: Belgrano 472. Arab dishes and regional cuisine. Very good.

Pepito: Jujuy 1180. A very popular *parrilla* (grill).

Balderrama: San Martín 1126. Regional food and show at nights ("peña folclórica"), worth seeing.

Tourist services

The **Tourist Office** is at Buenos Aires 93, very close to Plaza 9 de Julio. Its staff will be happy to provide you with maps, brochures, information about folklore performances, and assistance in finding inexpensive accommodations in private homes and hotels.

Jujuy

San Salvador de Jujuy was founded on April 19, 1593, and serves as the capital of Argentina's northernmost province of the same name. The town is divided by rivers, and the most interesting section for the tourist is the area bordered by the Río Grande on the north and the Río Xibi on the south. Jujuy is also built in a grid pattern, and the beautiful and well-tended **Plaza Belgrano,** with its fountain and citrus trees, serves as the focal point of the whole town.

On one side of the square is the imposing **Government Building**. Its second floor contains the **Hall of the Flag** (*El Salón de la Bandera*). On display in the purple and gold hall, in French Baroque style, is **Argentina's first flag**. It was designed by General Belgrano who gave the cloth flag to the inhabitants of Jujuy immediately after his victory in the battle of Salta in 1812, as a mark of appreciation for their contribution to his victory and to the struggle for independence.

Green Valley in the Jujuy region

On the other side of the square are **police headquarters** and the impressive **Cathedral** with its blue spire, dating from 1606 (the building has undergone many renovations and changes since then). Inside the cathedral is a breathtakingly beautiful carved wooden wall, the handiwork of local Indians. Downtown roads are narrow with many shops and old, two-story houses.

Jujuy does not offer the tourist much in the way of entertainment and in spite of a population of 140,000 people, is fairly quiet. There is the **Museum of History**, at Calle Lavalle 256, with exhibits of ancient pottery, weapons and portraits of governors of the town. It was here that General Lavalle was killed on October 9, 1841.

The area around Jujuy is blessed with interesting nature sites and landscapes, and dotted with small Indian villages where the ancient way of life is preserved down to the present day. The most famous of these is the village of **Humahuaca**, about two hours from Jujuy. It boasts an Independence Monument, a crafts market and various museums. If you're going on from here to Bolivia, don't spend time visiting these villages, since Bolivia has plenty of them.

Transportation
The **bus station** is in Ave. Dorrego, on the south bank of the

Xibi River. There are several buses a day between Jujuy and La Quiaca (on the Bolivian border), Salta, Tucumán, and the surrounding villages. The trip to La Quiaca takes about 10 hours. The road is paved but narrow, and the scenery offers much of interest.

Tourist services
Jujuy has a few hotels and pensions of intermediate quality. The **Tourist Office** on Calle Belgrano, corner of Lavalle, can give you details about them and provide brochures and maps, as well as explanations and suggestions for touring the area.

Where to stay
The infrastructure for tourism is still to be developed in northern Argentina, nevertheless the exisiting hotels are modest and clean.

Gran Hotel Panorama: Belgrano 1295, Tel. 22-832. Four stars, centrally located, swimming pools.
Augustus: Belgrano 715, Tel. 22688. Three stars; modern and very nice.
Alto de la Viña: Ruta 36, km 5, Tel. 26588. Only if you have a car, since it is in the outskirts. The view from this three-star hotel is magnificient.

On to Bolivia
La Quiaca can be reached by train as well as by bus, from the station which is situated two blocks from the square. The ancient train leaves late in the evening, and the journey is slow and tiring. You should arrive early at the station and find yourself a seat on the train well before it leaves, since it is usually full. The route is extremely dusty, and you should wear warm clothes since it gets very cold at night. The transition from an elevation of 1200 m to 3600 m causes shortness of breath, and you should be careful not to exert yourself, and to walk slowly so as not to suffer from the thinness of the air (for information on how to cope with high altitudes, see "Introduction").

The train reaches the border early in the morning, but you will have to wait till 8am for the border point to open. Only then will you be able to cross the old bridge that spans the dried up river and leads to the Bolivian town of Villazón. The frontier point closes for an afternoon siesta, and on weekends is open only half a day. The Bolivian immigration official will grant you a visa for only 30 days, but this can be extended for an additional 60 days without payment at the Immigration Office in La Paz.

Money can be exchanged in local shops, but these will take only cash dollars. Beware of moneychangers at the train station and check the exchange rate. Change only as much as you will need till you reach the next big town, where you will almost certainly get a better deal. There is daily train service from Villazón to La Paz — a journey of some 24 hours. For this route, the train is the most comfortable, fastest and cheapest means of transport.

The Lake District

Just as Mar del Plata is Argentina's most popular summer resort, the Lake District, which lies in the Andes some 1600 km southwest of Buenos Aires, is the country's favorite winter resort. Its distance from the capital means that it is less crowded than the seaside, but there is no self-respecting Argentinian who has failed to visit Bariloche, or at least does not dream of visiting there.

The fantastic scenery of blue lakes, forests and mountains offers vacationers a variety of nature hikes, ski resorts and up-to-date tourist services. All these together make the area very much like the Swiss Alps, and it is no wonder that the Argentinians refer to the place with pride and enthusiasm.

The Lake District extends almost the whole length of Patagonia, but the parks and main sites of interest are centered in the strip between San Martín de los Andes in the north and Esquel in the south, an area of some 500 km. The Lake District extends across the Chilean border, and a visit to the lakes on the Chilean side is recommended. Crossing the border presents no problems (for details, see below and the chapter on Chile).

This region is undoubtedly one of the most beautiful in Argentina, and has something for everybody: hiking trails, mountain climbing, camping and complete retreat from the world. You can go off to the islands, sail on the lakes, enjoy the beautiful scenery from the comfort of buses, or for those who just want to rest, enjoy the pensions that offer good food in a pastoral setting. It is impossible not to fall in love with the Lake District. You can find everything here in exactly the right proportion: beauty, comfort, things to do, a carefree, relaxed atmosphere, good food — and the prices are not too extravagant.

San Martín de Los Andes

This delightful town, some 200 km north of Bariloche, is composed entirely of small houses and straight streets and is surrounded by a number of interesting places to visit. The most important of these is the **Lanín Park**, which extends over a large area north of the town. In the center of the park is a giant volcano of the same name, which, reaching a height of 3740 meters, is

The Lake District

one of the largest and most beautiful of its kind in the world. The road north to Junin de los Andes and on to Chile passes through the park. If you wish to explore its hidden treasures, you can hike through its vast expanse dotted with lakes, or you can join a guided tour organized by one of the local tour companies.

Two roads link San Martín to Bariloche. The first is the paved highway used by the daily bus, and the second is the **Camino de los Siete Lagos** (The Seven Lakes Road). This tortuous road passes through beautiful scenery, including a desert where the wind and rains have carved the rocks into bizarre shapes resembling man and beast.

Traveling over this dusty track takes four hours. There are no buses and, as far as hitchhiking is concerned, you may travel this way at the rate of one lake per day. The tour companies run organized minibus trips, which are by far the best way (expensive) of visiting this area.

San Carlos de Bariloche

This popular holiday town, and the **Nahuel Huapi** Park which surrounds it, are the heart of the Lake District and contain the

BARILOCHE

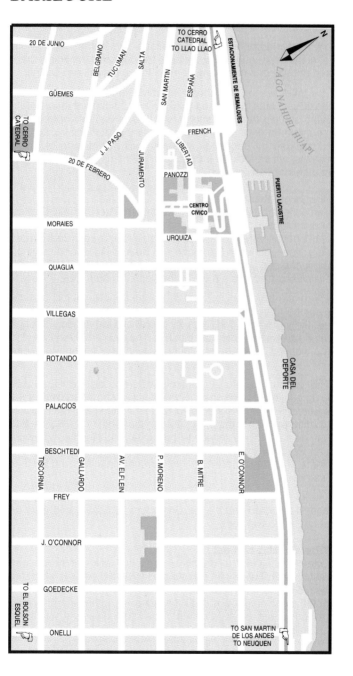

key to its magic. *Nahuel Huapi* means "Eye of the Tiger" in the local Indian language. Bariloche is the capital of the whole area, and the name is often used to refer to the entire Lake District.

The town lies on the shores of Lake Nahuel Huapi, which is the largest lake in the area (536 sq/km). Its picturesque streets climb steeply from the shores of the lake up the slopes of the mountain. In the center of the town is the Municipality Square, surrounded by chocolate factories built in the form of Swiss chalets, which look as if they have been snatched straight out of a children's fairy tale.

How to get there
Bariloche is the transportation and tourist hub of the Lake District, and there are frequent air and overland services between it and Buenos Aires. *Aerolíneas, Austral,* and *Lade* run frequent daily flights between Bariloche and Buenos Aires, and between Bariloche and Comodoro Rivadavia, and other cities in the south. *Aerolíneas* also has a route to the north, via Mendoza.

There is a train service from Bariloche (whose station is some distance from the town) to Buenos Aires several times a week, but the journey is long (over 30 hours) and exhausting, through the dusty and monotonous pampas. The train is not too crowded (no wonder!), and you should be sure to take enough food and drink with you.

The buses present an entirely different picture. They are luxurious, most have charming hostesses who serve beverages and snacks, and the journey is far more interesting and quicker (a difference of about 10 hours) than by train. Some bus companies provide service to the capital, and others to Mendoza and Córdoba in the north, and to Comodoro in the southeast. There are frequent buses to the surrounding towns and to Chile (see below).

The fastest and most convenient overland route to Patagonia and Tierra del Fuego is via Comodoro Rivadavia and then on south to Río Gallegos.

Where to stay and eat
One thing Bariloche definitely does not lack are hotels and restaurants. These can be found all over and cater to all tastes and budgets. Nevertheless, it is extremely difficult to find a hotel room during the peak seasons — summer and winter. In spring and fall it is quieter. The most pleasant hotels are actually situated out of town, on the lakeshores but these are more expensive, and inconvenient if you do not have a car.

Some of them are:

Edelweiss, San Martín 202, Tel. 26165. Five stars and all the facilities, including a fancy restaurant.
Tres Reyes, 12 De Octubre 135, Tel. 26121. Off the centro cívico, splendid view.
Mahuel Huapi, Perito Moreno 252, Tel. 26146. Four stars.
Nevada, Rolando 250, Tel. 22778. Four stars.
Aconcagua, San Martín 289, Tel. 24718. Three stars.

Somewhat cheaper recommended *Mosterías* are:
Nahuel, Gallardo 454. Warm and clean.
La Pileta del Pintor, 20 De Febrero 630. Very good.
El Manantial, 20 De Febrero 470. Friendly and nice.

When it comes to food, Bariloche's numerous restaurants specialize in all types of Argentinian as well as Italian cuisine. As for the famous Bariloche chocolate, see below: "what to buy"

What to see
The town itself offers the tourist mainly a chance to relax and take it easy. In the center is the **Municipality Square**, home of the **City Hall** with its **clock tower**, the **Tourist Office** (on the ground floor of the City Hall), and the **police station**, (to the right of City Hall). Most interesting of all, is the **Patagonia Museum** (Tel. 2-2309), which has a collection of stuffed animals including all species common to Patagonia, as well as geological specimens, ancient artifacts from the region and more. On the ground floor is a large exhibition of old military uniforms and weapons.

But the main attractions are to be found outside the town, in the natural beauty of the Lake District. The classic routes to follow are to **Cerro Tronador** and **Cerro Catedral**; the latter mountain is known for its ski slopes. A visit to **Victoria Island** is very enjoyable. This island is famous for its large red trees, the *Arrayanes*, and was chosen by Walt Disney as the inspiration for one of the best-loved children's films of our times — **Bambi**. You should book via one of the travel agents, since the boat fare alone is not much cheaper than the price of a complete guided tour, which includes visits to some of the other beautiful sites in the area.

There is also plenty of scope for walking tours over different and varied routes. You can go hiking from two or three days up to a month, provided you are properly equipped with camping gear and food. The Club Andino Bariloche will supply you with information and maps, and inform you of altered routes, weather conditions, etc. If you are taking a trip through the mountains,

Bariloche — the City Hall

A forest of Arrayanes trees

Cerro Catedral — summer and winter

you can spend the night in one of the hikers' *refugios* there, paying a small fee to the club to cover expenses.

Cerro Catedral

One of the most beautiful routes is the one through *Cerro Catedral* (Cathedral Mountain). The hike takes three days, and passes impressive green forests, bubbling streams, blue lakes and towering Andean peaks. The route starts at the foot of the mountain at Villa Catedral. Buses set out from Bariloche a few times a day. The climb to *Refugio Frey* on the shores of Lake Frey begins here, and takes several hours. The second day of the hike is the most difficult, and includes the crossing of two high mountain passes before you reach *Refugio San Martín* on the shores of Laguna Jacob. A short way up from the refugio is another enchanting lake, which is certainly worth the effort of the climb. The third day is devoted to the descent to Bariloche.

The best season for mountain hikes is in summer, December–March. Then the weather is pleasant, the skies are blue, and there is no snow to make walking difficult. In winter you can enjoy the ski slopes of Cathedral Mountain.

What to buy

The main street, leading off the Municipality Square, is lined with numerous shops offering a large selection of souvenirs typical of the locality, especially wood carvings, leather handicraft and wool products. Particularly noteworthy are the local sweaters, which are famous for their beauty and quality. You can find them in almost any store in town.

Bariloche is famous for its chocolate industry. The city and its outskirts are home to dozens of small chocolate factories, which produce an infinite variety of chocolates of unsurpassed quality. These chocolates are sold by weight in many shops. Just looking at their seductive displays will add to your waistline. Many shops sell home-made chocolate (*chocolate casero*), and generally speaking allow customers to sample the various kinds. The largest store, *Turista*, on Calle Mitre, is slightly more expensive than the others and does not allow you to sample their wares before buying. But you really can't go wrong! In a store like this, whatever you buy and however much you buy, you'll be sorry you didn't buy more!

On to Chile

There are several frontier points between Argentina and Chile and your choice will depend on your destination there. You can travel over a fast, paved, and quite ordinary highway, or choose a more interesting route and make an experience of the trip itself.

There is one bus a day from Bariloche to Temuco in the north. The trip follows a difficult route and takes 10 hours. The bus passes through the outstandingly beautiful **Lanín Park**. The road climbs through the Andes to the frontier point at **Truman**. The border check points on either side are several kilometers apart. Once in Chile, you will be traveling through beautiful forests, passing by small farms which are still plowed by oxen, and crossing rivers and streams over shaky wooden bridges. During the winter, the border is sometimes closed due to snow drifts that block the road.

The Bariloche-Puerto Montt route is far less impressive, but much easier to travel. Several bus companies serve this route, and the ride is fast and comfortable. The travel agencies offer one or two-day outings, which include a round trip to Puerto Montt, and provide a chance both to visit the city and to enjoy the lakes and landscapes en route. Another no less interesting possibility is to take a bus and then ride the ferry across *Todos los Santos* lake, considered by many to be the most beautiful lake in the south.

Bear in mind that crossing the border depends to a large extent on the clemency of the weather, as well as on the political climate. As tourists, we have little say in either matter, so it is advisable to check which way the winds are blowing before setting out — and decide accordingly.

El Bolsón

This picturesque little town, 124 km south of Bariloche, is attractive in its own right, both for the special charm and character of its streets, and for the pastoral countryside in which it rests. El Bolsón is chiefly known as the starting point for walking tours of the area, of varying lengths and difficulty. Its special feature is the fact that there are a large number of beautiful spots just outside the town. Even a short outing will give you a fair sample of them.

Esquel

This modern holiday resort located at an elevation of 540 meters above sea level, has a population of around 20,000 people. Esquel, too, serves as a starting point for various tours through the southern part of the Lake District, especially in the nearby

Los Alerces Park, which is considered less "touristy" than the others. There are comfortable hotels, a wide selection of restaurants, a local food industry of high quality (specializing in jams and chocolate), fishing spots, etc. The Club Andino Esquel and the **Tourist Office** in the bus station will be glad to give you advice and directions, and provide you with maps of recommended hiking routes.

There is a direct bus service from Esquel to Comodoro Rivadavia, and from there to the south. *Lade* also has flights to Patagonia in the south and to Buenos Aires in the north.

ARGENTINA

Patagonia

Almost devoid of vegetation, the ground bare and rocky, we set foot on the arid plains of southern Argentina — Patagonia. The climate here is extremely harsh throughout most of the year, and although the temperature never sinks below freezing, the biting cold and gale-force winds are enough to chase settlers much further north. No wonder then that Patagonia, which covers a third of Argentina, is sparsely populated (a population density of 2 people per square kilometer). The further south you go, the more virgin and undisturbed the landscape, until it becomes truly primeval. Unlike the jungle and other untamed spots, the horizon here is free of detail; you cannot fail to be overcome by a sense of infinite space. The outstanding beauty, the limpid sea in the east, and the lofty peaks of the Andes in the west, the awe-inspiring sunsets, the extreme contrasts of height and depth, and many other marvels of nature, as well as an abundance of birds and wildlife, combine to give this place a unique charm. Few settlements break up the vast open expanses, with large sheep ranches scattered among them.

Half of Argentina's sheep are raised in Patagonia and their thick, silky wool, as well as their meat and skins, provide the main source of income for the local population.

Traffic on the roads of Patagonia, most of which are unpaved, is sparse; on rainy days driving can be hazardous and difficult. The lack of industry means that most consumer goods must be imported from the north, and this is naturally evident in prices. The growing number of tourists over the past years has led to the development of tourist services, but these still fall short of what is needed. It can be very hard to find accommodation, especially during the summer influx of thousands of visitors.

How to get there
By air: *Aerolíneas*, *Austral*, and *Lade* all run scheduled flights between the towns of Patagonia and Buenos Aires. There are daily flights leaving Buenos Aires, some are direct and others with intermediate stops. The southernmost terminus of *Aerolíneas* and *Austral* is Río Grande.

Night flights are half-price, but these are heavily booked and you have to make reservations at least a week in advance. Although

Lade's flights are among the cheapest they are long and slow, with many stopovers en route. The planes are very old, most with piston engines, and there is usually no problem reserving a seat. *Lade* is the only company with local flights between the southern towns and to Tierra del Fuego, and these are no more expensive than bus journeys over the same routes. Reservations on *Lade* flights are not reliable, especially to remote destinations, and you will have to take this into account. Flights to and from Ushuaia are liable to be cancelled due to strong winds, which prevent planes from landing there.

Bus: The buses from Buenos Aires to Río Gallegos ply the coastal route (routa 3), and take at least two days to get there. The fare is only slightly cheaper than a night flight. Take a bus only if you want to visit places along the way.

Hitchhiking: If you have plenty of time on your hands and want to save, you can always hitchhike. You should allow 4-6 days, bearing in mind that this is one of the main hitching routes in the whole of South America. The gas stations along the route have showers and patches of lawn where you can set up a tent.

Come equipped with a good tent and sleeping bag, food, cooking utensils and most important of all — vast quantities of patience! The best lifts are from the huge trucks carrying goods south. Route 3 stretches for 3178 km from Buenos Aires to Ushuaia (Tierra del Fuego). Most of this length is paved.

Currency exchange
You will find it difficult to exchange dollars in the south. travelers' checks are virtually unacceptable, and cash is exchanged at a low rate and the commission charged is very high. You should try to exchange enough money before you leave the big city. If you nevertheless overspend and get "stuck", try changing in shops and private businesses rather than in official places. You'll find less beaucracy this way, and, more important, you'll get a better deal. Bear in mind that prices in the south run about 30% more than for the same items in the north.

Climate
The entire south has a harsh and treacherous climate. During the winter (April-September) it's very hard to get around on the muddy roads, flights are delayed and sometimes cancelled and access to most places is blocked. In other words, either come in the summer, or don't come at all. Since touring this area requires so much effort, it would be a pity not to derive the maximum benefit.

Always take with you a sleeping bag and the warmest clothes.

The notorious winds of Patagonia are frequent, and can reach a speed of 100 km an hour! During the summer the weather is slightly less hostile, and although the nights are cold, clear pleasant days are not uncommon. This is the peak tourist season, when accommodations are extremely hard to find.

Postal and telephone services
The large towns of Patagonia have post offices with letter and parcel service, as well as international telex and telephone services. However, the postal service is slow, so if you plan to return to Buenos Aires (in two or three weeks) hold on to your letters till you get there.

The Valdés Peninsula
Half way between Buenos Aires and the south is Península Valdés with its nature reserve, the center of an area rich in sea creatures and birds. The peninsula is a favorite haunt of sea lions, seals, penguins and whales, and these flock to its shores by the thousand. This rare concentration is what makes the nature reserve so interesting. It attracts tens of thousands of nature-lovers from Argentina and abroad each year. The best season to visit is September-December, in the spring, when you can see dozens of whales and thousands of other creatures. Sometimes you can get really close to these huge animals, even within a few meters. The whales, some of which are truly gigantic, swim near the shore and can be seen quite clearly. Especially impressive are the jets of water they expel from their spouts and the sight of their tails sticking straight up out of the water when they dive. It is one you will never forget.

Several tourist agencies in the nearby town of **Puerto Madryn**, some 100 km from the reserve, organize guided bus tours to the peninsula, incorporating visits to other sites in the area. Getting around the reserve itself is difficult if you do not have a car, and there is not much hope of getting a lift. You can hire a car in Puerto Madryn, but the prices are far steeper than usual. Those who stay over can find accommodations in **Puerto Pirámides**, at the entrance to the reserve, and a camp ground. Take food with you, since the restaurants are expensive and there are no stores. You can rent small boats, diving gear, water-sports equipment and the like in the vicinity.

The nearest airport is in the town of **Trelew**, and there are buses from there to Puerto Madryn.

Punta Tumbo
Punta Tumbo, situated about 100 km south of Trelew, has an

Enjoying the sun in Peninsula Valdés

enormous concentration of penguins which nest here during the summer. In the peak of the season, their numbers reach about three million! On the way to the penguin reserve you are likely to encounter other indigenous wild life, such as the *guanaco* (of the llama family) and the *ñandú* (of the ostrich family). In the huge reserve one can wander around among the penguins, and almost get close enough to touch them.

From Trelew one can hire a car or take a taxi, which is not expensive if one organizes a group of five people.

Comodoro Rivadavia

This town of 120,000 is the transportation, industrial, military, and commercial center of the whole of Patagonia. Some 1800 km south of Buenos Aires, Commodoro underwent an economic boom due to oil and gas finds in the region, and is now enjoying a prosperity that is truly enviable. The area provides about a third of the national oil supply; derricks and pipelines are everywhere. Large military forces are based around the city, and it was from here that the invasion of the Falklands Islands was launched.

The town's airport is the largest and busiest in the south. There are daily flights to Buenos Aires, Bariloche, and other towns in

Parque Nacional de los Glaciares

Patagonia. The highway to Tierra del Fuego passes through the city and makes it an important road for all the regional bus lines.

Río Gallegos

This southernmost town of Patagonia is the district capital for the tip of the continent. There's nothing particularly special about the place, and from our point of view its main importance is as a crossroads.

Río Gallegos has a small airport serving the few planes from Buenos Aires and elsewhere, including those half-price night flights we keep mentioning. *Lade* flies to Calafate, Río Turbio, and Tierra del Fuego, and north to the large cities, including irregular flights to Bariloche. *Lade* also flies to La Plata, close to Buenos Aires. This is also the end of the line for buses on southern routes.

There are two roads from Río Gallegos to Chile, one to Punta Arenas, and the other to the border town of Río Turbio. Route 3 from Buenos Aires continues south to the straits of Magellan and Tierra del Fuego, via Chile. Although buses travel these routes they are fairly expensive, in fact not much cheaper than *Lade* flights.

Parque Nacional de los Glaciares

Calafate

This small country town has thousands of visitors each year, arriving en masse in the summer to feast their eyes on **Perito Moreno** — the huge glacier which is the only one in the world that is still growing. The glacier, more than 50 meters high, is one of the many relics of the Ice Age that can be found in the vicinity, and is the main attraction of the **Glacier National Park** (*Parque Nacional de los Glaciares*). On hot, clear days (hot for the glacier, we are still freezing...), sections of the ice wall melt and fall into the water with a tremendous crash, creating huge waves. You may have to stand around for hours till this happens, but it's worth the wait.

Because of the harsh climate, the tourist season here is rather short, running from the end of October to mid-March. During this period the local tourist agencies organize guided tours to the glacier, and offer additional trips to more distant glaciers in the park, including trips in motor boats. Although the fare from Calafate to the park is expensive, there is really no other way to reach the glacier. You could try hitchhiking, but you will need lots of patience. Public transport does not run out of season, but there are taxis (expensive). Park-service cars leave Calafate every day for the park and with a little luck and a smile, you can usually persuade the driver to take you along. They do not leave at fixed times and there is not always room.

In the park itself there is an ACA bungalow site, but they are expensive and tend to be full during the tourist season. You can pitch tent, if you have a permit, several kilometers away from the glacier, alongside the road that leads to town. Calafate itself has several hotels and a camping site, as well as restaurants and grocery stores. If you plan to spend more than a day in the park, stock up on food in the town, since the restaurant next to the glacier is expensive.

Calafate is linked to all towns in the south via *Lade* flights. The tiny airport is within walking distance of the town center. Buses cover the monotonous route to Río Gallegos in 6 hours. Most other roads in the area are deserted, and hitchhikers run a risk of getting stuck. To get to Río Turbio, you should backtrack to Río Gallegos and then carry on from there, since there is hardly any traffic over the direct route west from Calafate.

Fitz Roy Mountain

Wild mountain scenery, majestic cliffs, glaciers and lakes — this is the Fitz Roy mountain region. Its peak is "only" 3375 m above sea level, but the cliff itself is a steep wall hundreds of meters high. Near Fitz Roy looms another imposing cliff, **Cerro Torre**, not quite as high as Fitz Roy, but no less impressive. The weather here is harsh, and it is only on a few days of the year, during the summer, that the skies are cloudless and the peaks of Fitz Roy and Cerro Torre exposed. Because of this combination of amazing cliffs and treacherous weather, these two peaks are considered by professional mountain climbers to be among the most difficult in the world to climb.

Access to Fitz Roy is complicated. It is a remote area, and the nearest settlement is Calafate, six hours travel away. There is no regular transport here, and very few cars travel the difficult road. The chances of hitching a ride are negligible. Farmers in the area depart from Calafate by truck from time to time, and will give you a lift for a fee. This is not a cheap option, but it may be the only way if one does not want to waste several days waiting for a lift which may never materialize.

At the site itself, there is an expensive *hostería* (hostel) and a camping ground nearby. From here there are a number of walking routes, mostly for one day. Among the most beautiful are the walk to the observation point over Cerro Torre (one day)

Perito Moreno Glacier

Cerro Torre

Fitz Roy

and the walk to the climbers' hut on Fitz Roy, where one should spend the night.

It is very important to bring enough food because there is no possibility of obtaining any at Fitz Roy, except in the hostería, where it is very expensive. Take into account that you might be delayed several days, until there is a vehicle returning to Calafate.

Río Turbio

This border town is the last stop in Argentina before you cross into Chilean Patagonia. You can get here by plane or bus, or by hitchhiking from Río Gallegos along a desolate road that passes through a few rather wretched settlements. The old-fashioned train that travels between the two towns carries coal from the Río Turbio mines to Río Gallegos and does not carry passengers.

It is possible to find overnight accommodations in the town, but your best bet would be to carry on immediately to Puerto Natales in Chile and stay there. There are direct buses from the center of Río Turbio (near the supermarket) to Puerto Natales. Another and cheaper alternative is to take a local bus to the Argentinian frontier point, cross the border on foot, and then board a Chilean bus.

A RGENTINA

The Argentinian and Chilean border points are several kilometers apart. Tourists crossing over from Chile to Argentina will sometimes be required to give a detailed list of their intended itinerary (see "Introduction" and "Documents").

Tierra del Fuego

The magical name of this exotic island at the southern tip of the continent cannot but awaken associations. The island was named by the famous Portuguese navigator, Fernando Magellan (1480-1521) who, in November 1520, sailed through the straits that today bear his name, on his way from the Atlantic to the Pacific Ocean, during the first circumnavigation of the globe in history. There are several theories as to the origin of the name. One theory claims that Magellan called the island "Land of Fire" because the local Indians lit bonfires in his honor. The better explanation is that the name was given on account of the red vegetation — especially the red tree-tops — which are due to the high concentration of iron oxide in the soil. It is impossible not to be impressed by the beauty of the foliage, which spreads like a lush, reddish carpet over slopes and valleys.

The island is divided between Argentina and Chile, and is sparsely populated. On the other hand, the area is famous for its abundance of fish and wildlife, including over 150 species of birds.

How to get there
Aerolíneas and *Austral* fly as far south as Río Grande, and *Lade* goes all the way to Ushuaia. Strong winds often cause serious alterations to timetables and even cancellation of flights. There are several buses per day from Río Grande to Ushuaia (3 hours). Hitchhiking is easy along this route: cross the large bridge south of Río Grande and wait at the next junction. On your way back, wait at the northern exit of Ushuaia, but bear in mind that many vehicles travel only as far as the industrial zone several kilometers away. Buses run several times a week between Río Grande and Puerto Porvenir in Chile (200 km — 5 hours). There are no problems crossing the border at San Sebastian. If you are traveling by car (Route 3), a ferry will take you over the straits between Patagonia and Tierra del Fuego. The road continues into Chilean territory, entailing the normal frontier road formalities. The ferry runs several times a day; the crossing takes about half-an-hour. There is also daily ferry service between Puerto Porvenir and Punta Arenas (3 hours).

Río Grande

This small town lies on the shores of the Atlantic, on the northern bank of the river after which it is named. Its streets are empty and neglected, its houses low and its places of interest — non-existent.

There are only a few hotels, and these are relatively expensive and full to capacity during the summer. If you are the sporty type, you can camp near the ACA service station on the beach (not to be confused with the expensive ACA luxury hotel in town). The station has showers and toilets, which are open all night. Outfit yourselves with warm, top-quality camping equipment.

Tierra del Fuego's proximity to the south pole results in drastic tidal flows; in the evenings, the sea recedes hundreds of meters. Make the effort to get up really early in order to see the waters "coming home" at sunrise, consuming the dry land once again.

Ushuaia

Welcome to the southermost city in the world! On the strength of its latitude, the remote, insignificant town of Ushuaia has acquired international fame. The town, with its wooden houses and tiled roofs, its hotels, restaurants, charming harbor and factories, bears the mysterious stamp of "the end". Throughout its history Ushuaia has been mentioned in this context, and has been visited by throngs of people wishing to include it as a landmark in their lives.

Where to stay

All the hotels in Ushuaia tend to be more expensive, and usually are fully booked, especially in the summer.

Ushuaia: Laserre 933, Tel. 2-2024. Four stars, the highest standard in town.
Canal Beagle: Maipú and 25 de Mayo, Tel. 2-1117. Three stars, good service.
Mafalda: San Martín 5, Tel. 2-2373. Near the navy base, recommended.
The *Ona Hotel*, on Calle 9 de Julio, is definitely **not** recommended. There is a cheap and good hostel on the road running parallel to the sea, in the red-turreted building visible from all points.

There are plenty of restaurants, but these are also not cheap. If you are partial to seafood, don't miss Ushuaia's king crabs, known here as *centolla*. Several shops serve hot chocolate, home-made chocolate, and excellent pastries.

Ushuaia

Tierra del Fuego

A RGENTINA

What to see

Avenida San Martín, which is the backbone of the town, contains the **municipality buildings**, the **tourist information office** (No. 524), **airline offices**, the best restaurants, duty-free stores, etc. Tierra del Fuego is a **duty-free zone** and as a result, many Argentinians do their shopping here.

Tourist agencies offer a wide selection of outings in the area, to look at the wildlife, glaciers and lakes. If you have a car you can stay in one of the motels along the Río Grande-Ushuaia road, or south of the town on the road leading to the national park.

The **National Park** (*Parque Nacional Tierra del Fuego*) is extremely interesting, with an abundance of wildlife. The most famous of these is the beaver, who is the pride of the park. The park rangers will enthusiastically direct you to a point where you can see it, or at least the amazing constructions of which the beaver is the architect and builder. This spacious park is situated south of the town, and can be reached by car, hitchhiking, or organized tour.

CHILE

Chile, a narrow strip of land between the western slopes of the Andes and the Pacific Ocean, is a land with a serene and pleasant folk tradition. Its variegated scenery — from desert in the north to glaciers in the south — offers numerous places to visit and routes to travel. The Chileans are friendly people, tolerant and always willing to help. Getting to know them — in the large cities and even more so in outlying areas — will undoubtedly be the highlight of your stay. All this, along with the clean, invigorating air, varied climate and well run tourist infrastructure, make a visit to Chile an enjoyable and unforgettable experience.

History

The Indian tribes, who populated Chile before the first Spaniards arrived in 1536, retained control of the country's southern region for many decades thereafter, leaving only the northern and central areas to the newly arrived conquerors. The Spanish attributed no great importance to Chile; for some time they refrained from moving south and clashing with the natives, who continued to maintain their ancient tradition without interference.

Eventually, however, Pedro de Valdivia (founder of Santiago) and the Spanish under his leadership did attempt to expand southward and lay claim to more territory, a move that met with fierce Indian resistance. Chilean history in the seventeenth and eighteenth centuries is a tale of the Indians' struggle to delay the inevitable and keep the Spanish out. A number of the important characteristics that typify Chile to this day took shape in that period — chiefly those pertaining to the country's demographic makeup and class structure. The Spanish immigrants excelled at winning the local women's hearts, and intermarriage between the two groups became a common occurance. Consequently, the mixed European-Indian *mestizos* quickly became the largest population group. In due course, most *mestizos* fell into the underprivileged working class which, until recent decades, had almost no rights at all. Since the Spanish generously apportioned Chile's land among themselves, a privileged class of wealthy landed gentry came into being. This stratum grew even more important when, after Chile declared its independence, it took the reins of government into its own collective hands.

CHILE

Chile's first independent government was established in 1810, but was ousted two years later by Spanish loyalists. Bernardo O'Higgins, Chile's national hero, and later its first President, left for Argentina, where he raised a joint Chilean-Argentinian army. This force, led by the Argentinian General José de San Martín, succeeded in expelling the Spanish and re-establishing Chilean independence. Though O'Higgins was appointed head of state in 1817, his liberal policies did not please the local population, and he resigned in 1823.

Seven years of social, political, and economic chaos set in and only when a military junta seized power, supported by broad groups in the army and the general population, did things calm down. The constitution of 1833 guaranteed control of Parliament to the landed gentry. A period of domestic tranquility and economic wellbeing ensued.

The discovery of natural resources and mineral deposits in northern Chile — which contributed to the development of trade with England, the United States, and even distant Australia — filled the coffers of the state, and led to an accelerated process of modernization. Roads were paved, railways laid, ports dredged, and the infrastructure of an educational system (even if restricted to the children of the rich) was set up. As trade and cultural relations with Europe broadened, the new winds blowing there also influenced many members of the ruling aristocracy and liberal tendencies critical of the conservative regime began to gain strength in social and political circles.

The momentum of industrial development produced a balance-of-payments deficit, and the Chilean Government went to war with Perú and Bolivia — which controlled a fertile region rich in mineral deposits — with the intention of taking over the mines and enjoying their proceeds. Chile, it is true, won the War of the Pacific (1879-1884), taking Antofagasta from Bolivia and Arica from Perú, and even reaching the outskirts of Lima. These conquests, however, sent the country into a severe internal and political tailspin, which culminated in a short civil war.

During the same period, important social changes were taking place. At the end of the nineteenth century, political parties began to organize and the government began to require their support in Parliament. In the early twentieth century, the lower and middle classes also began to accumulate power, and the regime's inability to satisfy them and offer solutions to pressing problems caused the social ferment to spill over into the military. The army seized power in 1924, held it for one year, and then returned it to President Arturo Alessandri who, despite all his efforts, could not restore tranquility.

CHILE

Political parties gained and lost political influence rapidly, chiefly because of the economic woes that became worse during the Great Depression of the 1930's. The recovery that took place during World War II (in which Chile joined the Allies in declaring war on Germany) marked a turning point of sorts, along with closer relations with the United States and encouragement of American capital investments. Nevertheless, inflation and unemployment persisted, and magnified yearnings for reform of the unfair social structure, in which the bulk of economic power rested in the hands of the traditional minority. As a result, Chilean regimes changed frequently.

In 1967, President Eduardo Frei introduced a far-reaching agrarian reform, including land expropriations from the estate owners, and improvements in the living and working conditions and wages of agricultural laborers. Numerous difficulties, however, impeded its fulfilment. The same period witnessed a rise in the power of the Left when leftist representatives of various parties combined forces to found a National Unity Party. Led by Salvador Allende, they won a plurality in the 1970 elections. An economic policy calling for nationalization of mines, among other tenets, damaged American economic interests and led the United States to impose sanctions. Allende reacted by drawing close to the Soviet Union and its allies.

In the 1973 elections, Allende was again victorious but was deposed and killed in a military coup in September of that year. A military junta headed by General Augusto Pinochet has run the country with unconcerned ruthlessness, until 1989. The Government's efforts notwithstanding, the upheaval has continued. With the return of democracy, many exiled Chileans returned, and the country is now passing through one of it's best economic periods, having received credit and investments from the U.S. and the EEC.

Geography and climate

Though it is the longest of the South American countries — extending more than 4300 kilometers from north to south — Chile's average width does not exceed 200 km, so that it is only the fourth largest country on the continent in terms of area (757,000 sq/km). Though Chile is divided for historical reasons into seven regions from north to south, a rough geographic reckoning may view the country as having three main sections: the desert in the north, the temperate center, and the cold, rainy south.

The Andes delimit the three regions to the east, with the Pacific Ocean on the west. In the north the mountains are very broad

CHILE

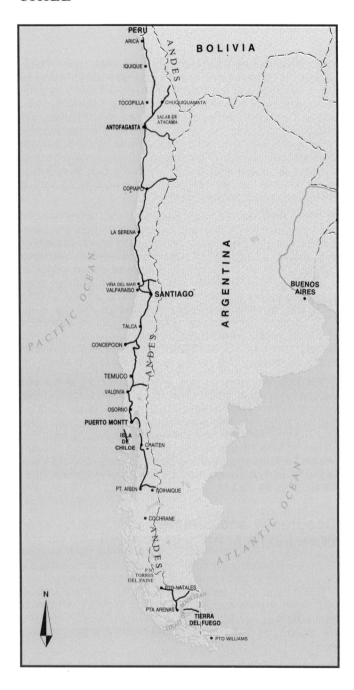

and have plateau-like summits; in the center they become narrower and higher (with peaks reaching some 7000 m); and in the south they are lower — "only" around 3000 meters. The Pacific Ocean washes a straight coastline in the north and center while in the south, the coast is broken up, ending in a far flung archipelago.

This unusual geography is accompanied by additional phenomena: The mountains have a high level of seismic activity, and earthquakes and volcanic eruptions have brought disaster with them more than once. The ocean too has destructive power and surging floods occasionally wash over the coastal cities and villages.

The northern region: Though it is a dry, rainless desert, temperatures here are moderate, and the weather is pleasant and comfortable even in summer. The average temperature (23 degrees Celsius, or 74 degrees Fahrenheit) and relatively low humidity make staying or working in this desert zone easier than in other deserts. Beneath it lie most of the natural resources and mineral deposits that serve as the central pillars of the Chilean economy.

The central region: This zone, extending southward to Puerto Montt, is home to about 90% of Chile's population and serves as the country's economic and social hub. Here the climate is comfortable and temperate; rainfall increases as one goes southward. Temperatures are moderate the year round, and only on mountaintops does the mercury drop to freezing point. This is an extremely fertile area with a wealth of flora — both wild and cultivated.

The southern region: This zone, stretching from Puerto Montt to Tierra del Fuego, suffers from an extremely harsh climate. Given the combination of fierce winds, rain and cold, it's no wonder that the area is uninhabited save for a few cities. Despite the harsh conditions, temperatures do not drop below freezing. The numerous glaciers found chiefly in the southernmost tip of the region are mute survivors of a bygone geological epoch.

Population, education and culture

About 300,000 Indians with no European blood still survive in Chile. Almost all of these are concentrated around the southern city of Temuco. Most of Chile's other 15 million citizens are *mestizos* — of mixed Indian and Spanish descent. The European immigrants, who left their imprint on the demographic makeup of Argentina and Uruguay, never reached Chile, either because of the country's distance from Europe or because of the barriers posed by the towering Andes. Whatever the reason, they account for a mere 1.5% of the country's population.

More than 90% of all Chileans live in the central region, with about a third of these in the capital of Santiago, which is growing at a rate of 4% per annum. Nor has the trend of accelerated urbanization passed over the less attractive northern and southern sectors; there, too, the population is essentially city-based. A drop in mortality and a high birth-rate are the principal factors behind Chile's 2.5% annual population growth rate; 40% of the population are children below the age of 10.

Chile's educational system is one of the most advanced in South America. In addition to elementary and secondary education, Chile boasts numerous universities, which offer diverse curricula.

Economy

Chile's economy is based first and foremost on exploiting the numerous mineral deposits and natural resources with which the nation has been blessed. Copper, of which Chile supplies about 10% of world consumption, accounts for about half of the nation's total exports. Though its price has fallen, it still retains pride of place in the national economy. Other metals found in the rich veins of northern Chile — mainly iron, and some gold and silver — are mined in smaller quantities. Another important export industry involves lumber and wood products (paper, etc.), which are derived from Chile's vast forests. Deep-sea fishing is another important sector, and places Chile among the world's leading fish-exporting countries.

Agriculture, the second-ranking industry, employs more than 20% of Chile's manpower. Even so, local farms do not meet the domestic demand and Chile imports great quantities of foodstuffs from other countries. Three million head of cattle and about seven million sheep make up a significant portion of the agricultural field with most meat and meat products earmarked for export.

In recent decades, Chilean governments have implemented a policy to encourage accelerated industrial development. This is concentrated around the large cities, and employs close to 25% of the workforce. Because of the low technological level and the lack of capital, most industrial plants are labor-intensive, producing textiles, food products and simple, low-quality consumer goods. Recent years have seen a trend towards technological expansion and development and more sophisticated factories, producing machinery, motor vehicles, and even petrochemicals are being constructed at a steady pace. From its own reserves Chile produces less than half of its national consumption of oil, natural gas and coal.

When General Pinochet seized power, he introduced the economic system championed by the well-known economist Professor Milton Friedman, stressing freedom of capital, free competition and reduced import duties. Credit was granted with great flexibility by non-governmental agencies and foreign investments received special assistance and encouragement. Though inflation, which reached 341% in 1975, was halted for a time, unemployment swelled and violent social ferment was reawakened. The government has struggled desperately to stifle the resulting unrest.

In 1979, Pinochet began trying to maintain a fixed dollar exchange rate for the peso. Economic pressures, however, forced him to desist. In 1982 he devalued the Chilean peso and adopted a series of economic measures which in effect ended the Milton Friedman era.

The economic crisis has only intensified over the years. Unemployment has risen, reaching up to 25% of the local work force in some areas. Many Chileans emigrate to other countries, particularly Argentina, searching for work. Inflation levels which are causing much dissent and resentment in business and public circles, also burden the Government, crippling its attempts to repay outside loans, and to continue internal development. Their inability to raise foreign capital or to receive international credit adds further to Chile's economic difficulties.

Inflation levels caused much dissent and resentment in business and public circles, but since the return to democracy, there is an economic boom.

General Information

How to get there
By air: Close to twenty airlines link Santiago with the important cities of Europe, the United States and the Far East, as well as the other countries of South America. Some flights include stopovers in Brazil, Argentina, Perú, etc.

Lan Chile, Air France, Iberia, Sabena, KLM, Lufthansa, SAS, Swissair and other airlines fly from Europe, while *Eastern* and *Lan* fly from New York and Miami. All the South American flag carriers maintain regular routes between their respective capitals and Santiago.

By land: The Pan-American Highway (*Carretera Panamericana*)

Chile — south

and north

traverses the length of Chile and links it with Perú. Numerous roads cut across the mountains to Argentina and Bolivia (details concerning each road and border crossing will be provided as we proceed). Buses connect Chilean frontier towns with their counterparts across the borders, and Santiago with the capitals of the neighboring countries. Trains travel from Antofagasta to La Paz, Bolivia.

Documents

Passport holders from the following countries require visas: most of the Arab countries, Central American countries, East European countries, New Zealand, Luxemburg and France; the rest can enter with only a valid passport. As this changes, ask the nearest consulate before you plan a visit. Upon arrival you get a 90-day visit permit, with an additional 90-day extension issued with no problem at the Immigration offices in Santiago.

On arrival in Chile you will need a tourist card, issued by the air line or obtainable at the border point. The immigration officers will attach the tourist card to your passport, and you must carry it at all times and surrender it when leaving the country.

Visitors from various countries are obliged to pay tax, when entering Chile. It changes from one country of origin to another, but is generally not more then a few dollars.

Accommodation

Chile has many hotels of all categories. Their overall quality is satisfactory and the cheaper ones, too, are usually clean. A number of cities have youth hostels, but most of these are open only during the tourist season. An ever-growing number of campsites are being set up throughout Chile, most providing convenient facilities.

Hotel rates, posted in every room by law, include a 10% service fee and a 20% tax. It's important to check if the tax is also added to the tab for meals when the bill isn't paid on the spot. If so, it's better to pay there and then to avoid paying tax.

Wining and dining

The superb flavor of Chilean cuisine undoubtedly stems from its succulent seafood. Most restaurants serve the standard fare of meat and its familiar side-dishes (beware of raw fruit and vegetables, which may not have been washed!), but the seafood overshadows them. Fish, crabs, oysters and their numerous cousins from the briny deep are served in various forms: roasted, boiled, fried, etc.

Chile's excellent wines, unquestionably the best in Latin America, complement these dishes admirably. Chile's three hundred wineries produce some one thousand varieties of wine, an inexhaustible selection. Some are ranked by quality: *vino reservado* is the best of all, followed by *vino especial*.

Most restaurants customarily offer a four-course table d'hote menu: appetizer (usually salad or vegetables), soup, entree and dessert. This is much less expensive than ordering each course separately (a la carte), and the quality of the food is definitely adequate. Chileans eat lunch between noon and 3pm, and dinner after 9pm. It is customary to leave a 10% tip.

When to come; national holidays
Summer — from October to April — is the best time to visit Chile, both the cities and the countryside. During the winter — July through October — the excellent ski areas near and south of Santiago are open.

The major holidays are January 1, May 1, August 15, September 18 (Independence Day), October 12 (Columbus' Day), November 1 and December 25.

Currency
The local currency is the *peso*. Lately restrictions have been placed on the foreign exchange market, but there is no black market. Cashing travelers' checks is slightly more complicated than dealing in cash, especially outside of Santiago, but no significant difference in exchange rates is involved. Bank drafts are paid in local currency only, as are cash withdrawals against credit cards.

American Express and *Diners Club* cards are widespread and accepted in most of the exclusive hotels and restaurants.

Domestic transportation
Buses run between all the major cities, from Arica in the north to Puerto Montt in the south. If you have a student card you're entitled to a sizable discount, though you may have to demand it forcefully (though politely) at times, since drivers are not too eager to give it.

Passenger trains currently operate only in the Santiago region, on a line between the capital and Puerto Montt. The trip is fast and pleasant, though tickets must be purchased in advance. Second class is crowded and uncomfortable. *Lan Chile* Airlines provides frequent air service between all major cities.

You can continue south of Puerto Montt in three ways: via

Argentina, by air, or by ship (see "Puerto Montt"). It is easy to find your way in a rented or private car, for the roads are good and, with the help of the up-to-date maps supplied by the local Auto Club, you can go almost anywhere without difficulty.

The Chileans' friendliness is expressed on the highways, too. Hitchhiking is more commonplace here than anywhere else in South America. Drivers will often volunteer to take hitchhikers to their destination, even if they have to make a detour to do so. It usually won't take you long to flag someone down, and the overall experience is a pleasure!

Measurements, electricity, time
The metric system is standard. Electrical current: 220V.

The Chilean hour is GMT-4 (GMT-3 in summer)

A suggested itinerary for touring Chile
Due to Chile's length, there is no point in covering the country from end to end. It is better to combine your visit to this interesting country with trips to nearby sites in the countries to the east. In accordance with your general route, you can cross the Andes in various places, "pop in" at adjacent sites, and head back. Tourist sites in Chile are concentrated in the following regions:

North: between Arica and Antofagasta
Center: Santiago de Chile and its vicinity
South-central: the area between Temuco and Isla Chiloé, including the lake area.
South: Patagonia and Tierra del Fuego; Puerto Natales, Punta Arenas, and surroundings.

Central Chile

Santiago de Chile

Chile's capital was founded by Pedro de Valdivia in 1541, when he arrived at the site with a group of Spanish settlers. The city developed slowly, evolving gradually into an economic, social and political center of great importance and, in due course became the national capital.

Its location in the geographical center of Chile, between north and south, close to the ocean (100 km) on the one side and to the Andes (50 km) on the other, also aided Santiago's development and helped turn it into the bustling nerve center of the entire country. Alongside the splendid scenery and exceptional design, Santiago's altitude — 556 m above sea level — gives the city an ideal climate both summer and winter.

Close to one third of all Chileans — about 5 million — have chosen to live in Santiago and its environs and with good reason: The region is in a state of constant expansion and development. Santiago's elegant upper-class east side is home to the rich elite. The poorest citizens — who have migrated from the countryside in search of fortune in the big city — live in the overcrowded and depressed south side, which is also the industrial and commercial zone (about 60% of Chile's industry is concentrated here). The city's commercial, political and cultural heart flaunts an untidy melange of building styles, with grand Colonial-style facades from the sixteenth to nineteenth centuries standing alongside modern office buildings, shopping centers and the like. But the promising exterior cannot hide the economic depression afflicting Chile: streets and avenues abound with peddlers, hawking their wares on every corner.

Its rare scenery, tourist sites, comfortable climate and hospitable citizens combine to make Santiago an interesting and pleasant city to visit.

How to get there

By air: The modern Arturo Benitez Airport is 24 km from Santiago. A fast, comfortable Aerobus Tours Express bus sets out for the city every hour, with other buses plying the route at irregular intervals. Taxi fare to the city is fixed, irrespective of the number of passengers.

SANTIAGO

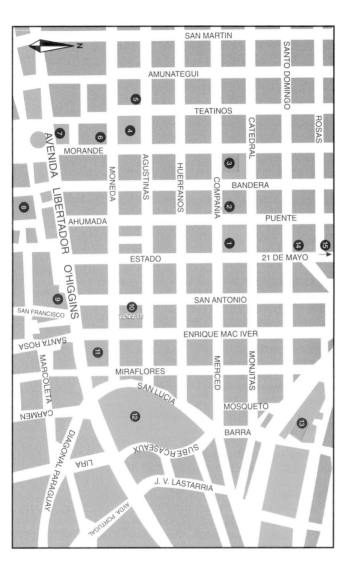

CHILE

By land: Numerous bus lines link Santiago with the north and south. Most of these arrive at and depart from the Alameda Bus Terminal, on Alameda O'Higgins. Buses arriving from Argentina also stop at this station. From here the subway takes you downtown in a matter of minutes. Buses from Uruguay, Perú, Brazil, Ecuador, Colombia and Venezuela operate from the offices of their respective companies, all located downtown.

The central train station, too, is situated on Alameda O'Higgins. Several trains set out daily, all headed south, stopping at the large cities until they reach Puerto Montt (an eighteen-hour trip). Though a second-class ticket is cheaper than bus fare, second-class cabins are crowded, uncomfortable and not recommended for long trips. To secure a seat, you must buy your ticket in advance at the railway offices (not at the station), at Alameda O'Higgins 853 (Tel. 398247), open Mon.-Fri. 8:30am-7pm and Sat. from 9am to 1pm.

Where to stay
Most of the hotels in Santiago are located downtown, within walking distance from a metro station. In Las Condes you can find some Apart-hotels.

Very expensive
Carrera: Teatinos 180; tel. 6982011, fax 6721083.
Holiday Inn: Av. Bernardo O'Higgins 136; tel. 381042, fax 336015.
Sheraton San Cristóbal: Av. Santa María 1742; tel. 2335000, fax 2341729.

Expensive
Tupahue: San Antonio 477; tel. 383810, fax 395240.
El Conquistador: Cruchaga 920; tel.+ fax 6965599.
Aloha: Francisco Noguera 146; tel. 2332230, fax 2332494.

Moderate
Libertador: Av. Bernardo O'Higgins 853; tel. 394212.
City: Compañias 1063; tel. 6954526.
Santa Lucía: Huérfanos 779, 4th floor; tel. 398201. Recommended.

Inexpensive hotels are located some distance from the city center, mainly in the vicinity of the train station and Alameda O'Higgins. Most are reasonably clean and provide very basic services (though it's a very good idea to check for hot water — its availability should not be taken for granted). One such hotel is the *Souvenir* at Calle Amunategui 850, near the Mapucho Station.

What to eat, where and when

Breakfast, lunch, and *once* — rather like afternoon tea, taken between 5 and 7pm — can be had at any of Santiago's many restaurants. Most offer standard Continental fare during the day. These restaurants-cafés open in the early morning hours and are packed at meal time. In the vicinity of the train station, the markets and the city center, there are many such restaurants, most rather inexpensive. In places where you eat at the counter, prices are about 25% lower.

As for dinner, the picture is altogether different. It's customarily not eaten before 9pm and is served in restaurants of various sorts, with regard both to menu and to prices. Supper is a quick, informal affair in popular restaurants, but can easily turn into a sumptuous feast in the excellent luxury restaurants, which you'll find downtown and in the big hotels. Most such establishments serve superb seafood, along with meat and poultry.

The seafood is of rare quality; washed down with the excellent local wines, it is a pleasure you must not miss. We'll mention only one of the most special restaurants, *Los Adobes de Argomedo*, on the corner of Argomedo and Lira (Tel. 229794), which serves excellent meals at reasonable prices. The large restaurant is decorated in ranch-style, and the waiters are dressed accordingly. Each evening at 10 o'clock there's a rousing folklore performance with songs and dancing. Los Adobes specializes in steaks, seafood and popular Chilean dishes.

Transportation

Santiago's modern subway makes getting around downtown much easier. And although the lines are short (the longest is 11 km), it saves a great deal of travel time since it passes under the congested city center. It operates from 6am till 10:30pm during the week, and from 7am till 10pm during weekends. Buses and minibuses also run with great frequency, but are usually jammed. Taxis — a very large fleet — are painted black and have yellow tops. They charge by the meter, adding a 50% surcharge after 9pm and on Sundays.

Tourist services

The Government Tourist Bureau, *Sernatur*, at Avenida Providencia 1550 (tel. 6960474), can provide a wealth of information about Santiago and the entire country. The office is located opposite the Congress building and is open from 9am-6pm (half-day on Saturday).

Explanatory material is available at the Auto Club, Calle Pedro

CHILE

de Valdivia 195. Topographic maps may be obtained at the *Instituto Geográfico Militar*, at Alameda 240.

Airline offices are located downtown on Agustinas, Moneda and Huérfanos, between Morandé and Estado. The central office of the national airline, *Lan Chile*, is at Calle Agustinas 640 (tel. 6323211).

Tourist sites

Anyone wishing to get to know Santiago should begin at the beautiful central square, **Plaza de Armas**. This marks the edge of the downtown area which stretches from it to the Alameda — Avenida O'Higgins. The lovely plaza, the heart of the entire city, is the site of some of the most important municipal institutions: The **Post and Telegraph Office** at its northern end, houses a small **Postal Museum** (Mon.-Fri., 9am-5pm). The building to the right is the **Palacio de la Real Audiencia**, where the local government gathered during the last years of the colonial period. Today it houses the **Museo Histórico Nacional** (National Historic Museum, open Wed.-Sat., 10am-5:50pm, and Sun., 10am-1:45pm). The next building is the **Municipalidad** (*City Hall*); the original building was founded in 1670, and served as *Cabildo*, and later as a prison. Destroyed by a fire, the actual building was erected in 1892-5. In front of it, we can see the monument to the founder of Santiago, Pedro de Valdivia.

On the western side of the square, are the beautiful **Cathedral** and its **Museo de la Catedral** (open Mon. 10am-1pm, and 3:30-7pm; during the summer also on Wed.). The main commercial streets branch off from here, as does the handsome pedestrian street **Ahumada**, which extends as far as Alameda O'Higgins.

East of the plaza, on Calle Merced toward the corner with San Antonio, we find the **Casa Colorada** (Red House), built in 1769 for the most prosperous businessman of the period, don Mateo de Toro y Zambrano. Later it became the governor's residence and the Presidential mansion; today we can visit the **Museo de Santiago** (open Tues.-Sat. 10am-6pm, Sun. and Holidays 11am-1:30pm).

The Ex-**Congress Building** is located two blocks west of the plaza on the corner of Compañía and Morandé; today it serves the Ministry of Foreign Affairs. The garden is open to public. A left turn onto Calle Morandé takes us to **Plaza de la Constitución**, where we find the Chilean Finance Ministry. The magnificent building to the north is the **Hotel Carrera**. On the plaza's southern side, the official Government Palace — **La Moneda**, built in 1805 — stands in all its splendor. The magnificent palace was damaged during the 1973 military coup, and here the President was murdered. Every second day, between 10 and 10:30am, you can watch the **Change of Guard**.

From here it's only a short stoll to Santiago's main avenue, **Avenida Bernardo O'Higgins,** called the **Alameda** by the local citizens. This boulevard, about a hundred meters wide and more than three kilometers long, is in fact the southern border of the commercial district. It is adorned with gardens, statues, fountains and scores of public institutions. Hundreds of peddlers hawk their wares — highly varied, mostly cheap — up and down the sidewalks. Turning right, westward, we head toward the train station and unremarkable residential quarters; a left turn, eastward, will bring us to some of the most beautiful and impressive sites in town.

As we walk down the Alameda, we first discover on our right the grand structure which houses the **University of Chile**, founded in 1842, and the largest and most important of the country's seven universities. Powerful spotlights illuminate the magnificant structure by night, and the vicinity pulses with life until very late.

Three blocks onward, on the same side of the street, is Santiago's oldest church, the **Iglesia San Francisco**, topped by a tall red spire. Built between 1586 and 1628, it houses the interesting **Museum of San Francisco** (open Wed.-Sun., 10am-1pm, and 3-6pm) with pieces of Colonial and Religious Art; paintings from the seventeenth and eighteenth centuries are displayed alongside some of the nation's most important national-religious treasures. Particularly interesting are 54 large paintings describing the life of St. Francisco. The museum is arranged in good taste and certainly merits a visit.

Crossing the Alameda opposite the Church and walking down Calle San Antonio for about two blocks, we reach the **Teatro Muncipal** (Muncipal Theater), Chile's most important center for the performing arts. Major musical and theatrical performances take place here often, and it is recommended that you go to one of them.

Continuing down the Alameda, but now on its northern side, two blocks past Iglesia San Francisco, we find on our left the impressive **Biblioteca Nacional** (National Library), a majestic French-style building built between 1913 and 1924. With over 6 million volumes, and the National archives, this library (open Mon.-Fri. 8am-9pm) is one of the largest in South America.

Past the Library rises **Santa Lucía Hill**. It was near this spot that the Spanish seafarer Pedro de Valdivia founded Santiago 450 years ago. The well tended hill is undoubtedly one of the loveliest and most pleasant places in Santiago, and the

CHILE

view it affords is unforgettable. Trails and numerous flights of steps (or an elevator) lead to its top, where a small church and modest **Archaeological Museum** repose (open Tue.-Sat., 10:30am-2pm and 3:30-7pm; during the summer also on Sun. 11am-2pm). Benches and fountains scattered among the flower beds and trees add a touch of tranquility to the hill. A visit here is unquestionably a "must", and you can time it to coincide with a relaxing afternoon *siesta*, with the bustling city at your feet.

North of Santa Lucía Hill, on the bank of the Río Mapocho, lies one of the most beautiful and best kept of Santiago's parks — the **Parque Forestal**, designed in its present form in 1901. The **National Museum of Fine Arts** (Museo Nacional de Bellas Artes) is situated here (in the corner with Calle Miguel de la Barra, open Tues.-Sat., 11am-8pm, Sun. 10am-6pm). It is an impressive institution with an extensive permanent collection of paintings and sculptures by Chilean Artists. Undoubtedly the most important of its kind in Chile, the museum is well set out and properly maintained and a visit here is highly recommended. (Part of it is currently closed, as restorations of parts damaged during the earthquake of 1985 are under way.)

Another central site not to be overlooked is the park on **San Cristóbal Hill.** The steep hill (880 m above sea level, 340 m higher than the Plaza de Armas) stands out against the backdrop of the city, and its summit is Santiago's highest point. The hill is located north of the Rio Mapocho, within walking distance from downtown (about 1.5 km), not far from Santa Lucía Hill, Parque Forestal, and the Art Museum. The cablecar will take you to the hill's summit, where an enormous **statue of the Virgin Mary** looks out over the splendid view below. The statue is illuminated in the evening, and the panorama of Santiago's lights is most impressive.

The well tended **park** on the hill offers a wealth of amusement and recreation facilities, including restaurants and a swimming pool. Halfway up the hill is the **Municipal Zoo**, with more than one thousand animals (open Tues.-Sun. 10am-6pm). The cablecar has a station at the zoo entrance. In the park's upper section the statue of the Virgin is kept company by an interesting **observatory** (run by the Catholic University), restaurants, and park benches. These are dispersed among lawns and shrubbery, groves of shade trees, fountains and other graceful attractions which lend the park its special charm.

While in the park, be sure to see the **Enoteca** (Wine Museum). This handsome Colonial building has been lovingly restored and displays many of the wonderful Chilean wines. A visit here is no substitute for visiting one of Chile's wineries, where one can see the wine-making process; however, the Enoteca is interesting for its own sake. What's more, the friendly waiters will invite you for a little drink, on the house, at the end of your visit!

Parque O'Higgins, another special place, is located between Avenida Tupper and Avenida Rondizzoni (buses 19 and 20 from downtown, or subway line 2 to the *El Parque* station). A small, Colonial-style village — *El Pueblito* — has been built within the park. Among its eighteen houses are restaurants that specialize in the cuisine of Chile's different regions. Alongside the restaurants are displays of local crafts, and you can see artists at work. The park is open Tues.-Sat., 8am-8pm. Here you'll also find South America's largest amusement park, with modern and exciting rides laid out with great care amid rich greenery and small pools. The facilities at Fantasilandia are open Wed.-Fri. from 3:30pm, and on Saturdays and Sundays from 10:30am.

Not far from the park, on Avenida Blanco Encalada, is the **Club Hípico**, Santiago's major sports club, founded in 1869. Its swimming pool and recreational facilities are for members only, but the racetrack, where races are held on Sunday and holiday afternoons, attracts crowds of spectators.

Finally, we should also mention the interesting **National History Museum**, located in Parque Quinta Normal (bus 5) with its entrance behind the church. This museum is open Tues.-Sat. 10am-1pm and 2-6pm; Sunday 2:30-6pm; closed Mondays. The museum has a collection of mummies, fossils from all over Chile including a small dinosaur, displays from Easter Island, and more. The most famous exhibit is the frozen body of a child who lived more than five hundred years ago, found in the early 1950s at an elevation of 5000 m above sea level on the peak of El Plomo. The corpse, amazingly well-preserved, is the subject of many studies and theories as to its origin, the culture to which the child belonged, and the circumstances of his death. Some scholars claim that the boy did not die a natural death, but was rather frozen in the ice after having been offered as a human sacrifice to the local gods.

Entertainment, culture, and nightclubs

What with two symphony orchestras, a ballet company, fifteen theaters, scores of cinemas, and more, there's no doubt that Santiago is an important cultural center.

Major cultural events generally take place in the **Teatro Municipal**, Calle San Antonio 149. These include operas, concerts, ballet, and plays. Try to attend a performance if you can. Most of Santiago's other theaters are also located downtown, and so are the many cinemas, which show the latest American releases.

Naturally, we shall not overlook nightclubs and discotheques. These are active chiefly on the weekends, when the various **cafe-concerts**, too, burst into action. In the latter you may spend an enjoyable evening listening to the strains of a small and colorful ensemble, *muy simpatico*. **Barrio Bellavista**, north of rio Mapocho, is the bohemian center with numerous restaurants and cafés. Its atmosphere is vivid and colorful.

Clubs put on folklore shows including the *cueca* — Chile's national dance — for the general public. The most famous and prestigious of these is *El Pollo Dorado* at Calle Agostinas 881, where the excellent show comes with an equally excellent dinner — and at an even higher price! The show starts after 10pm and it is best to make reservations.

Currency exchange
Foreign currency can be changed at banks and through moneychangers (*cambio*). Banks customarily charge a commission, especially for cashing travelers' checks. Many moneychangers will cash travelers' checks into dollars, and you should avail yourself of their services if you are continuing on to countries where a black market operates and cashing these checks can be a sticky and complicated affair.

Most moneychangers are located downtown, on Huérfanos and Agostinas. They are closed in the afternoons, and for most Saturday is a half-day. Luxury hotels have in-house moneychangers; be sure to deal with them and not with hotel cashiers! Compare rates before changing currency, for the differences may amount to several percent.

Postal and telephone services
The central Post Office is situated in a large building on the Plaza de Armas. Here you can mail letters, send packages, and make international phone calls.

Shopping
Santiago's largest and most important shopping district is along the streets that border the Plaza de Armas, and those leading from it toward Alameda O'Higgins. Two streets in this area — Huérfanos and Ahumada — are pedestrian malls, lined with stores that offer merchandise ranging from miscellaneous souvenirs to the latest in consumer goods.

Speaking of souvenirs, the government shop (*CEMA*) at Avenida Portugal 351, undoubtedly offers the broadest selection. This store, housed in an impressive colonial-era building, is the main branch of a specialty chain set up by the Government aimed at providing tourists with one central "address" for most types of souvenirs and products typical of Chile. Bear in mind, of course, that prices here are higher than elsewhere; if you're exploring the entire country, you'll do well to buy your souvenirs outside the capital. Nevertheless it's certainly worth your while to pay the government store a visit for a first impression — it's got everything.

Chile is especially noted for metal crafts. Since mining is so important to the economy, it's only natural that Chilean artists and craftsmen make use of a variety of metals as their raw material. Accordingly, you can find silver, copper and bronze artwork of many types and tastes, from decorative housewares, ashtrays and candlesticks to coffee tables and other furniture. The silver jewelry, studded with locally produced gems, is truly special.

Embroidery, ponchos, rugs, clothing and various leather goods are produced outside of Santiago, primarily in southern Chile, and are likely to be much cheaper there. The lovely pottery prominently displayed in shop windows is also "imported" — from a small town named Pamaire, located some 60 km from Santiago in the heart of a region rich in clay. Those with a taste for the potter's craft will certainly wish to visit Pamaire and watch the craftsmen at work in their homes.

Chilean wines are excellent and inexpensive. You should try them at every opportunity — as the saying goes — wine is proof that God loves men!

The area surrounding the Hotel Carrera is packed with stores that offer a variety of souvenirs, handicrafts and jewelry. This is certainly the place for you to do your shopping. For one, it's where the locals go; for another, prices are reasonable (there's probably a connection here!). For clothing and footwear go back to the city center, where the large stores sell the latest fashions — at appropriate up-to-date prices. High quality shoes, purses and leather briefcases are relatively inexpensive.

A new and modern shopping center is located in Providencia, ten minutes from downtown. Here you'll find dozens of boutiques and nice little shops that offer a huge selection of merchandise of all kinds, at various prices.

Weather
The Santiago area enjoys a relatively comfortable climate. Summer is hot and dry, with the afternoons and evenings particularly pleasant. Winter is cold, though temperatures rarely

fall below freezing. Most of the rain falls in winter, though scattered showers may occur in spring and autumn as well.

Important addresses and phone numbers

Immigration Department (for extending your visa): Moneda 1342; Tel. 6725320.
Ambulances: Tel. 2224422
First Aid: Tel. 342291
Police: Tel. 133
Firemen: Tel. 132
Skiers Emergency Rescue: Tel. 136
Sernatur (Tourist Information): Providencia 1550; tel. 6960474
Lan Chile: Agustinas 640; tel. 6323211
Ladeco: O'Higgins 107; tel. 338343

Embassies

Germany: Agustinas 785; tel. 335031
Australia: Gertrudis Echeñique 420; tel. 2285065
Belgium: Av. Providencia 2653; tel. 2321070
Canada: Ahumada 11; tel. 6962256
Italy: Clemente Fabres 1050; tel. 2232467
Spain: Av. Andrés Bello 1895; tel. 2352755
U.S.A.: Agustinas 1343; tel. 6710133
France: Av. Condell 65; tel. 2251030
U.K.: Av. El Bosque Norte 0125; tel. 2313737

On to Argentina

In addition to the air service described above, many companies provide overland service between Santiago and Argentina — chiefly to Mendoza. For details, see the chapter on Argentina (Mendoza). The most reliable companies, as far as schedules and service are concerned, are *Nueva O'Higgins San Martín* (recommended), Calle San Francisco 30 (Tel. 380-410), and *Cata*, Calle Huérfanos 1147 (Tel. 65845, 69502).

Around Santiago

Since Santiago is halfway between the mountains and the sea, it's only natural that vacation and getaway sites of various sorts are relatively close by — the seashore to the west and ski resorts to the east. Viña del Mar, the western resort town, is Chile's most popular summer vacation spot, while the various ski slopes in the soaring Andes have achieved international fame, and are equal in quality to similar resorts in Europe or the United States.

CHILE

Viña del Mar

Viña del Mar (pop. 310,000) is one of the most beautiful and picturesque of South American cities; it has become Chile's most popular vacation resort for good reason. With its broad avenues and their rows of towering palm trees, its well tended plazas full of shrubbery and flowers, its bustling promenade, open air cafés and white beaches, Viña del Mar welcomes the visitor to its relaxed, carefree atmosphere. Add the excellent climate and a wealth of hotels and restaurants, and you've got all the ingredients for a successful resort town.

When to come and how to get there

Viña del Mar is only a few kilometers from Valparaiso, Chile's second largest city. Buses from Santiago leave the Mapucho station frequently; the 135-km trip takes about two hours. The official season at Viña del Mar runs from September 15 until March 15. However, the city is buzzing from late August through the end of April. During this period it is almost impossible to find a room unless you book well in advance.

Where to stay

Viña del Mar has countless hotels and guest houses at various levels of price and service — from luxury hotels to cheap hostels to campgrounds.

Miramar: Av. Marina s/n, Caleta Abarca; tel. 626677, fax 665220. Five Stars, superb.
O'Higgins: Plaza Vergara s/n; tel. 882016, fax 883537. Four stars, recommended.
San Martín: Av. San Martín 667; tel. 689191, fax 689195. Four stars, out of town.
Hotel de Viña: Viana 619; tel.882953. Small, three-star hotel, moderate price.
Hotel Von Schroeders: Von Schroeders 392; tel. 660081. Three stars.

A great many cheap hotels and pensions (*residenciales*) are dispersed throughout the town; most are reasonably clean. The youth hostel, near the Sausalito stadium, admits only card-carrying members of the Youth Hostel Association.

What to see

The Chilean Tourism Ministry has an Information Bureau at Avenida Valparaiso 507, third floor, suite 303 (Tel. 882285).

Viña del Mar makes no pretenses of offering anything beyond rest and recreation, and has no special "tourist sites". Wander through town — on foot, by car, or in a horse-drawn carriage — and pass the luxury hotels, fancy villas, and handsome

167

residences built around the plazas, and surrounding Laguna Marga Marga in the town center; keep going until you reach the floral clock at the seashore. A tour such as this will afford you a basic familiarity with Viña del Mar, and thereafter you'll probably prefer to spend your daylight hours stretched out on the soft, clean sand at the beach. The well-maintained public beaches run the full length of the city, and are packed with thousands of bathers in a colorful, merry tumult. On the beaches and in the city itself you will find abundant opportunities for recreation activities such as golf, tennis and water sports.

In the afternoons and evenings, nothing beats the promenade for a relaxing stroll, during which you can comtemplate the sun as it sinks bewitchingly into the western sea. Here you can also enjoy the enticing aromas that waft from dozens of restaurants and cafes, and savor the ice cream, fruit juices and the like — high-calorie pleasures to be sure (beware — you'll have to reappear in swimwear the next day...). You can, of course, choose one of the superb seafood restaurants and enjoy an evening feast in the fresh sea air. Afterwards, Viña del Mar offers you its multifaceted nightlife: cinemas, discotheques (the most famous is *Topsy Topsy*, one of the most beautiful in South America), concerts and ballet (intermittently), and,of course, the municipal casino, housed in a large building approached by a bridge over Laguna Marga Marga.

Viña del Mar is surrounded by small resort towns that benefit from the large city's tourist "spillover". The most attractive and interesting of these is **Renaca**, five km north of Viña del Mar, with hotels, restaurants and beautiful beaches. If you find that Viña del Mar is booked up — or, alternatively, if you want to rest in a quieter place — go to Renaca; a totally enjoyable experience is guaranteed.

Ski resorts
Several dozen kilometers east of Santiago, a number of the most interesting and beautiful ski areas in South America are hidden away among the snow-capped peaks of the Andes. Taking advantage of the topography and comfortable climate of the region, the Chileans have built resort towns that provide skiers with service of international caliber. This, along with excellent slopes for skiers of all levels, from beginner to world champion, has proven a powerful magnet for the skiing set.

When to come and how to get there
Because the seasons are "reversed" in South America, winter, the best ski season, runs from June through October, when the ridges are covered with more than six feet of gleaming snow

that makes for superb skiing. Accommodation is hard to find during the ski season, though possibilities abound in the various towns. It is best, of course, to make reservations, but a little patience and perseverance will probably find you a place to lay your head even at the height of the season. The farther south you go, the longer the ski season lasts, and in southern Chile you can usually go skiing even in late November.

Ski slopes can be reached by rented car (depending on the conditions of the road on snowy days), bus and train. Buses of the Grez company (Calle Ahumada 312, suite 315, Tel. 83997) leave Santiago several time a day. The trip lasts up to four hours each way. Several companies specialize in package excursions to the ski slopes, supplying transportation, lodging, meals, and lift tickets. These deals are rather expensive; if you can reach the Andes on your own you'll probably save quite a bit. Reservations can be made at the Chile Ski Club in Santiago, Calle Compañía 1068, suite 1009 (Tel. 81247).

Special shops and ski clubs on the slopes rent out all kinds of ski equipment. You must remember to bring warm clothing, a woolen cap, gloves and, of course, sunglasses to prevent snow-blindness.

Portillo
Chile's most famous and best developed ski area is Portillo, site of the 1966 world ice-skating championships. It's a nice little town, 144 km from Santiago and 2865 m above sea level. Picturesque Portillo, surrounded by snow-covered and treeless mountains, is the primary ski area and one of the most popular resorts in all of South America. Here many ski lifts will carry you to the slopes, which are well-appointed both in quantity and in quality. Skiing instruction and other services are also available. Portillo's snow is smooth; even beginners will find it easy to ski here. Even so, be careful to choose the course which best suits your proficiency. On the village edge is a long, narrow lake — *Laguna del Inca*. Frozen over during the winter, its glassy surface serves as a skating rink and playground. The *Hotel Portillo* is the town's largest and grandest, but its prices appear to stand in direct proportion to its altitude. There are, to be sure, other hotels, but these are rather expensive as well.

Farellones
The resort area of Farellones (elevation 2300 m), which has grown more popular in recent years, is a mere fifty kilometers from Santiago. Only ninety minutes from the capital, Farellones is surrounded by a number of small resort villages (the most

famous are *La Parva* and *El Colorado*). Taken all together they offer vacationers a broad range of winter sports. The hotels and restaurants here are less expensive than those in Portillo and are in ample supply. The weather is great; the sun beams down and the ski runs are clearly marked and well designated. Many lifts, a skiing school and equipment rental shops are at your service, making it easy for you to get organized. Many young skiers prefer Farellones because of its relaxed, informal atmosphere, reasonable prices and rare beauty. Santiago's two universities — the General and the Catholic — operate inexpensive hostels for those of limited means. Although they are situated slightly out of town, you will find their atmosphere pleasant. Recommended.

The Northern Deserts

Chile's northern third is a vast, arid, and desolate desert which, apart from a few medium sized cities and small oases, shows absolutely no sign of life. The sun, which beats down mercilessly 365 days a year, and the nearly total absence of rain, prevent the existence of any sort of flora, and because of the lack of water there is no wild life. Settlement here is therefore based on a continual supply of water and food from central Chile, and the inhabitants derive their income mainly from the abundant natural resources with which this part of Chile has been blessed.

Arica

Chile's northern border town, 2340 km north of Santiago, lies on the Pacific coast near the border with Perú, and serves as a transit point for those arriving overland from Perú and also from Bolivia. Arica's 100,000 residents engage in commerce and services, for most of the exports and imports of neighboring landlocked Bolivia pass through the town. Arica, Chile's "city of perpetual spring" with an annual temperature of 22 degrees Centigrade (72 degrees Fahrenheit), is steadily gaining in popularity as a resort. Its fine beaches and excellent location, the desert scenery with sand dunes stretching as far as the eye can see, the blue ocean to the west, and the Andes delimiting the eastern horizon, provide sufficient reason for this.

How to get there

Arica's airport links the city with Santiago and Antofagasta (from where you can reach the rest of the country), and with La Paz, capital of Bolivia. The Pan-American Highway, running the length of South America, passes through Arica and links it with Perú to the north and Antofagasta and Santiago to the south. Traffic on this road is rather sparse, gasoline stations are few, and settlements are separated by many long hours of travel.

From Arica, regular bus routes run north to Perú and south to Santiago. The southern route is traveled by several companies — some provide meals on the way — and the fare is high. It is twelve hours from Arica to Antofagasta, and twenty-eight to Santiago. Hitchhiking on this road is rather difficult, due

CHILE

Parque Lauca

to the light traffic. But if you've decided to try anyway, be sure to keep your head covered and bring plenty of water, as you're liable to spend long hours waiting in the hot sun. If you plan to drive, check with the Tourist Bureau as to whether you'll need special permits at checkposts along the highway; furthermore, be sure to take along enough fuel and an extra container of water.

On to Bolivia
A train runs between Arica and La Paz only twice a month, but buses set out daily for Charana, the Bolivian border town. The road climbs to heights of 4000 m above sea level, and crosses **Parque Lauca**. From Charana there is a train twice weekly to La Paz, and the line is full and crowded. One must take warm clothes for the trip because even on clear days it is cold at these high altitudes.

An entrance permit for 30 days is issued at the Bolivian border, and can be extended, if necessary, in La Paz.

Food and lodging
Since Arica became a popular resort town, hotels, pensions and restaurants have sprouted like weeds. The rustic Hotel *El Paso* is delightful, and moderately priced. The *Hotel King* is

Arica — the cliff of Morro de Arica

slightly cheaper, and provides good service. There are numerous pensions (*residenciales*) in Arica — clean, comfortable and very inexpensive — along with a simple campground at the southern end of town, along the seashore.

Arica's restaurants and cafés are mostly located around the beaches and provide tasty, inexpensive fare. *Residenciales* serve especially inexpensive three-course meals. The prestigious restaurants are open in the evening; most specialize in fish and seafood. You'll find an expensive and very good restaurant in the casino building.

What to see

Arica's **Tourist Bureau**, at Calle Prat 375, second floor, tel. 232101, will provide you with up-to-date information about events in town and places to visit in the area.

The wonderful beaches are Arica's main attraction. Along the many miles of clean golden beach you can get a tan, frolic in the cool water the year round, and enjoy the company of other vacationers.

The prominent attraction downtown is **St. Marcos Church** in **Plaza de Armas**, built on an iron frame to the design of the French engineer Gustav Eiffel, designer of the Parisian tower bearing his name.

Fresh fish is sold near the pleasant **fishing port**, where flocks of pelicans rest on the breakwater and feast on the abundance of fish. From the cliff which extends south of the city, there is a good view of the city, the shoreline and the desert inland, and one can also see birds of prey gliding above.

There is a **history museum** built on the cliff which commemorates the glorious battle of the Chilean conquest of Arica from the Peruvians at the end of the 19th century, during the Pacific War. The fine panorama from here is a good reason by itself for the short climb.

There isn't much of a night life here, the most bustling and exclusive place is the **municipal casino**.

As for shopping, Arica offers a choice selection at low prices, since many items are duty-free as part of Government policy to encourage people to live in the region. Photographic equipment and supplies are cheaper here than in Santiago.

Excursions

Arica is the starting point for two interesting places: the town of Tacna on the Peruvian border and Lauca National Park on the road to Bolivia. Each is a short trip from Arica, and you can either return to Arica or keep going to the neighboring countries.

Tacna

The Pan-American Highway out of Arica passes through Tacna on its way to Arequipa, in Perú. You'll cross the border a little before you enter town; if you're going to return to Chile after visiting Tacna, tell the immigration officials before you cross over. There are several buses each day on the 55-kilometer route between Arica and Tacna; the trip takes about an hour and a half. The town has no particular attractions, but it does have a tax free market for electronic and photographic equipment, and it is worth comparing prices with those in Arica.

Parque Nacional Lauca

On a plateau among the snow capped Andes, 140 kilometers east of Arica and about 4000 meters higher, a large area has been set aside for a unique national park.

In this region, administered and supervised by Chile's National Parks Authority (*CONAF: Corporacion Nacional Forestal*), lives one of the largest concentrations of *vicuñas* in the world. This member of the llama family was hunted nearly to the point of extinction for its soft wool and delectable meat. The United Nations intervened and the *vicuña* was declared a protected species. In the countries where they live in relatively large numbers (chiefly Chile and Bolivia), their habitats were declared nature reserves, and off-limits to hunters. Another rare animal which exists in large numbers in the park is the *vizcacha*, a creature which resembles a rock rabbit.

Parque Lauca, however, offers more than lots of *vicuñas* and hundreds of species of birds and animals. Its wonderful location, exquisite scenery, and lovely blend of blue lakes, green plants and snowy white peaks will make your visit there a special experience.

There aren't too many ways to get there, however, since transportation to Lauca is not well organized. Tour companies in Arica offer one-day outings to the park, but these are naturally rather expensive. Those with time on their hands will be interested in hiking Lauca's wonderful trails for a few days and then going on to Bolivia. Ask about transportation at the CONAF offices, since CONAF sends a supply truck to Lauca several times a week, and you can often hitch a ride. There are several *refugios* — little wooden cabins for tourists who need a place to sleep — scattered about the park.

Be sure to keep in mind that you may encounter difficulties in breathing because of the high altitude (guidelines for coping with high altitudes are given in the Introduction).

Iquique

Iquique, the capital of Chile's northern region, 316 km south of Arica (500 km north of Antofagasta), is an important center of Chilean fish industry. It reached its peak at the turn of the 19th century and beginning of 20th century, as a salt mining center. At this period impressive buildings were built. As prices of salt went down, the fish industry gained importance. In 1975 Iquique was declared "Zona Franca" (free port), known as Zofri, and since then commerce has flourished. Today 150,000 people live in Iquique.

The most impressive buildings are at the historical quarter, around the main plaza. There is a fine clocktower and the Municipal Theater, which was built in 1890 as a symbol of richness and power. The regional museum (open Mon.-Fri. 9am-1pm, 4-8pm, weekends 10.30am-1pm) is at Baquedano 951, and displays the archaeology and anthropology of the region.

At the Zofri, north of town, you might find different products at attractive prices. Open Mon.-Fri. 10am-1pm, 4-9pm, Sat. 10am-2pm.

Antofagasta

The port city of Antofagasta (pop. 200,000) is the largest town in northern Chile. Life here is centered around the harbor, where a massive breakwater protects the anchorage from ocean storms. This port, from which most Chilean copper is exported, is the most important one to the national economy and Antofagastans are proud of the fact. Along with an excellent climate, Antofagasta boasts broad beaches studded with stones carved into wondrous forms by the pounding surf. Because of its industrial nature, however, Antofagasta is not known as a resort town or tourist attraction. Its great economic importance notwithstanding, the city actually has no substantial economic base of its own, and even drinking water is piped in from streams in the foothills of the Andes.

How to get there

Antofagasta's airport links the city with all parts of Chile, plus Argentina, Bolivia, Perú, and even the United States. The most frequent service is to Santiago.

Buses, too, connect Antofagasta with Santiago, Arica, La Paz and Argentina. The Pan-American Highway passes through the city and is its main street. The train runs from Antofagasta to La Paz, the capital of Bolivia. The difficult trip takes more than a day and half, with the train climbing to elevations where the thin air makes breathing difficult. The nights are extremely cold;, so if you're planning a night trip, bring along a sleeping bag in addition to warm clothing!

Where to stay

Inasmuch as Antofagasta is an industrial city, it's only natural that most hotels there are intended for business travelers. The best is the *Antofagasta*, Balmaceda 2675, tel. 224710, which offers its guests a broad range of services and rest and recreation facilities. The *San Martín*, at San Martín 2781, tel. 263503, is an intermediate-class hotel. Inexpensive hotels are located near the bus terminal, around the train station, and along Calle San Martín.

Restaurant menus are reasonably varied, but the seafood is especially good. In the large hotels, at the Automobile Club at the edge of town, and at the seafront restaurants you can eat well without too great an financial outlay. Fish and seafood are cheaper than meat which, along with most of the merchandise in Antofagasta's shops, must be brought in from Santiago, and is therefore somewhat more expensive.

What to see

The city itself does not have much to offer from a tourist's viewpoint. If you find yourself here on business (unlikely), or en route to somewhere else (far more likely), take advantage of your brief stay to take a walk downtown. Visit the **Clock Tower** in the central plaza (a gift of the British community in Chile), and the beautiful **University** and adjacent **Museum**; see the bustling **port** and go out to the seashore.

The most popular beach is **La Portada** where, in addition to swimming and sunbathing, you can contemplate the effect of seawater on the rocks. Restaurants abound near the waterfront and nearly all of them specialize in fish and seafood. Their atmosphere is pleasant and their prices affordable.

For evening hours you'll find cinemas, discotheques, and a theater downtown.

The Tourist Ministry is located at Baquedano 360, second floor, tel. 264044.

Excursions

Chuquicamata

Some 220 kilometers northeast of Antofagasta, at an elevation of 3011 meters above sea level, is the largest open-pit copper mine in the world. Until the Allende Government nationalized such industries in the early 1970s, this mine (like many mines and factories) was American-owned. Now it is run by government representatives and the workers, and in the heart of an arid and desolate region, thousands of laborers dig out immense quantities of copper, which is transported first to Antofagasta and then to all corners of the world. Most of the 34,000 residents of the town of Chuquicamata earn their living from mine-related activities.

The guided tour of the enormous pit and the equipment used for excavating and transporting the ore is fascinating. These excursions set out from Antofagasta, but tourists who reach the site by themselves — by public transportation or by hitchhiking — are received at the Tourists' Center at the mine entrance and can join a group there. Lodging possibilities are limited. There are inexpensive workers' restaurants in the mine area and in town.

San Pedro de Atacama

One of the most interesting places in northern Chile is the little village of San Pedro de Atacama, in the heart of the Atacama Desert. This remote hamlet, home to fewer than two thousand people, was a God-forsaken oasis until not many years ago, when fascinating archaeological relics were discovered here, dating from the early Stone Age (the Paleolithic period, 10,000 BC) until the period immediately preceding the Spanish conquest (sixteenth century).

To reach the village, you must go via the city of Calama, 116 kilometers northwest. Buses make the trip several times each week in approximately two and a half hours. On days when there's no bus, you can go by truck or by hitchhiking. There are several hotels and inexpensive pensions in the village, and you can proceed directly — though it's complicated — to Argentina.

The road to San Pedro de Atacama passes through unique "badlands". Here, unlike other such valleys, the strange giant shapes are formed, not of stone, but of salt. Geological changes in this area caused an uplifting of the mountains, which consist of a large quantity of salt; these, once hardened, created a unique and dazzling sight.

On the slopes of the mountains surrounding the village you can make out strange stone formations. These appear to have been ancient redoubts; troves of tools, fabrics, ceramics, jewelery and other artifacts have been found in them. All of these, together with dozens of mummies, skeletons, and skulls, have been put on display in a fascinating **Archaeological Museum** (open daily, 8am-noon and 2-6pm) on the site. Here you may behold the relics of a bygone culture, preserved in exceptionally good condition by the dry climate. The pride of this museum is its collection of mummies of women, whose clothes — and even their hairstyles — have been preserved in an almost perfect state.

Within hiking distance of the village you'll find the remains of what has been called "the lost world". This site, with thousands of ancient graves, strongholds, and settlements, is rich in artifacts more than fifteen centuries old. Here, in addition to mummies and skulls, an abundance of weapons, wood carvings, tools, and various other types of interesting finds have been discovered.

Once you've completed your visit to these sites and seen the museum and its exhibits, there are additional possibilities for short outings in this area, to remote oases populated by Indians, ancient cities of stone, and the volcanic geysers of **El Tatio**, which erupt each morning.

C_HILE_

The South-Central Region —

Land of lakes and volcanoes

Of all the exquisite natural treasures on Earth, not many surpass those of southern Chile's lake district in beauty, grandeur and charm. The rich blend of lakes, dense greenery, small villages, picturesque houses, grazing cattle and volcanoes billowing forth white smoke, creates a wonderful landscape of sublime tranquility.

A trip to southern Chile is one of the most exhilirating experiences a traveler can look forward to while touring South America. Though you must take care to choose the right season (winters here are rainy and unpleasant) it is hard to imagine a more interesting and enchanting place. To absorb the spirit of the area, it's not enough to organize a hasty scramble from site to site. If you mean to cultivate a real affection for this region, you must blend into it at a natural, somewhat slow pace, and conduct yourself with patience, tolerance, attention and sensitivity.

The superb cherries which grow here are another feature of this splendid area, and anglers will enjoy the good fishing in the lakes.

Temuco
The commercial center of this fertile region is Temuco (pop. 200,000), 672 km south of Santiago. Founded only in the 1880s, Temuco is one of Chile's "young" cities, which is evident in its commercial nature, its architecture, and its people. Temuco is located in the heart of the area where most of Chile's surviving Indians dwell, and it serves them as a marketing center for the wares they produce in the surrounding villages and small towns.

Temuco's immediate surroundings are rich in interesting sights and enchanting scenery and there are seven national parks here.

How to get there
Temuco, too, is situated on the Pan-American Highway, and many buses run north to Santiago and as far south as Puerto Montt. The train, running parallel to the highway, is very

THE LAKE DISTRICT

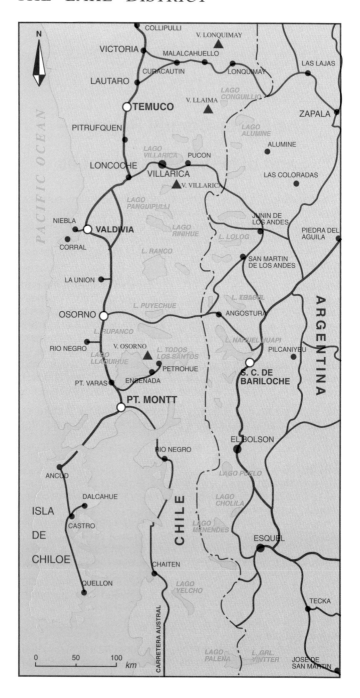

comfortable (especially in Pullman class) and we recommend that you take advantage of it. The trip to Santiago takes about ten hours. Buses set out for Argentina very early every morning, traveling by way of San Martín de los Andes to Bariloche (concerning this lovely route, see "Argentina — the Lake District"). Two companies, one Chilean and the other Argentinian, take turns to travel the route each day. In winter, when the snow builds up at higher elevations, the pass is blocked and the only way to reach Argentina is via Puerto Montt (see below).

Where to stay

The *Hotel Bayern*, at Avenida Prat 146, tel. 213915, and the *Nicolas*, at General Mackenna 420, corner of Portales, tel. 211813, are the best in town. The *Turismo*, at Luis Claro Solar 636, tel. 210583, off the central square, is moderately priced and very nice. Lots of inexpensive pensions are located near the market and the train station. As for food, there's nothing exceptional about Temuco, and the city's many restaurants serve typical Chilean fare. Like the other cities in the south, Temuco offers a wealth of fish and seafood, in addition to the meat and vegetables that grow in this region.

What to see

Temuco's rather narrow main streets are lined with houses, most two stories high, fronted with shops, shops and more shops. The city center has no special attractions apart from Indian men and women in their multicolored dress. With no special sites that one "must" visit, all we can do is amble quietly along the streets, at Temuco's relaxed tempo and make friends with the locals. In order to meet the natives, especially the Indians from the surrounding villages, it's worth your while to visit the large, covered **market**, located downtown on the corner of Rodríguez and Aldunate. Here you'll find foodstuffs, vegetables and meat, along with artifacts, jewelry, handicrafts, weaving, etc. — all made by the Indians. Many of these items are more beautiful and of higher quality than those offered in most South American markets though prices are in accordance. The beautiful ponchos, wall hangings, sweaters, woodcrafts and metalcrafts, all reflect the unique style of this region, though if you're on your way to the Andean countries (Bolivia, Perú, Ecuador) bear in mind the tremendous variety which awaits you there, at much lower prices.

Speaking of marketplaces, we should mention Temuco's **cattle market**, one of the most famous in South America, which operates on Thursdays and Fridays between 1 and 4pm. Dozens of ranchers come into town, bringing hundreds of head of

cattle for sale. Cattle merchants and other interested parties
congregate on a special platform, and the cattle are put up for
auction one by one. Hundreds of cattle are jammed into corrals
next to the train station, and the *huasos* (Chilean cowboys)
then drive them into a small arena where the buyers observe
them and set a price. The prices shouted out by the caller are
per kilogram of meat; once an animal's price is so determined,
the beast is led into a pen to be weighed and have its final price
set. The traders, usually dressed in the traditional ponchos and
wide-brimmed hats, sit as if frozen to their seats and their bids
are indicated by slight gestures apparent only to the auctioneer.
Visitors can watch the proceedings from a roofless terrace.

A stop at the **Museo Araucano** will reward you with further
acquaintance with the Indian community. Here you'll find an
interesting collection of Indian handicrafts from various periods
and of various types. The second floor houses a library on the
subject and the staff will be delighted to answer your questions
and tell you about the local population, their history, customs,
and so forth. After visiting this museum, you can learn more
about the Indian's ways of life by personal experience, and go
out to tour the nearby villages, where you'll meet the Indians in
their daily routine.

If you favor a panoramic view, you'll certainly want to climb
Nielol, a hill which affords a splendid view of the city and its
surroundings. A peace treaty between the Spanish from the
north and the Araucano Indians, who controlled the area until
then, was signed on this hill more than one hundred years
ago and Temuco was founded in the wake of the accord. A
round Indian-style house has been reconstructed on the hill,
and not far away, there is an exhibition of the local flora.

Excursions in the area

Lonquimay — and active volcano
In the late 80's Volcan Lonquimay errupted and created a new
crater. This trip allows us to enjoy a unique experience — to
view this fantastic natural phenomena from a distance of a
few hundred meters only!

From Temuco or Victoria there are buses to the village of
Malalcahuello, from which tours are organized to the volcano.
Make sure that the guide that brings you to the place stays until
dark, when the sight is most impressive.

Indian villages
Several dozen kilometers west of Temuco are a number of
villages populated by Indian tribes. Anyone who expects to see

war-painted Indians is in for a disappointment, since nothing of the sort is at hand. The local residents may perhaps be descendants of such Indians and at times one may even observe traditional ceremonies that have been preserved — but on normal days they listen to the radio, wear sneakers and accept dollars. Nevertheless, their handicrafts, behavior and way of life is extremely interesting.

To reach the villages, either take a taxi or hitchhike about sixty kilometers through lovely scenery (on a far less lovely road) to the coastal town of Carahue. The route passes through small settlements, but only from Carahue onwards, both to the south and up the Rio Imperial, will you encounter communities where life still goes on in a pattern that is slowly vanishing.

Skiing

The Andes rise east of Temuco and their peaks are lower here than they are in the Santiago area. Abundant rainfall and cold climate join forces, with the result that some of Chile's most beautiful and pleasant ski areas are located here. As if to add charm to the idea, some of these ski centers are spread over the snow covered slopes of volcanoes — including some active ones.

Villarica (see below) and Llaima are the most important ski areas. Llaima, 185 km east of Temuco, is at the foot of the volcano bearing the same name. The mountain soars to an elevation of 3060 m, though the highest point in the ski area itself is about a thousand meters lower.

Conguillio National Park

Volcan Llaima is located in the center of the Conguillio National Park. This wonderful park abounds in forests, lakes and snow capped peaks. A dirt road passes through the park and one can tour by car or do some of the walks and hikes. One recommended possibility is the climb to the summit of Llaima, whose crater continuously gives off white smoke. This is a full day's climb, and demands suitable preparation. Another much easier route, which is also enchanting, is the hike along the Sierra Nevada trail, which takes only a few hours. In both cases, one must begin the hike at the camping area in the center of the park, on the shores of the beautiful Lake Conguillio. Those who wish to visit the park without a car can catch a bus which travels the route from Temuco to Melipeucio, a quiet and remote Indian village. From here it is a day and a half of pleasant walking to reach the central camping area, but it is not difficult to hitch a ride along the way.

Mt. Villarica

Villarrica

Villarica is a charming and tranquil town seventy-five kilometers southeast of Temuco. Many buses travel from Villarica to Temuco daily. The trip — south on the Pan-American Highway to the town of Freire, and from there east to Villarrica — takes almost two hours. (The journey is longer and more complicated by train, and is not recommended.) The bus from Temuco to Argentina picks up passengers in Villarrica and Pucón. Villarrica, with a population of 25,000, lies on the southwestern shore of Lake Villarrica and serves as a popular resort and ski center. The lake — twenty kilometers long and eight wide — is one of the most beautiful in the area, and its shore, rich in greenery, provides recreation and resort sites that both tourists and locals love. In summer, throngs of visitors pass their time at water sports — sailing, swimming, fishing — while skiing takes over in the winter.

CHILE

Villarrica has restaurants and a number of hotels, of which the best is the *Yacht Club*, housed in a handsome building surrounded by small houses. The *Hotel Parque*, like the Yacht Club, is located on the lakefront, but is less expensive. In the town itself you'll find cheaper hotels and pensions, though as a rule you must remember that it's a resort town and that prices are quite high, especially during the tourist season.

Pucón

The pleasant town of Pucón (pop. 18,000) hugs the southeastern shore of the lake some twenty-four kilometers east of Villarica. The wonderful climate, the gorgeous scenery and the giant Villarrica volcano, which looms behind the town, have helped make Pucón an exclusive and ever-in-demand resort — a fact reflected in its prices. While it's true that the people who live here should be grateful for the natural delights that have turned their town into such a sought-after place, they should also thank the Queen of England for their prosperity. Since Elizabeth II stayed here during a state visit to Chile in 1968, Pucón's reputation has spread far and wide, and hordes of visitors flock to it. The subject of Pucón's prices is like the question of which came first, the chicken or the egg: whether the Queen's visit caused prices to skyrocket, or whether the prices are so high that one must be the Queen of England to vacation here ...

But we mustn't panic. Anyone who doesn't insist on staying at the lakeshore *Gran Hotel Pucón* or the *Antumalal*, where Her Majesty stayed (tel. 441011), has a reasonable chance of finding cheaper accommodations. Other possibilities are the *Hotel Araucarias*, Caupolican 243, tel. 421286, the motel *Cabañas*, Av. Bernardo O'Higgins, tel. 441122, and the *Hostería Suiza*.

For cheap and pleasant accommodation ask for *Casa Familla Sonia*, where you can rent the necessary equipment — crampons and axes — if you plan to climb the volcan Villarica (see below). Here you can also ask for a guide (ask for Joaquin).

City dwellers will certainly be delighted to spend the night in one of the comfortable and inexpensive campgrounds between Villarrica and Pucón. As for food, apart from the restaurants in town you can try your luck at fishing. Lake Villarrica is packed with fish, and even the inexperienced fisherman can expect to land a satisfactory lunch.

A very pleasant walk is at the little peninsula, where rich chileans built nice houses and have their golf club, within a rich greenery and a fine view of the volcano.

You can hire bycicle from El Pollo, at the corner of calle Palguin and Brazil, for enjoyable trips in the vicinity.

The Volcano

Behind Pucón, Mt. Villarrica rises to an elevation of 2940 m above sea level. Its lovely crater, which erupted most recently in 1985, gives off a constant stream of white smoke and lava particles, and on a clear day can be seen from great distances. The mountain's upper portion if perpetually snow clad; the black stains on it are actually scattered patches of lava. The ski area, thirteen kilometers from Pucón, is reached by a charming dirt road. Before you reach the mountain you'll pass a park rangers' station; the rangers can inform you about the weather, as well as climbing and skiing conditions. During the skiing season a bus leaves from Pucón each morning, though you can always hire a taxi if you so desire (it's also an easy, enjoyable four-hour walk). At the foot of the mountain, near the lower end of the lift, there's a *hostería* that provides accommodation for skiers, but it's quite expensive and open only during the ski season. About one kilometer before you reach it are two *refugios* (cabins) where you can stay for nothing, though these lack water and beds.

Climbing the active volcano at Pucón is stunning, yet difficult and dangerous. It takes more than six exhausting hours to reach the rim of the crater, from which one discovers the awesome sight of molten lava bubbling out of the bowels of the earth.

In order to climb the mountain you've got to get there the day before and spend the night in one of the *refugios*. Bear in mind that the weather is quite treacherous and that the climb is out of the question in winter because of the snow pack covering the mountain. During the rest of the year the weather swings between extremes from one day to the next and it's hard to predict when climbing will be possible.

The mountain's innocent appearance is highly misleading and it doesn't take too long to find this out. You should climb up the left side, which isn't as steep as the right; it's easier though longer. Tremendous lava flows cleave the path leading to the slope, and you must cross them one by one. To add to your burden, the basalt rock is not solid, but consists of layer upon layer of volcanic sand and particles of tuff (porous sedimentary rock). For every twenty centimeters you climb, you're liable to slide back eighteen, as if you're climbing sand dunes. All of this happens in the first four or five hours of the climb. Then you reach the ice belt, a glacial strip that surrounds the crater like a collar. It is very difficult to cross and you should avail yourself of crampons and axe. The glacier is steep and slippery.

With no rocks to grab hold of and no obstacles to break your fall, a slip is liable to end in disaster! **Be very careful!** Once across the glacier, you come to the rim of the crater, which is three hundred meters in diameter and fifty meters deep. Here you'll behold a breathtaking sight. As you stand there, look straight down into the center of the crater, into the gaping green, red and yellow hole in the ground, from which globs of molten lava and grey-white clouds of smoke pour continually. It should be noted that this crater disgorged millions of tons of lava only a few years ago.

The way down is also hard. Be careful not to step on broken chips of ice and don't slide between them; treat lava rocks and downhill slopes with similar caution. Try to go down on exactly the same path you used to go up, and remember to do so by daylight. If you take too long to climb up or spend too much time at the top, you won't have enough time to come down by daylight — an extremely dangerous proposition.

Note
It is true that climbing to the crater of an active volcano is an unparalleled experience, but it involves considerable effort and great danger. Accordingly, if you're considering it, you should give the matter careful thought. To have enough time to reach the crater and return before dark you must set out by 6am the latest, and be prepared for twelve hours of non-stop, exhausting, complicated climbing with neither trail nor path, on porous tuff and slippery, extremely dangerous patches of ice. Dress warmly, for the mountain gusts are bone-chilling despite the exertion of the climb. You **must** wear strong hiking shoes and take along food and water. Crampons and axes are very important.

Do not go without a guide; many have lost their lives on this volcano!

Valdivia
The enchanting town of Valdivia, some 150 km south of Temuco, has a population of 110,000 habitants. It was founded in the 16th century where two rivers join to create the Rio Valdivia. Only in the 18th century it gained its importance, as German immigrants settled in the place and made it an important industrial center. Valdivia was damaged in 1960 by an earthquake, and many edifices were rebuilt. Valdivia enjoys a special atmosphere thanks to its university — Universidad Austral.

The main street is Av. Ramon Picarte, which leads to the main Plaza. At the plaza is the cathedral, and continuing on to the river you pass by the municipal market. Across the street, by the river, is the Floating Market (Mercado Fluvial), where fishermen sell their products from their boats, every day 8am-2:30pm. Most action here is on Wednesday and Saturday.

Cross the river by Pedro de Valdivia Bridge to the **Isla Teja**. Here is the "ciudad universitaria", where you can enjoy the charming parks and edifices and visit the Botanical garden. The Museo Austral (closed 1-3pm) has a fine collection describing the history of the town and region. The edifice itself is interesting and it offers a fine view of the river and town.

A recommended excursion from Valdivia takes you west to **Corral**, on the other bank of the river. You can get there either by boat from Valdivia, or by bus to **Niebla** (18 km west), and cross the river from there. You will enjoy the scenery of green hills and blue water. In Corral you can visit the Castillo de San Sebastian, which is one of many castles built here in the 17th century in order to guard the town and its port.

The scenery of the whole district is splendid, with hills, rivers, lakes and the ocean. From Niebla you may wish to continue 20 km north along the coast of the ocean, to enjoy the scenery and the beaches, before returning to Valdivia.

Osorno

The town of Osorno (pop. 110,000), 260 km south of Temuco, was founded by German immigrants as an agricultural colony. Despite struggles with the Indians who controlled the area — which resulted in the town's abandonment for a short time — the immigrants managed to build a settlement that, over the years, became a large regional agricultural center, where the German influence is evident to this day. Many of the numerous hotels, restaurants, shops and clubs in Osorno bear German names, and German is still spoken in many places.

How to get there

That lengthy thoroughfare, the Pan-American Highway, reaches Osorno, too, on its way from Temuca via Valdivia to Puerto Montt. Daily *Lan Chile* flights link Osorno with Santiago, as do many bus lines. Buses for neighbouring cities set out frequently from the market area. The Santiago-Puerto Montt train stops in Osorno and the trip, in Pullman or first class, is very comfortable.

There are two major ways of going to and from Argentina: the highway from San Carlos de Bariloche, and the bus-ferry route across **Lago Todos Los Santos** ("All Saints' Lake"). The bus (several times weekly in winter, daily in summer) passes through beautiful countryside, though during winter one should expect to be delayed due to snow. The lake route takes a full day, and some bus companies include night accommodation by the lake. Crossing the lake, one of the loveliest in the region, is a very impressive experience. If you've got time on your hands, don't miss it.

Where to stay
The *Gran Hotel Osorno* on the central plaza is ideally located and moderately priced. The *Inter Lagos*, at Cochrane 515, tel. 234695, one block from the square, is a nice three-star hotel. There are two clean campgrounds on the outskirts of the town, the *Olegario Mohr* and the *Trumao*.

In the culinary field, the local products are prominent, though the residents' German ancestry contributes its influence as well. Many restaurants specialize in German food: lots of meat, marinated in oil and roasted, are served alongside seafood and typical Chilean dishes. The best of German cuisine can be tasted at *Peter's Kneipe*, Manuel Rodríguez 1039, two blocks from the square through Calle Matta. The less expensive restaurants are located in the vicinity of the bus and train stations.

What to see
Osorno generally serves only as a transit point for people going to the lake district and actually there is no other reason for staying there. Except for the Spanish Maria Luisa fortress and two small museums, Osorno, although a pleasant city, has little to interest the tourist. Even the **Tourist Bureau**, next to the Provincial Government building on the central plaza, finds it hard to provide information about city attractions, and the staff will generally content themselves with talking about the town's surroundings, where there's lots to see.

Lakes
In summer the lakes in the region are popular with vacationers, though there's no feeling of crowding. From Osorno, many buses head each day for the lakeshore, where you can get away from it all, spend several days hiking, and visit small towns and picturesque villages still not connected to the national power grid, where wooden ox-drawn plows remain the norm. Lakes **Rupanco** (sixty kilometers from Osorno) and **Todos Los Santos** are the most famous and popular in the area.

Parks
Puyehue National Park is situated eighty-one kilometers east of Osorno in the heart of a forested area. The park centers around

hot springs — the **Termas de Puyehue** — and the adjacent massive, old Gran Hotel. A swimming pool and hot baths are situated next to the hotel, near mineral water springs whose output is bottled and sent into town. One bus a day makes the two-hour trip from Osorno.

The **Antillanca** ski area, which has become popular in recent years, is located within the park's confines, a circumstance which has spurred development of the region. Hotels, hostels and restaurants have been built (such as the Osorno Andes Club which has opened a hostel at the base of the ski area with the capacity to accommodate two hundred). The park itself is drenched in greenery, interspersed among small lakes. You can camp out for days, just resting up, or hiking through the serene and undisturbed countryside.

The volcano
Mt. Osorno soars to a height of 2600 m above sea level on the shore of **Lake Llanquihué**, the largest of the southern lakes. On clear days a marvelous view can be seen from the slopes of this volcano. If you're a good hiker, we recommend that you make the climb. Getting all the way to the summit is a difficult and complicated undertaking; one has to climb through thick forest and the mountaintop itself is snow covered even in summer.

During the winter, the entire mountain is enveloped in deep snow and its slopes turn into an active, bustling ski area.

A hike
Apart from the normal route from Osorno to the charming town of Puerto Varas ninety-nine kilometers further south, good hikers have the fascinating option of making their way on foot through one of the most beautiful hiking areas in the world. Head east from Osorno in the direction of Puyehue Park, and from there make your way southward from village to village toward **Lake Rupanco** and from there to **Lake Todos Los Santos**. There's a pleasant little town called **Petrohué** on the lake's western shore and from there you can go sailing on the limpid waters.

If you wish, you can take a ferry from here straight to Argentina. If you stay in Chile, you can continue westward to the town of Ensenada on the shore of **Lake Llanquihué** and then on to Puerto Varas. This area abounds in trails and paths that pass through lovely towns and villages. For part of the way, of course, you can use public transportation or hitch. Elsewhere you can take a boat or walk.

Almost any route you choose will meet your expectations and provide an extraordinary experience. Plan for a week on the road and take along suitable camping equipment and plenty of food. You'll have no trouble finding water along the way.

Puerto Varas

The town of Puerto Varas (pop. 30,000) lies on the western shore of **Lake Llanquihué**, the largest of Chile's lakes, nineteen kilometers north of Puerto Montt. The town is called the "City of Roses" for the rosebushes that adorn its short street. Across the lake you'll see Mt. Osorno in all its glory, the white crown stunning in its perfection.

Near the town, unique archaeological remains have been found, which testify to human habitation from very early days. These are the most ancient archaeological finds anywhere in the Americas and scholars claim that they provide proof of human settlement here, in periods far earlier than had been commonly supposed. Excavations have gone on for a number of years. Though final conclusions have yet to be drawn, the "dig" is undoubtedly interesting. A road from Puerto Varas circles the lake along which there are places to relax, fish and enjoy the vivid greenery. Buses make the trip from Puerto Montt several times a week on the Pan-American Highway.

On to Argentina through Lake Todos los Santos

The main route from Puerto Montt to Argentina passes through Puerto Varas and continues on to Lake Todos Los Santos and the lakeshore town of Petrohué.

A few kilometers before Lake Todos Los Santos are the beautiful and turbulent **Petrohué Falls**. From Petrohué there is a ferry which crosses the lake to the village Peulla. The cruise, which takes two and a half hours, is exceptionally beautiful. From Peulla one reaches the Argentinian border, 18 km away, by dirt road, and from there another cruise crosses **Lago Frias**, whose enchanting scenery is reminiscent of Norwegian fjords. Tourist buses travel daily along the road between the two lakes. They are expensive, but one has no hope of hitching here. Those who wish to do the route on foot are advised to do so in the reverse direction — from Argentina to Chile — because then most of the way is downhill. The start of the route on the Argentinian side is at Puerto Blest on **Lake Nahuel Huapi**.

Petrohué Falls

Puerto Montt

The Pan-American Highway reaches 1057 km south of Santiago de Chile to the lovely port city of Puerto Montt, on the northern edge of the Gulf of Ancud.

Puerto Montt was founded in 1852 by a group of German immigrants whose descendants still live there. As time passed, the city developed and became a center for agriculture, fishing and tourism, which has achieved ever-growing popularity in recent years. The 100,000 people who live here make their living from the sea, from tourism and from services they provide to the small towns of the region. The city effectively constitutes the southern extremity of Chile's unbroken settled area; south of here stretch more than a thousand kilometers of a sparsely populated archipelago which suffers from a harsh, rainy, wintry climate most of the year.

Transportation

Like the Pan American Highway, the railroad from Santiago reaches its terminus here at a noteworthy station, if only because it is the southernmost train station in the world. Trains from Santiago arrive here eighteen to twenty hours after setting out, with many intermediate stops. A daily express sets out for

Lago Frias

Santiago, while a "milk-run" follows the same route at a more leisurely pace, stopping at every village and city along the way. A timetable is posted at the train station, which also offers baggage-checking service and a restaurant.

The modern bus terminal is some distance from the city center. There is bus service to Santiago (several times a day), to cities in the area — Puerto Varas, Osorno and northward (approximately once an hour), to Isla Chiloé (every two hours) and to Argentina. Buses to the latter destination depart every morning and go either directly to Bariloche or via Puerto Varas and Lake Todos Los Santos (see above). Students are eligible for a considerable discount on bus travel, but sometimes one must insist on getting it. A Student Card isn't always enough and one who requests a discount must stand up for his or her rights firmly — though politely. It helps. *Lan Chile* flies daily to and from Santiago and Punta Arenas.

Where to stay and eat
One of the best hotels in Puerto Montt is the *Vicente Pérez Rosales*, Antonio Varas 447, tel. 252571, fax 255473. The hotel *Burg*, P. Montt 56, with Portales, tel. 253813, and the *Residencial Angelmo*, Angelmo 2196, tel. 257938, are cheaper.

There are many hotels, some quite expensive, on the main

street next to the train station. On the side streets, the pensions and hotels get less expensive the farther you get from the shore. Many residents will accommodate guests in their homes for a small fee. Negotiations with some pension-owners may result in permission to sleep on a mattress in the attic — very cheap. The rate in some pensions includes use of the kitchen. A small youth hostel is open during the summer.

Puerto Montt is famous for its superb seafood. Even experienced and knowledgeable gourmets will find themselves surprised at the abundance and quality of Puerto Montt's fare. In the city's numerous restaurants — especially those in the Anjelmo area — strange looking monsters of the deep are laid on your plate, and you'll need a stiff upper lip and a broad mind to overcome your instinctive horror and get the fork into your mouth. Anyone who can't take it, of course, can choose fish, crabs and other offerings that are easier to digest, if only in the psychological sense ...

Beef, *empanadas*, rice and the other familiar Chilean dishes are also served in plentiful portions and good quality, so there's no need to bring along canned food and even those who can't work up the courage to take a chance on the seafood will not die of hunger.

What to see
The **Tourist Bureau** is in Edificio Intendencia, 2nd floor, tel. 254850. The staff will be delighted to assist you with maps and information, and will help you in matters of accommodation and transportation.

Puerto Montt is a quiet, pleasant town, and its residents are kindly disposed toward tourists. The tranquil landscape, the small wooden houses, the clean sea and the surrounding greenery create a relaxing atmosphere. You'll enjoy wandering along the streets and observing the wonderful, slow paced life they lead here. The little fishing port Angelmo, about a kilometer out of town, is a colorful jewel of a place, bustling in its own way with small fishing boats, lots of fishermen, tourists and — in their wake — simple fish restaurants, stands with handicrafts for sale, and more. One of the finest times to visit Angelmo is at low tide, for in these high southern latitudes the water ebbs considerably, leaving scores of meters of moist sand on which the lovely fishing boats are calmly beached. The local market offers a selection of superb, reasonably-priced local *artisania* (handicrafts). This is one of the best places in Chile for purchases of this sort.

Apart from being a lively tourist spot, Puerto Montt also serves as a point of departure for many sites in the vicinity:

Small towns: We highly recommend that you wander around the port area and try to hitch a ride on one of the little supply ships that make their way among the settlements in the area. If you succeed, you can expect the marvelous and unique experience of a visit to remote places reached by few outsiders, where the natural beauty has not yet been marred by the tourist plague.

Fjords, lagoons and icebergs: The entire region south of Puerto Montt, especially south of Isla Chiloé, is a beautiful uninhabited area where primeval nature reigns undisturbed. The weather is usually harsh, greyish, rainy and cold, what makes the experience doubly moving.

Chiloé Island

Isla Chiloé, one of the most charming jewels of Chile, lies a short distance south of Puerto Montt. This enchanting island bursts with greenery. Its houses are tiny and picturesque and its atmosphere pastoral and serene. The whole scene, calm and relaxing, appears to have been taken out of a beautiful Impressionist oil painting. There are two major towns on the island — Castro and Ancud — plus fishing villages spread up and down the coast.

Buses set out for Chiloé from Puerto Montt every two hours or so and, after about an hour's ride on Route 5 as far as Pargua, a ferry takes the bus across the narrow strait separating Chiloé from the mainland. Then you continue, first to Ancud and then on to Castro.

Ancud, the smaller of the two towns, is located on the shore of a bay which is left half-dry at the evening low tide. The small and colorful houses of the town nestle in a valley situated between two green slopes.

Possibilities for accommodation in Ancud are numerous and inexpensive and the town is an interesting place in its own right. The central square, the little port, the handsome streets and lovely houses undoubtedly merit a visit.

Castro is a pleasant town, linked to Ancud by a concrete highway that winds through forest and meadow, between bay and village. It has a strange character all its own. Since Chiloé was low on the Spaniards' list of objectives and was subsequently the last district to join the call for independence from Spain, the remnants of past cultures have yet to disappear and the residents of Chiloé in general and Castro in particular, are known for their tendency toward superstitions — as expressed in their somewhat odd behavior ...

*C*HILE

Laguna San Rafael

The houses on Chiloé are built of wood, and only in recent years have they been connected to a power grid and water system. The men generally wear dark plastic hats while the women are clothed in bulky and graceless woolen attire.

On the waterfront, the buildings are erected on wooden piles so as not to be flooded; their images reflect in the clear, motionless water. This is one of the most interesting sights of human settlement in all of South America. Places that deserve a visit include the **seaside market,** the friendly **Tourist Bureau** on Plaza de Armas, and the tiny **museum** adjacent to it. The **cemetery** on the hill overlooking town is colorful and rather special; you should visit it, too.

Castro offers a number of inexpensive little hotels, most near the Plaza de Armas. The *Residencial Mirasol*, at Calle San Martín 815, is very nice and recommended.

From Castro you'll find it worthwhile to take an excursion through the little fishing villages in the vicinity. It's best to go off the main road and penetrate the rural areas, if only a little way. If you do so, an unforgettable experience of visiting a "living museum" — the last remnants of a vanishing way of life — awaits you.

On Sundays, the little fishing village of Dalcahue, 20 km north of

Scenery in Chiloé Island

Castro, holds a special kind of market. A bus sets out from Castro before daybreak, and the trip is an entertaining experience in its own right. Castro residents load goods and food on to the bus, in quantities that would normally require three buses or more. These goods are put on sale at the market, where you will find various foodstuffs, a large selection of wool products, sweaters, wall hangings and much more. Recommended.

Given all the wonders of this vicinity and its attractions, one shouldn't miss the opportunity to visit Chiloé Island.

If planning to continue south from Chiloé to Carretera Austral and Coihaique (see below, "South to Patagonia"), you don't have to go back to Puerto Montt. There are ferries from Chonchi and Quellón on the island to Puerto Chacabuco and Chaitén (a few hours), and from there you will find a frequent transport south to Coihaique. From Quellón there are also ferries to Puerto Aisén, 70 km from Coihaique, but it is a long and expensive journey.

South to Patagonia

There are a number of ways to proceed South to Patagonia, some very expensive and others not so; the matter requires lots of luck and perseverance.

During the summer, passenger ships ply the route from Puerto Montt to Punta Arenas — a captivating voyage through exceptional scenery of fjords and icebergs. A tourist boat makes the trip in four days or more, while a cargo ship may take up to ten days. Passenger ships have three classes; third class is definitely satisfactory for young tourists. In addition to the passenger ships, many cargo ships operate on this route and their captains will often agree to carry passengers for pay. This is an interesting and inexpensive way to make the trip, which we can recommend highly. Its only drawback is that you may be delayed in Puerto Montt for quite some time until you find a suitable ship. Should you find it hard to locate one in the Puerto Montt harbor, try your luck at the port in Chiloé.

Another way, of course, is by plane. *Lan Chile* flies south and back several times each week. The Chilean Air Force also flies southern routes. Though these flights are cheaper, it is quite difficult to obtain a ticket and their frequency and timetables change constantly.

The only possibility of reaching south Patagonia by land is via Argentina. You can cross the mountains and proceed south from San Carlos de Bariloche. The fastest (though lengthy) route is from Bariloche to Commodoro-Rivadavia, then to Rio Gallegos and westward to Rio Turbio and the adjacent border crossing to Puerto Natales.

Another option is to continue south by the "**Carretera Austral**". This road, connecting Puerto Montt with Puerto Aisén, Coihaique and Cochrane, was completed in 1988. Traveling by this road offers superb views of forests, lakes and mountain peaks.

It is more than 600 km from Puerto Montt to **Coihaique**. This town of 40,000 inhabitants is the region's capital. From here you can go by road and ferry to **Chile Chico**, and to cross the border to Perito Moreno in Argentina.

Laguna San Rafael
The boat trip to Laguna San Rafael takes you through wild landscapes of archipelagos and canals to this lagoon and to the great San Valentin Glacier. The lagoon and its glacier are exquisitely beautiful, and many icebergs, seals, dolphins and birds are seen from the boat.

The best start point for this trip is Puerto Aisén (70 km from Coihaique), a port town with a population of 15,000. The trip takes 3-4 days, depends on the kind of boat you take. You can take one of the organized tours, which are very expensive, but you can make it cheaper by inquiring among the fishermen in the port.

The Far South —
Patagonia and Tierra del Fuego

At South America's southernmost extremity, where dry land comes to an end, you'll find some of the wildest, most astounding and stunning regions on earth. Among the icebergs, fjords, lakes, lagoons, ice fields and gigantic mountains that make up nearly one third of Chile's total area, you'll find less than 3% of its population. This is an open area of primeval nature, where the works of man are hardly discernible. Chilean Patagonia is a land enchanting in its beauty, stunning in its virgin glory.

Most of the region's tourism and commercial activity is concentrated around its two major cities — Punta Arenas and Puerto Natales. The two towns also serve as points of departure for wonderful trips into the countryside. Words cannot describe the scope and power of the experience that awaits you here: the sensitive visitor cannot help being moved by everything and everyone he encounters. While plant life is almost totally lacking, Patagonia abounds in wildlife. Llamas, foxes, pumas and many more species inhabit Patagonia's vast expanses while innumerable birds, including the condor, fly above.

Patagonia's climate is harsh most of the year; not many plants, as we've noted, can grow here. Fishing and sheep-herding are the main activities. Rain falls the year round, and the driving winds can reach speeds of 100 kph and more!

In summer, the sun shines twenty hours a day — because of Patagonia's latitude, and the high and low tides, characterized by extreme differences in the water level, are something to behold. The tourist season is summer, between November and February. Few visitors come to Patagonia the rest of the year, especially between April and September, and most forms of transportation to the various sites of interest are unavailable. You must bring along warm clothing at any time of year. Furthermore, if you intend to sleep under the stars in parks, pack an excellent sleeping bag and a strong, reliable tent!

Since it's harder to change money here than elsewhere, you should bring pesos from the north and as for foreign currency, stick to cash dollars. Travelers' checks can be cashed only after

Landscape of Southern Chile

some effort on your part and at a poor rate. Since Patagonia is remote and isolated and almost everything has to be brought in from the north, goods usually cost about 50% more than they do elsewhere in Chile, a fact you must take into account.

Punta Arenas

Punta Arenas is not only Chile's southernmost city, but also one of its nicest. This city of 110,000 people, located 2200 km south of Santiago, has served as an important regional center since 1584, when the first settlers arrived. Due to its strategic location — on the northern shore of the Strait of Magellan — settlement here has always been regarded as vital, even more so in recent years following the discovery of significant quantities of oil. This has added impetus to urban development: many homes have been built and new streets paved, and new settlers have arrived in droves. The area currently supplies much of Chile's consumption of oil, natural gas and coal.

How to get there

Punta Arenas is connected by land to neighboring Argentina and by air and sea to northern Chile. *Lan Chile, Aerolíneas,* and other commercial airlines, as well as the Chilean Air Force, provide excellent air service to and from Santiago, Puerto Montt and Buenos Aires. In summer tickets must be reserved well in advance. As for reaching Punta Arenas from the lake district, see "Puerto Montt".

Two good roads link Punta Arenas with Rio Gallegos in Argentina. The shorter and more convenient runs along the coast of the Strait of Magellan, provide a beautiful and interesting trip that takes from five to seven hours, depending on border-crossing difficulties. Buses run several times a day in summer and several times a week in winter. Buses leave Puerto Natales several times a day for the four-hour trip along a good highway. A ferry provides daily service to and from Puerto Porvenir in Tierra del Fuego, setting out from a harbor about five kilometers from downtown Punta Arenas (take the bus to Zona Franca and then walk about a kilometer). Tickets can be purchased on the ferry itself for the three-hour trip across the Strait of Magellan. Departure times vary according to the time of year and day of the week. Check at the Tourist Bureau in Punta Arenas as to the exact schedule on the day you want to sail.

Where to stay

Hotels and restaurants of various standards are scattered throughout Punta Arenas, especially downtown along the streets around the Plaza de Armas. On the square itself you'll find the largest — the *Cabo de Hornos*, Plaza Muñoz Gamero 1025, tel. & fax 222134. Other are the *Los Navegantes*, Menéndez 647, tel. 224677, with a 4-star standard, and the more moderate *Plaza*, José Nogueira 1116, tel. 221300.

A very inexpensive hotel is located above the *American Service Restaurant* at Calle Roca 953. The owner of the restaurant, lets out little rooms on the second floor. Though they're rather miserable, they've got everything you need: a bed, a closet and a gas heater. The price is very reasonable, and in a town where accommodation is so expensive this option is quite satisfactory. The Tourist Bureau can provide you with information about accommodation in private homes.

There is no shortage of restaurants in Punta Arenas. Though the accent is on seafood, lamb is no less commonplace. Vegetables, eggs and the like are expensive, for most such foods are brought in from the north. The downtown area has a number of sandwich-and-hamburger places, which serve the fastest and cheapest fare available.

What to see

The municipal **Tourist Bureau** is in the **Provincial Government Building** at Calle Waldo Seguel 689, tel. 224435. The friendly staff will give you a map of Punta Arenas, background material and explanations concerning the city, its attractions, outings in the area, transportation and hotels.

Punta Arenas has been favoured with a great many interesting sites that deserve a visit.The streets are laid out in a grid pattern, making it easy to find your way around. The **Plaza de Armas**, with its **statue of Magellan** (the European discoverer of the area), is the heart of town and most activity in Punta Arenas is concentrated in its vicinity. If you want to assure yourself good luck, try kissing Magellan's enormous foot; local tradition attributes wondrous powers to this act. In the plaza you'll also find a small and interesting **museum** with displays of local history, animal life and natural resources.

The city lies on the shore of the broad strait through which the famous Portuguese navigator Fernando Magellan made the first passage in November, 1520, thereby confirming Columbus' hypotheses about the way to the Indies, by finding a direct route from Europe to East Asia. The coastline essentially serves as Punta Arenas' eastern border, with the city spread out along it. From the shore there is a lovely view of the island across the strait — Tierra del Fuego.

On the eastern side of town there's a unique graveyard which is certainly worth a visit. The carefully tended **cemetery**, enclosed within a high stone wall, abounds in greenery and trees that have been pruned with exemplary precision into a variety of interesting shapes. The numerous house-like structures are in fact family mausoleums, where each member of the family is entombed in an individual sarcophagus, around which many ornaments and religious icons have been scattered. Some of these graves possess especially weird shapes — such as one tomb shaped like a ship with the "upper-deck" on ground level leading down directly into the "hold", where family members are buried in the walls.

North of the cemetery, and 2.5 km from downtown, you'll find the **Patagonia Institute** on the left hand side of road, with its museum of work tools, handicrafts, textiles, wool products and pottery typical of the Patagonia area. The Institute also offers a shop in which lovely, charactistically Patagonian ornaments are sold (but at very high prices!). A small **zoo** housing animals native to the region is located in the Institute's courtyard. Of interest are the *guanaco* (wild llama), the terrifying puma, and the condor, impressive for its size and wingspan. In front of the Institute, on the lawn between it and the main highway linking Punta Arenas with the ferry terminal, there is an **exhibit** of railway locomotives and rolling stock, and old agricultural machinery, for which there was probably no other place anywhere in Chile.

Across from the Patagonia Insititute is a bustling modern **shopping center.** As one of the Government incentives to encourage setîlement in Patagonia, a free-trade zone (*zona franca*) was established in Punta Arenas. Here you can buy a wide variety of luxury items — from exclusive clothing, to all sorts of photographic equipment, liquor and imported chocolate, to state-of-the art electronics. The *Zona Franca* was set up here, a short distance from the center of town, and it contains a long row of modern shopping centers, built with care and filled with dozens of shops. Even if you have no intention of buying a stereo system or a color TV, you'll certainly be interested in visiting this fascinating place, which is reached from town by taxi or numerous bus lines. If you want to stock up on film, lenses and other photographic equipment, or to treat youself to some Swiss chocolate, this is certainly the place. Prices are similar to those in New York, and the variety is adequate. The self-service restaurant on the premises is expensive and not very good.

Excursions in the area

Isla Magdalena and sea cruises

A two-and-a-half-hour cruise south from Punta Arenas in the

Red vegetation of the "Land of Fire"

Strait of Magellan brings you to Isla Magdalena, home to tens of thousands of penguins, seals and sea lions, and an abundance of birds and animals that depend on the region's icy waters for their sustenance. In the waters around the boat you'll easily spot dolphins and, at times, even small whales splashing innocently around the island.

Sailing to Isla Magdalena is but one facet of a broad and generally expensive variety of cruises offered by agencies in Punta Arenas. Some organized excursions go as far as Antarctica, in an area where the marine scenery, rich in fjords, lagoons and massive icebergs, is among the world's most fascinating.

Tierra del Fuego
A ferry sails every day between Punta Arenas and Puerto Porvenir, the Chilean town in Tierra del Fuego (see also "Argentina"). The western, Chilean half, of the island is slim pickings for tourists and is liable to be disappointing and your main interest is in passing through to get to Argentina.

The bus from Puerto Porvenir to Rio Grande, Argentina, runs several times a week, crossing the border at the San Sebastian checkpost. Here you may encounter problems with the authorities and you must be patient and careful.

Puerto Natales

Puerto Natales (pop. 20,000) is 254 km north of Punta Arenas. This quiet town, situated on the shore of an enchanting lagoon amidst splendid pastoral scenery, is frequented by tourists mainly during the summer on their way to the natural attractions in the vicinity. The border crossing to Rio Turbio, Argentina (see Argentina — "Rio Turbio") is close by, a 30-minute bus ride away.

Small boats set out from Puerto Natales' little port for nearby bays, and a cruise on one of these is recommended. On less frequent occasions, and with no fixed schedule, a ship on its way north (to Puerto Montt) pulls into port and here it's easier than in Punta Arenas to persuade the captain to be so kind as to let you aboard.

In and around town you'll find many hotels and small pensions, but their prices are high. With a little initiative you can pitch a tent in a corner of town and spend the night there. At the *Secretaria de la Juventud* (Youth Secretariat), next to the plaza, you can sleep cheaply — in a sleeping bag on the floor. There's no shower, and you must get permission from the person in charge if you want to shower in the adjacent school. Those setting out for a trip in the vicinity would do well to leave all spare gear here, for unnecessary weight is liable to be an unbearable nuisance.

To and from Punta Arenas there is a fast, comfortable bus service several times daily. A student card gives you a discount, though some persuasion may be required. Hitchhiking opportunities abound and this form of transportation should present no problems.

The main attraction that has put Puerto Natales on the tourism map is the Torres del Paine National Park, 130 kilometers northeast of the town.

Parque Nacional Torres del Paine

To the south of Argentina's Parque de los Glaciares a number of strange mountain ridges with sharp peaks look like gigantic towers touching the sky. These are the *Torres* (Towers) *del Paine*. Although they soar to "only" 2670 m, the sharp uplift is impressive because the region from which they rise is not much above sea level. As if this did not suffice, the mountains are blessed with a number of lakes, glaciers and unspoilt countryside, and an abundance of animal and bird life and a tempestuous climate are added.

The *Paine* has become a powerful attraction in recent years due to its beauty and fascinating hiking trails. To visit the park you must come well-equipped with camping gear and, of course, food.

When you stock up on food, pack a 50% reserve to allow for unplanned delays. True, food is available in the park itself at a shop in the administrative center — at high prices — but since you'll probably be miles from there, except for the first and the last day, you won't want to rely on this, so come equipped. The weather is very pleasant during the summer but terribly cold during the rest of the year. Temperatures plunge at night, and there's nothing unusual about sleeping in heavy clothing inside your heavy sleeping bag.

Reaching the park is no simple matter. Since it is far from Puerto Natales, with only one village between it and the town (Costelo, about seventy kilometers away), transportation is meant mainly for tourists. During the summer, when most of the visitors come, a bus runs several times a week and goes as far as the Park Office. Hiring a taxi is expensive, but in the transitional seasons — before October and after February, when the park is almost devoid of visitors — it's almost the only way to get there and back. You must make arrangements with the driver about the return trip, otherwise you're liable to be stranded for days after your hike in the park. *Torres del Paine* is cut off in the winter and there's no way of reaching and exploring it. Trucks do set out for the park from the CONAF (Parks Authority) office in Puerto Natales at irregular intervals and, at times, especially during the off-season, they are willing to pick up hitchhikers.

A hike around the park's periphery, encompassing the "towers", takes from six to ten days at six to eight hours' walking per day, and this is the most popular route. If you like, of course, you can stay in the park for weeks on end and hike the approximately two hundred kilometers of marked trails of the immense park.

You'll have to pay an admission fee and register at the entrance, and you'll be given a map on which the hiking trails have been marked. The perimeter hike itself may begin in a *refugio* (a hut set aside as a shelter for hikers) about fifteen kilometers from the entrance, or at the *Administración*, several kilometers farther down the path along the southern shore of Lake *Pehoe*. At the *Administración* compound you'll find a **visitor's center** with a relief map of the park and information concerning its history, geology, flora and fauna, etc. — all very interesting, arranged in good taste and worth a visit. The somewhat "dry" scenery of the route leading here changes suddenly, the moment you actually begin to hike amidst the wild foliage, past gorgeous lakes, around steep mountains, alongside glaciers and beside

Parque Nacional Torres del Paine

churning streams. Numerous wild animals — *guanacos*, foxes, hares and many more — will cross your path. With special luck, you may get a close-up view of a giant condor hovering in the air, or some pumas — which, though not dangerous (at least that's what the park rangers say) should be treated with great caution.

The hiking trails will lead you between colorful lakes, each at a different elevation. These came into existence as a result of the melting glaciers from the last Ice Age. But if you stick your hand into the water, you'll discover that it does not appear to have had time to heat up much since then... The waters are cold, pure and good to drink, and each lake is of a different hue.

The greatest experience of all is your encounter with the massive mountains of ice, especially the Grey and Dickson Glaciers. As you approach these giant glaciers, you hear a dull groaning sound emanating from beneath them, caused by the movement of water seeping underneath and melting them. The great weight of the ice gives the glaciers a sharp blue coloration and generates tremendous pressure which changes the crystalline structure of the glaciers, an astonishing and incredibly beautiful sight to behold. These glaciers are in a state of continuous melting and are only a "little" behind schedule, when compared with the many other glaciers that once covered the region.

There are a number of *refugios* (log cabins for visitors) along the route. In a *refugio* you should try to sleep on the upper bunk, and to hang your gear in the air — because of the mice. These too have discovered the pleasures of the *refugio*, and many of them make their homes there, so that you must keep all equipment and food out of their reach. *Refugios* have large wood-burning stoves. The custom is that the first to arrive goes out to gather wood. The wood you find in the *refugio* should not be used, since it's meant for visitors who may be delayed on the way and therefore arrive after nightfall. Given the length of the trail and the chances that the number of hikers will exceed the facilities offered by a *refugio*, be prepared to sleep in a tent. Also consider the possibility of rain, in any season. Charming wooden houses are located throughout the park. The experienced and polite park rangers (*Guarde Parque*) who live there will be delighted to offer reliable and up-to-date advice concerning hiking possibilities on the various trails, the condition of bridges, etc. Let them be of assistance to you.

PARAGUAY

When you enter this South American state, it may seem that you have reached a forsaken country where ignorance and economic backwardness prevail. This first impression, even if not totally incorrect, is rather superficial. Anyone who spends some time here will discover a unique country. Paraguay's name comes from the *Guaraní* language, and means "a place with a great river". The reference is to the confluence of the Paraguay and Pilcomayo rivers, where the capital city of Asunción stands.

Paraguay has known many wars, whose destructive results are evident to this day. The country has been ruled tyrannically by a president who was in office for some thirty years. The economy has been devastated by financial power brokers from within and without the country. It was conventional to think of this land, where the percentage of surviving Indians is the highest in South America, as a giant "farm" run by the former president as if it were his personal estate. Paraguay is home to an international business community which has taken shelter there because of the country's flexible and unconstricting economic laws.

In recent years, since the fall of Stroessner, a process of accelerated development has evinced itself in many fields, funded by outside capital channeled into Paraguay in recognition of its increasing importance, and this obviously has social and political consequences. For the tourist, Paraguay is one of the few countries where one is impressed by the simple way of life, and the tranquil and friendly population.

History

Paraguay was initially populated by the Guaraní tribe, extending from Brazil in the east, to the slopes of the Andes in the west. When the first Spaniards arrived in 1525, the Indians refrained from fighting them. The lack of hostility, led the Spanish to begin frequenting the area and laying foundations for settlements. In 1537, Juan de Salazar founded the capital city of Asunción. This was the start of a nation building process exceptional in Latin America, in which the native Indians integrated harmoniously with the Spanish newcomers. The slight importance which the Paraguay and Pilcomayo Rivers had in relation to the gold and silver centers of Bolivia and Peru, and the obstacles the Indians in northern Argentina set in the path of those

PARAGUAY

navigating these waterways, led to the isolation of Asunción's Spanish community. The colonists quickly assimilated into the local population, and the community that developed was but slightly influenced by its subjugation to the Spanish viceroy in Peru. In 1776, when a viceroy based in Buenos Aires was appointed for the La Plata region, Paraguay was attached to the new jurisdiction. In May 1811, Captain Pedro Caballero led a rebellion against Spanish rule. He and his men routed General Belgrano, who had been sent from Argentina to Paraguay to ensure the latter country's continued ties with Buenos Aires. About a month later, a junta was formed which headed the young state. Paraguay, in contrast to its neighbors, won its independence with almost no struggle and nearly no casualties. In 1814, José Rodriguez Francia declared himself sole ruler.

José Francia, known as El Supremo, led Paraguay for 26 years, until his death in September 1840. His rule was rigid and unbending; employing terror against his opponents and isolating Paraguay from the outside world. No one was allowed to enter Paraguay or to leave it, and trade with other countries was banned altogether. Only when he was replaced by Carlos Antonio López, a professor of philosophy, were the borders opened, and Paraguay's relations with its neighbors allowed to develop. Various disputes soured relations with Brazil, Argentina, and even the United States, Great Britain and France. However, the momentum of accelerated development — and Carlos López's political tolerance — ushered in a period of growth and prosperity that lasted until López's death in 1862. He was succeeded as dictator by his son, General Francisco Solano López. Three years later, Paraguay became entangled in a terrible, destructive war — the war of the Triple Alliance.

This conflict, which began in a dispute with Brazil, and a subsequent invasion of Uruguay in pursuit of the Brazilian Army, became more and more of an entanglement, lasting five full years. Argentina, Brazil and Uruguay formed an alliance devoted to destroying López's army. When it ended, Paraguay was utterly routed, and casualties amounted to one million men! As the war drew to an end, Solano López seized often with attacks of madness and rage, was killed in the battle of Cerro Corá on March 1, 1870. Even so, he is still regarded as one of the greatest national heroes.

At war's end, Paraguay tried to rise from the ashes, but a prolonged border conflict with Bolivia over control of the Chaco (Paraguay's western section) led to another war, which broke out in 1932 and lasted three years. In its course, the Bolivian army was repelled and Paraguay secured control of the entire area. A cease-fire and peace treaty between the two combatants were achieved with the mediation of the neighboring countries and the United States. An arbitration panel consisting of the presidents of these countries awarded three-fourths of the Chaco to Paraguay.

During the following two decades, Paraguay knew a series of tyrants who created social, economic, and political havoc. In 1954, backed by the army and the *Colorado* party, General Alfredo Stroessner seized power and ruled the country with an iron fist. In the course of his rule a trend towards development was evident, but not in the required measure.

In the course of his rule, Paraguay's isolation has slightly lessened — its currency has stabilized, roads have been paved, air routes developed, and accelerated industrial and economic development has begun to manifest itself. In 1967 the regime loosened its grip somewhat, and a new constitution, slightly more liberal than the previous one, went into effect. General Stroessner has been continually re-elected to additional five-year terms, for a total of more than thirty years.

Sroessner was overthrown in 1989. Since then Paraguay started to stroll in the path of the democratic nations, waiting with optimism to see the results of the slow entrance to the international community. The *Mercosur*, the South American Common Market, is expected to help in the development of the required infrastructure.

The period started by General Andrés Rodríguez, formerly Stroessner's right-hand man, is known in Paraguay as *"la transición"*. To everyone's surprise Rodríguez called for the first free elections the country ever had; due to leave office in mid-1993, if the threats to democracy from some military sectors are not fulfilled, Rodríguez's administration is changing many of the national institutions from the very root.

Geography and climate

Paraguay, 407,000 sq/km in area, is divided by the Paraguay River into the "Eastern Region", about one third of the country, and the "Western Region", the Gran Chaco.

More than half of Paraguay is forested, and the remainder serves chiefly for cattle grazing. Only 6% of the land is devoted to agriculture, and almost all of it is concentrated along the Paraguay River.

Massive rivers surround Paraguay, and their tributaries spread a network of veins throughout the country. The harsh tropical climate places great obstacles in the path of orderly and organized agricultural development. The immense Chaco region remains desolate, as if waiting for a redeemer. Apart from cattle grazing, it is of little value to the country's economy. The Eastern Region, geographically an extension of the Brazilian lowland, is home to about 90% of Paraguay's population, who engage mainly in agriculture under almost feudal conditions. Several hundred immigrant families hold close to 300,000 sq/km of land, some three-fourths of Paraguay's total area, whereas more than 100,000 native families must share only another 30,000 sq/km amongst themselves. Most of the latter have neither title deeds nor permanent rights to their land.

The subtropical climate in Paraguay is harsh and uncomfortable. Little rain falls in the Chaco region, though humidity is very high. Summer in the Eastern Sector and Asunción is very hot; temperatures soar as high as 40 degrees Celsius (104 degrees Farenheit). Rain falls an average of eighty days, spread throughout the whole year. Winter temperatures are significantly lower, but the humidity is high and really cold weather is rare.

Population, education and culture

The proportion of native Indians in the local population is higher in Paraguay than in any other South American nation. Although only 60,000 "pure" Indians have survived, some 75% of Paraguay's 4,500,000 inhabitants have Indian blood, so that even the relatively small European immigrant community has assimilated into them. Paraguayans are noted for their mutual tolerance, as evinced in the areas of religion, language, and customs.

Most of Paraguay's population lives off the land, chiefly in the country's Eastern Region. Asunción (pop. 650,000) is the only large city. The high proportion of Paraguayans of Indian descent who preserve the ways of their ancestors has caused the Guaraní language to remain the country's primary spoken tongue. The use of Spanish is common mainly in Asunción, and serves mostly for official requirements.

The slaughter of men in Paraguay's wars has left its imprint to this day: the rate of out-of-wedlock births is the highest in Latin America. It is accepted practice for a man to have a number of "wives" in addition to his lawful spouse. Their number is determined by his ability to support them and their children.

Although elementary education is ostensibly compulsory and free, Paraguay's illiteracy rate approaches 25%. The educational system has expanded in recent years, and about 75% of school-age children are enrolled. Higher education is offered mainly in Asunción, home to the country's two universities. The variety of subjects taught there is rather restricted, and many Paraguayans go abroad for higher education.

A very interesting case is the Western region, the Chaco. After it was conquered in a bloody war against Bolivia, the area was kept under military rule until 1967, and even today the uniformed presence is very high, civilians preferring not to cope with the very harsh conditions. A fifth of the 65,000 inhabitants of the arid region are Mennonites, spread in 20 settlements. Members of a pacifist sect originated in Central Europe in the 16th Century, they settled here in the late 1920's, and run a kind of "state-within-a-state", with their own educational system (which uses both, a German dialect and Spanish), maintain their own roads, etc. Their importance is far greater than their number, but in the last years, locals are claiming their rights to the land, a subject with far-reaching implications for the future of the country.

Economy

Since his rise to power, Rodríguez has striven to stabilize the local currency, to calm economic conditions, and to bring about growth. The government appreciates the economic importance of industrialization, as well as the massive initial investment and high cost of the energy required to run an industrial system. With these factors in mind, the government has undertaken a variety of activities to encourage capital investment from abroad, mainly from the U.S., Europe, and Japan, which have lately discovered Paraguay's latent potential. In recent years investment has been concentrated in mammoth power plants that Paraguay is constructing along its river borders with Brazil and Argentina. In due course these will produce several times as much electricity as is required for domestic consumption and the surplus will be sold to Paraguay's neighbors for hundreds of millions of dollars annually. These construction projects on the Parana River place great pressure on the local economy and cause fluctuations and shifts in its make-up but the government is making efforts to prevent any negative impact.

Industrial development has accelerated in directions other than the traditional branches such as meat and meat products. (The meat industry has seriously deteriorated in recent years and is no longer a prominent factor in the national economy.) Large plants are now being built for essential products as well as for consumer and export goods. Export of wood and wood products, for example, accounts for a healthy slice of the national income. Nevertheless, Paraguay still lives by working the land. About half of Paraguay's population engages in agriculture, working only

PARAGUAY

PARAGUAY

6% of the country's land! Yet the agricultural sector accounts for most of Paraguay's export revenue.

Folklore

Paraguay preserves ancient and undisturbed Indian folklore. The relative scarcity of tourists and outside visitors helps to preserve the native culture, which remains authentic.

Handicrafts, chiefly weaving and embroidery, are highly original, as is the local woodwork. As for music, the characteristic Paraguayan instrument is the *lyre*; the folk songs are wistful and quiet.

PARAGUAY

Asunción

Paraguay's capital, more than an interesting tourist city, is a genuine reflection of this unique and strange country, whose population congregates around Asunción. As you walk about the downtown section, through Plaza Uruguaya and the narrow streets nearby, you will find it hard to believe that this is the center of a capital city with more than a million inhabitants in its metropolitan area. The relative tranquility and the absence of typical urban phenomena such as cramped quarters and overcrowding are perhaps the best expressions of the easy-going and placid nature of the Paraguayan, as well as his special grace and charm.

The city is marked by low houses that seem to have known better days. The serene face this city presents casts a calming spell on the visitor. This, to a great extent, compensates for the city's lack of special tourist sites, the harsh and humid climate, the plague of mosquitoes (described by Gerald Durrell in his book *The Drunken Forest*) and the poverty of the natives.

Transportation
By air: The Silvio Pettirossi International Airport is 16 km from downtown. Transportation into town, by bus, minibus or taxi, is fast and comfortable.

The national airline, *LAP*, flies weekly to Madrid, Frankfurt, and Miami, and offers numerous daily flights to neighboring countries — Argentina, Uruguay, Brazil, Peru, Chile, Bolivia, and Ecuador.

Iberia flies from Madrid via Brazil, and *Eastern Airlines* reaches Asunción by way of Peru and Bolivia. Most South American airlines fly to Asunción several times a week.

By land: The train ride between Buenos Aires and Asunción is rather exhausting, the trip takes more than two days. Asunción's train station is in Plaza Uruguaya. Buses make the trip several times weekly in half the time. The *La Internacional* and *Nuestra Señora de la Asunción* companies operate buses to and from Brazil several times each day via the Iguacu Falls (see "The Iguazú Falls" in the chapter devoted to Argentina).

The *COIT* company runs buses to Montevideo twice weekly (office in Plaza Uruguaya, corner of Antiquera Street, Tel. 48274, 47290) — a 26-hour trip in modern buses. The enjoyable ride takes you past the scenery of the Chaco through Argentina. There is no bus service to Bolivia; one must go by way of Argentina.

Asunción's central bus terminal is located on the eastern side of Plaza Uruguaya.

Automobiles and hitchhiking: One can get to Asunción from Brazil with no difficulty via the Iguaçu Falls on Route 7 (Ruta 7) as far as Coronel Oviedo, and then taking Route 2 to Asunción. From Argentina, one crosses the river from Posadas to Encarnación; from there it is 730 km on Route 1 to Asunción.

The desolate and rather difficult Trans-Chaco Highway leads to Bolivia. Hitchhikers should bring along enough food for prolonged waiting, and twice as much patience. Crossing the border here is also more complicated than usual. In the absence of an official and orderly transit point, the Bolivian soldiers may well require you to report to the immigration offices in La Paz to obtain a visa. Travel along this route, through extremely monotonous landscape, is nonetheless a singular, unusual experience.

Where to stay
As a rule, hotels in Asunción can be considered expensive, even those defined as "inexpensive". It is very difficult to find one which is clean and centrally located, as well as reasonably priced. A very important accessory is the air conditioner, since during the humid nights it can be extremely hard to sleep.

Continental Hotel: 15 de Agosto y Estrella; tel. 493760, fax 496176. Five stars, three blocks from the Plaza de la Independencia, excellent location.
Paraná: 25 de Mayo y Caballero; tel. 444236, fax 494793. Between the Plaza Uruguaya and the Plaza de la Independencia, excellent location.
Chaco: Caballero 285 (in the corner with Mariscal Estigarrabia), tel. 492066. One block from the former, one of the best in town.
Guaraní: Ind. Nacional y Oliva; tel. 491131. On the southern side of Plaza de la Independencia, very popular with businessmen.
Zaphir: Estrella 955, between Colón and Montevideo; tel. 490025, fax 447278. Three stars, modern, good location.

Smaller, cheaper hotels, near the train station and Plaza Uruguaya, are called *residencial*, distinguishing them from the more expensive hotels.
Residencial Rufi: Cerro Corá 660, next to the corner with Antequera two blocks from Plaza Uruguaya. Recommended.

PARAGUAY

ASUNCIÓN

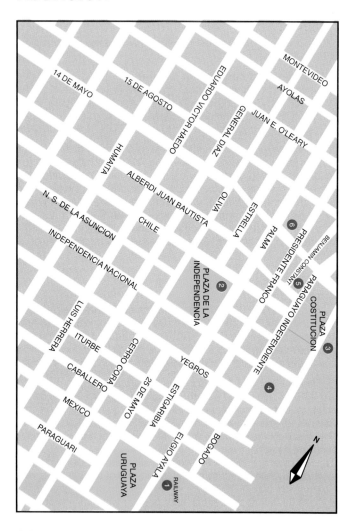

Index
1. Train Station
2. Pantheon
3. Congressional Palace
4. National Cathedral
5. Central Post Office
6. Independence House

PARAGUAY

Asunción — Plaza Uruguay

Where to eat

The large hotels offer good restaurants; others can be found in the town's main thoroughfares. Prices can be high and do not include taxes and service charges.

The typical dishes, *empanadas*, pastries filled with cheese, meat, vegetables, etc. are sold on the street. The local specialty is the *chipas*, a small tasty cake made of cornmeal dough mixed with cheese and egg. Don't eat one unless it's fresh! Although the flavor is usually excellent, the hygienic conditions under which they're made are not the best.

Paraguayans love soup, and it's served in every restaurant, stand, bar, and wherever. Fruit is excellent but expensive, and is usually sold by peddlars along downtown Asunción's main streets. The city's water service is the newest in South America, but the habit of washing fruits is still not very rooted among the sellers.

Formosa: España 780. Chinese
Acuarela: Mariscal López y Teniente Zotti, Brasilian food.
El Tirol: Estados Unidos and Cerro Corá. Central European.

El Antojo: Ayolas y Haedo. Spanish cuisine.
Le Flore: San Martín 815. Italian.
Spaghettoteca: San Martín 893. Italian.
Brunch Menu: Estrella y O'Leary. Vegetarian.

Urban transportation

The small, colorful buses that drive along the narrow streets are the most popular way of getting around Asunción. One may find the buses here a never-failing source of entertainment: even the old yellow school buses, with the protruding, front-mounted engines, are glorious specimens in comparison to the noisy crates of Asunción. These buses are apparently powered by the residual inertia of a push given them in the thirties... that is, the 1830s, when they marked their hundredth birthday! It's hard to describe the situation any other way. The bus drivers, too, make a living in an unusual fashion. On some lines there are no tickets, and the driver reports the number of passengers as he wishes and pockets the rest of the money, whereas drivers on lines for which tickets are provided receive a certain percentage of the proceeds. It follows logically then that the bus spends most of its time just waiting for passengers. You don't have to stand at a bus stop, since the driver stops for anyone who waves. It may also happen that someone flags down a bus from 200 meters away, and the driver may simply park and wait until the would be passenger covers the distance at his own leisurely pace.

An Asunción bus has not only a driver but also a conductor, whose function is to pull people aboard and push them inside to make room for more. The buses have rather low roofs, and anyone of average or above average height cannot stand erect. Riding these buses, in sardine can conditions and with bent head, is therefore an unforgettable experience...

Tramcars have been returned to service, but they operate only along short lines in the city center. Taxis, too, are mostly found downtown. Their prices are moderate, and it is customary to add a 10% tip.

Tourist services

The Government Tourist Ministry is located in Palma 468, next to Alberdi St., tel. 441530. It is closed during the afternoon *siesta*. The office offers the tourist explanatory material, maps (better maps in stores), etc. — in Spanish.

Tourist sites

Most of the sites of particular interest to the tourist are found within walking distance of one another, in the vicinity of the central plazas. **Plaza Uruguaya** is the transportation center; the bus and train terminals are located there. It is only natural that the inexpensive hotels are nearby as well. The plaza, square in shape and sheltered by large shade trees, is almost always swarming with children, senior citizens, soldiers and peddlars. During the afternoon *siesta* one can hardly find a place to sit down. The long streets leading away from the plaza are lined with closely built two-story buildings housing innumerable shops. Next to the plaza, at the very beginning of Mariscal Estigarribia Street, is the **Museum of Fine Arts** (*Museo de Bellas Artes y Antiguedades*, tel. 447716), which houses a disappointing and neglected collection of works of art.

Five blocks northwest of the plaza is another square, no less important: the beautiful and well kept **Plaza de la Independencia**. At its northern end is the impressive **Pantheon**, where the nation's heroes are buried. An honor guard of Paraguayan soldiers is stationed here. Buried here are the remains of dictator Francisco Solano Lopez, of Estigarribia (a hero of the Chaco war of the 1930s), and of two "unknown soldiers".

A right turn on Chile Street brings us to **Plaza Constitución**. It is bounded on its eastern side by the **National Cathedral**, whose grand, impressive facade belies its plain interior. Across the plaza is the **Congressional Palace**, the seat of delegates making their first steps in the new democracy.

Continuing down El Paraguayo Independiente Street, which leads away from the plaza, we reach the **Government Palace**, a sort of imitation of the Louvre in Paris. In front of this building, guarded on all sides by armed soldiers, is a well kept garden and large floral clock. Here the President of Paraguay oversees all affairs of state. Visitors are not permitted to enter it, nor can they come too close.

Close by, on the corner of 14 de Mayo and President Franco Streets, is the **Casa de la Independencia**, which houses displays from the annals of Paraguay's history.

Palma, **Estrella** and **Oliva** Streets are Asunción's main arteries; along them you will find respectable businesses, banks, restaurants, and the like. A stroll here during rush hour is an interesting experience, although it is crowded then.

The impressive **Botanical Gardens** are located 7 km from downtown, along the Paraguay River on grounds that were formerly the private estate of the Lopez family. The gardens are very well kept, and offer an impressive variety of flora and a small zoo. The Lopez mansion itself, not far from the Gardens,

PARAGUAY

The Government Palace

has been converted into a museum of Paraguay's history and of its Indian population. From downtown, take bus 40, 36 or 2, and be sure to ask which way the bus is going when you get on.

From the Botanical Gardens, a dirt road about 2 km long leads to the river. Crossing the river in a small boat, we reach the **Indian reservation**, home to members of the *Maca* tribe who were brought here from the Chaco to serve as a tourist

*P*ARAGUAY

attraction. Apart from the plague of mosquitos, it's hard to say that we're dealing with an especially fascinating site. True, the aging Indians are adorned with massive feather headdresses, but they also wear sneakers. From their straw huts — protected from the rain, of course, with sheets of plastic — we hear Western music blaring from state-of-the-art radio sets... Pretty girls and wrinkled old women will approach you, more than willing to be photographed topless, for a fee of course. In short: skip it.

Entertainment
Asunción is not much for nightlife. Shortly after dark, the streets fall silent and people vanish into their homes. Only in a few places is there any late hour entertainment, and these are meant chiefly for tourists and the young generation, mainly local students.

The downtown offers several rather antiquated cinemas. A number of nightclubs and discotheques — some located in the large hotels — are also in operation, but they are generally empty on weekdays.

General information

Currency and foreign exchange
The national currency is the *guaraní*, its dollar exchange rate is set by the government. Bank notes are easier to exchange than travelers' checks, for which the banks charge a high commission. Bank transfers are paid out only in local currency and according to the official rate. Moneychangers offer a higher rate than do the banks, but be very cautious and count your money carefully! Moneychangers at border points offer a lower exchange rate than in Asunción, so try to exchange only the amount required for your immediate needs until your reach the capital.

In Asunción the best place to change currency is the area of Palma and Alberdi Streets, where most of the moneychangers *(Casa de Cambio)* are located. Not only do they offer slightly more than the bank rate, there is less bureaucracy.

The *guaraní* is considered a stable currency and wide fluctuations in its rate are rather uncommon. Outside Asunción — even in hotels and restaurants — it is hard to change dollars. Stability notwithstanding, *guaranís* are not sought after, and it's best to get rid of them before leaving Paraguay.

Postal and telephone services
Telephone service links Paraguay to most countries of the world,

though collect calls are not always available. Postal service is very slow and letters take a long time in transit. The central post office is on Alberdi Street, corner of Benjamin Constant Street. A branch is located in the Hotel Guaraní (Plaza de la Independencia) and provides most services.

Business hours and holidays
Most shops, businesses, banks, and government offices open early, and close for the *siesta* as early as 11am. The major public holidays, when everything is closed, are May 1, May 14-15 (Independence Day), and December 25.

Measurements; electricity and time
The metric system is used throughout the country.Paraguayan electricity is 220V.

Paraguayan time is GMT-4 (GMT-3 in summer).

Weather
Hot and muggy. The summer is particularly harsh and an extended stay in this subtropical climate is highly unpleasant. The temperature difference between day and night is not great; the nights, too, are very hot and humid. Winter is slightly cooler, but still not pleasant. During the afternoon hours the temperature drops and fresh breezes blow, making these hours the most pleasant.

Cotton clothing is the most suitable, since synthetics become distinctly uncomfortable.

Personal documents
Every tourist entering Paraguay must hold a valid passport and a visa (except for Americans and citizen of the neighboring countries). Upon arrival you get a tourist card, which allows a 90-day stay. When leaving the country, you'll have to pay a tax (about 10 US$).

Important addresses
First Aid: Tel. 204800
Red Cross: Tel. 204900
Public telephone cabins: Presidente Franco, corner with Nuestra Señora de la Asunción.
Taxis: Tel. 333737
Automóvil Club del Paraguay: 14 de Mayo St., corner of Brasil St.

Embassies
Germany: Avda. Venezuela 241; tel. 24006

Austria: Gral. Diaz 525; tel. 443910
Belgium: O'Leary 409; tel. 444075
Canada: Avda. Artigas 2006,; tel. 2293301
Spain: Yegros 437; tel. 490686
U.S.A.: Avda. Mariscal López 1776, tel. 213715
France: Avda. España 213
U.K.: Presidente Franco 706; tel. 444472
Italy: Avda. Mariscal López 1104; tel. 25918
Switzerland: O'Leary 409; tel. 490848

Excursions

San Bernardino

This resort town on Lake Ypacarai, 55 km from Asunción, is frequented during the summer by Paraguay's rich. It offers a variety of vacation services including hotels, restaurants, and sports facilities. As in Asunción, mosquitoes thrive here. Those planning a lakeside vacation should take them into account and equip themselves accordingly. You can reach San Bernardino quickly by bus from Asunción, or by driving down Route 2.

Itauguá

A visit to Itauguá, 30 km east of Asunción, is highly recommended. This picturesque little town, more than two hundred fifty years old, is the center of an embroidery and weaving industry that produces unique fabrics which greatly resemble spiders' webs. Some handcrafted specimens are of stunning beauty and complexity, the result of years of work. They may be seen on public display in stores and workshops along the road through town. The unique tablecloths, blouses, dresses, ornaments, and so forth are impressive and their high price is justified. These embroidery works are known as *ñandutí*.

In the center of town is a neglected square bounded on one side by an ancient church. The entire plaza, with its white houses and red shingled roofs, has a special charm.

The bus trip from Asunción to Itauguá takes less than an hour, and a visit here requires no more than another two. Accordingly, Itaugua is just right for a short day trip from the capital.

Ciudad del Este

The border town with Brazil, about 13 hours by bus from Asunción, has tremendously grown in the last few decades. It was founded in the 1950's, and since it was declared a "Zona Franca" (free of tax zone), Ciudad del Este became a bustling town of 150,000 inhabitants, the second largest in Paraguay, and it attracts many people from Paraguay and its neighboring countries, who come to buy here goods in low prices. Its former name, "Ciudad Presidente Stroessner", was changed after his fall in 1989.

The nearby Rio Paraná forms the Brazilian border. A bridge ("Friendship Bridge") connects the two countries, and another 30 minutes drive bring you to the Brazilian town of Foz do Iguaçu and to the Iguazú Falls (see Argentina — "The Iguazú Falls).

You can also visit the **Itaipu Dam**, the largest hydroelectrical project in the world. The 20 billion dollar project was a joint venture of Paraguay and Brazil, and its capacity is more than 12,600 megawatt.

If you plan to visit the Iguazú Falls, you better spend the night in the Brazilian or the Argentinian towns, which are more pleasant to stay.

U RUGUAY

Uruguay is among the least known countries in South America. Its official name is the Oriental Republic of Uruguay.

During the 1970's the country was ruled by a military regime, something foreign to Uruguay's liberal character, in order to cope with armed subversion. In the early 1980's democracy was restored, bringing along political and economical stability.

From a tourist point of view, Uruguay's potential is not fully exploited. Visitors usually visit the capital, Montevideo, and the prestigious resort of Punta del Este.

History

The *Charrúa* tribe which occupied Uruguay before the arrival of the Spanish did not relinquish their ancestral land without a struggle. The Spanish explorer Juan de Solís, who landed at Montevideo in 1516, was killed by the *Charrúa* and for many years these Indians succeeded in preventing Spanish settlement on their land. Only in the late seventeenth century, when the Spanish (in Argentina) and the Portuguese (in Brazil) both displayed increased interest in Uruguay, was the first settlement established, at Colonia (1660).

Settlement activity became truly significant only after Montevideo was founded in 1726, and fifty years later, in 1776, when a Spanish viceroy was appointed for the Rio de la Plata region, Uruguay was included in his jurisdiction. In addition, both Brazil to the north and Argentina to the south sought to annex Uruguay. The small province was bounced between the Spanish and the Portuguese. For a short period, in 1806, it was controlled by the British, who withdrew, following defeat in their attempt to conquer Buenos Aires.

In 1811, the Uruguayan national hero, José Artigas, gathered an army which forcefully opposed the Portuguese invasion from Brazil, enjoying some Argentine support in this endeavor. Somewhat later, after Brazil took Montevideo in 1817, Artigas was forced to flee to Paraguay. In 1825 a group of fighters known as "33 Orientales" (the band of 33 Easterners) began to fight the Brazilians, with the aid of neighboring Argentina. Two years later, victory was theirs. In August 1828, Uruguay effectivly achieved its independence, and a constitution was adopted two years

U _RUGUAY_

later. But Uruguay, with a population at the time of 74,000, was split between the urbanites, or _Colorados_, who tended toward liberalism and social progress, and the landowners, or _Blancos_, who favored the economic interests of the local aristocracy.

The conflict between these two groups, who developed into the country's largest political parties, was accompanied by violent struggles which peaked in a twelve-year civil war that broke out in 1839. The hostilities came to an end only through the intervention of the neighboring states, and without a clear-cut victory for either side. The involvement of Brazil and Argentina in Uruguay's internal affairs, led Uruguay to take part in a war against Paraguay as the third partner in the so-called War of the Triple Alliance (1865-1870). In these and following years, the urban Colorados took firm control of the Government, while the Blanco party of the land owners failed in all its efforts to gain power.

Commercial contacts with Europe began to solidify during this period. European demand for meat and meat products, which Uruguay produces in abundance, contributed to the country's rapid development. Waves of immigration flooded Uruguay's shores and in the last quarter of the 19th century its population multiplied several times over, reaching one million by 1900.

The most significant change in Uruguay's national life began in 1903, with the election of José Battle y Ordóñez as president. During his first term this talented leader enacted a series of legal and social reforms which led to the political stability that would characterize Uruguay for decades to come. After a four-year hiatus between terms, Ordóñez laid the foundation for Uruguay's progressive constitution, a document nourished by a democratic spirit rare in this part of the world. Its provisions included articles ensuring social welfare, a liberal system of government in which all citizens are equal in the eyes of the law, proportional representation in the legislature, and total separation of Church and State. Ordóñez' successors continued in his spirit, sustaining this process: a Supreme Court was appointed, a method was devised for overseeing elections, and social welfare and pensions were established.

The First World War led to accelerated economic development. Western Europe purchased meat and related products in tremendous quantities, and Uruguay, in turn, imported many consumer goods. Post-war developments in Europe, along with changes in the investment channels of Western capital, brought about an economic depression which hit rock bottom during the 1930's. The depression forced President Gabriel Terra to declare himself dictator and to suspend the nation's elected institutions and constitution. He ruled Uruguay with an iron fist for five years, enjoying public faith and support, and was able to undertake comprehensive legal reform. General Alfredo Baldomir, an opponent of Terra's, was elected President in 1938, and Uruguay entered the World War II era under his leadership.

Like its Latin American neighbors, Uruguay maintained a moderate, neutral position during the war. Although it carried out a number of actions against Germany (such as seizing German vessels and interning Germans and Nazi agents), Uruguay's unequivocal decision to align itself with the West was taken only in 1941, when the President placed the country's ports at the disposal of the United States Navy. In 1942 relations were broken with Germany, and in 1945, just before the war's end, Uruguay declared war on Germany.

While the war raged, Uruguay again enjoyed a period of prosperity. European orders for its products led to extensive renewed growth, the principles of liberal democracy were again applied in the government, and a flourishing economy contributed to parallel improvement in the educational and cultural spheres.

The 1940's and 1950's were noteworthy for political tranquility and the continuation of liberal social trends. At the end of that period, however, a severe recession caused noticeable social ferment. This was expressed in the 1958 elections with the election of the Nationalist Party, the Blancos, their first victory in ninety-three years! Even so, the hope for improvement failed to materialize. Blanco economic policy lacked efficient means for bringing about economic recovery and halting inflation, and the Uruguayan economy progressively deteriorated. The Colorados returned to power in 1966 and undertook a constitutional reform that separated the powers of the branches of government, while greatly expanding the President's authority. Strikes, riots, and terrorism erupted in the early 1970s, leading to increased military involvement in government, with the president constantly relying on the army to prop up his regime.

But in 1984, the trek towards democracy began. In December of that year, Uruguay conducted general elections bringing her back to the exclusive club of democratic nations. The Colorados party received the majority of votes and their leader, Julio Sanguinetti, became president. He quickly began rehabilitating the social and economic fiber of the country. During his office, stability was restored and many Urguayan refugees, residing in Europe, returned to their homeland. Sanguinetti was warmly received by world democracy leaders who have promised to assist Uruguay both politically and economically. In 1990 Alberto Lacalle was elected President.

URUGUAY

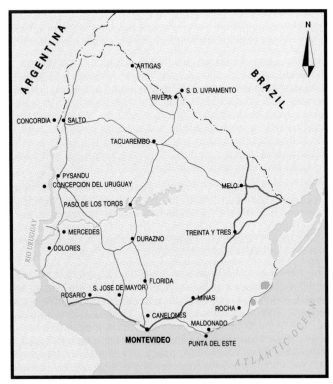

Geography and climate

Uruguay is the smallest country in South America, with an area of 177,000 sq/km. On the east it borders the Atlantic Ocean, on the north it shares a border with Brazil, while in the west the mighty Uruguay River (1850 km long, and up to 10 km wide) separates it from Argentina. The Rio de la Plata, 420 km long, serves as Uruguay's southern border. Uruguay is divided into 19 provinces, which enjoy a large measure of autonomy.

The flat pampas in the south constitute most of Uruguay's territory, while the north is largly an extension of the Brazilian highlands, with hills and low mountains. The land is generally rocky but highly fertile. Forest regions are found only near the Brazilian border and in some areas along the river. Although

URUGUAY

Uruguay is poor in natural resources and mineral deposits; little has been done to exploit what does exist.

Uruguay's subtropical climate is noted for instability, which stems from sudden and variable winds — one moment from the sea, and the next from the interior. The winters are wet, with the average annual rainfall at 900 mm. The Rio Negro is the largest river, and its tributaries drain the entire country. It joins the Uruguay River before the latter empties into the Rio de la Plata.

Population

Uruguay is home to about three million people, mostly of European extraction, whose ancestors arrived during the 19th and 20th centuries. The vigorous opposition of the native Indians to Spanish settlement led to struggles that ultimately brought about the obliteration of the Indian community. The proportion of people of Indian descent is one of the lowest in all of South America.

Eighty percent of Uruguay's population reside in urban areas. Half of all Uruguayans live in Montevideo, while the rest are concentrated in cities along the Rio de la Plata and the Uruguay River. The birth rate has remained stable for years: fewer than one-third of Uruguay's citizens are under the age of fifteen, and eight percent are sixty-five and over. This should be compared to the norm of the rest of the continent, where the proportion of children can reach 50% and life expectancy is far lower than in Uruguay.

Uruguay's official language is Spanish. Education, including higher education, is free, and the illiteracy rate is low (less than 10%). The great majority of Uruguayans are Catholic.

Economy

Like its larger neighbor Argentina, Uruguay has an economy essentially based on agriculture. Some 80% of its land is arable, and it is only natural that the economy has developed in this direction. Some 60% of the cultivated land is devoted to raising livestock, which accounts for 75% of Uruguay's export income. This important branch of the economy began with 100 head of cattle and the same number of horses, sent to Uruguay by the ruler of Paraguay in 1603, to breed in Uruguay's empty expanses. The pampas are divided into huge sheep and cattle ranches. Beef is Uruguay's chief export. Other agricultural activities are few; wheat and similar crops are mainly for domestic consumption and not for export.

The absence of natural resources such as oil and coal, combined with the lack of a developed industrial infrastructure, result in a heavy burden on the national economy. Uruguay is forced to import most of its energy sources as well as many consumer goods — from textiles and plastics to machinery and cars. Despite encouragement of productive sectors, customs rules and exchange rate policies to support export and hinder imports, Uruguay still has to cope with economic crises.

Due to historical dependence on its neighbors, lack of efficiency and inflexibility in the managing, it is very hard to rechannel production to suit the changing demands of the world market, and that is why many Uruguayans are so confident about the possibilities which the new *Mercosur* (South American Common Market) can open. Uruguay enjoys foreign aid and tourism, especially from Brazil and Argentina.

General Information

How to get there

By air
The Uruguayan national airline, *Pluna*, flies both within the country and to neighboring countries. Madrid is its most distant destination. *Lufthansa*, *KLM*, *Air France*, and *Iberia* fly to Montevideo, either with a stopover in Rio de Janeiro or on the way to Buenos Aires. *Eastern* flies here from New York. *Aerolíneas* and *Pluna* have frequent flights to Buenos Aires' Aeroparque Airport. *Cruzeiro do Sul* flies to Rio daily, and *Varig* makes the trip several times per week.

Pluna runs a shuttle bus service from Carrasco Airport to Montevideo (a 30-minute trip), and from the company offices on 18 de Julio Avenue to the airport, at unscheduled intervals. The airport, 20 km from the capital, is small and outmoded, and offers a nice restaurant on the second floor.

By land
From Argentina: The bus trip from Buenos Aires to Montevideo lasts eleven hours. The *COT* company (offices in Montevideo: Plaza Cagancha 1126, tel. 921605) has a fleet of modern, comfortable buses. The most pleasant, interesting, and inexpensive way to make this trip (10 hours) is on the passenger ship that crosses the Rio de la Plata. The ship has cabins of various classes and restaurants. A deck ticket, the cheapest of all, includes a bed in a cabin shared by eight passengers. The city of Colonia serves as the major border crossing between Uruguay and Argentina. Colonia and Buenos Aires are linked by frequent air service (15 minutes) with the Argentinian metropolis

visible across the Plata. A hydrofoil crosses the Plata several times daily — an interesting trip in a unique vehicle, though the potential traveler must bear in mind that it is noisy and apt to be accompanied by an unpleasant sensation. A ferry takes passengers and cars across the gulf more cheaply. Convenient bus transportation from Colonia to Montevideo (a 3-hour ride) is provided by several companies.

From Brazil: The buses from Rio, São Paulo and Porto Alegre are luxurious, comfortable, and fast. A number of companies provide service several times daily; several of them switch buses at the border. The *CYNSA* company's offices in Montevideo are located in Paraguay 1311; tel. 905321

From Paraguay: The *COT* company operates two buses weekly between Asuncion and Montevideo via Argentina (26 hours). The passenger enjoys luxurious and comfortable buses, soft drinks, light refreshments, and the passing scenery of the Chaco region. The *CYNSA/Brujula* offices are located in Paraguay 1311; tel. 916619.

Documents
North Americans and Western Europeans with valid passports do not require a visa and may enter Uruguay for up to 90 days. This stay can be extended for an additional 90 days at the Immigration Office in Montevideo.

When to come; national holidays
Summer (November-April) is the main tourist season; and the hotels are full and beaches are crowded. Winter is not as nice, though not much rainier than summer.

The important holidays are January 1, Easter, May 1, July 18 (Independence day), August 25 (Artigas' day), and December 25.

Currency
Uruguay has no foreign currency restrictions, and use of credit cards is common and convenient. The same holds true for travelers' checks, with only a small difference in exchange rates when compared with cash. Many places will exchange travelers' checks for cash dollars for a small commission, an important service for a visitor planning to continue on to Brazil or Argentina, where the difference in the exchange rate for cash and travelers' checks can reach 20%!

Business Hours
Stores are open on weekdays, with an afternoon siesta. On

U RUGUAY

Saturday shops are open half day. Everything is closed on Sundays except for food stores, which are open a half day. Banks are open weekdays, from around noon, with individual hours for each bank.

Transportation
Onda provides nationwide bus transportation with very frequent service. Trains run several routes on an antiquated, slow, and uncomfortable British rail network. *Pluna* provides air transportation between major cities. Automobile travel — rental or private — between the large cities is comfortable, since a network of paved roads links all the central sections of the country.

Measurements; electricity and time
The metric system is used exclusively. The electric network is 220V.

The Uruguayan time is GMT-3.

Montevideo

In addition to being Uruguay's capital and largest city, Montevideo is the country's major tourist center. This city, founded in 1726, is home to approximately one and a half million Uruguayans.

Montevideo is not a "tourist city" in the accepted sense of the word. Unlike Rio de Janiero and Buenos Aires, it is not noted for a bustling tourist infrastructure. In contrast to Paris, London, or New York, it has no special sites that attract visitors intent on making the rounds from place to place. Montevideo is undoubtedly a city to which people come primarily to enjoy a general impression of it, its residents and — above all — its beaches.

Accommodation

Most of Montevideo's hotels are concentrated downtown, between Plaza Independencia and Plaza Libertad, along the Avenida 18 de Julio, which is the main artery of the city; and on nearby streets from Canelones to Mercedes. Along Mercedes Street we find inexpensive hotels, while the expensive and prestigious ones are situated on Plaza Independencia. The old quarter of Montevideo, in the vicinity of Plaza Constitución and chiefly on Buenos Aires, Sarandí and Rincón Streets, is home to scores of inexpensive pensions, though some are dirty and run-down. Many hotels of intermediate price and quality can be found along Avenida 18 de Julio. The following are recommended:

Victoria Plaza: Plaza Independencia, Tel. 914201. One of the best in town, occupies an impressive 21 story building.

Hotel Lafayette: Soriano 1170, Tel. 922381. Somewhat expensive, well located.

Internacional: Colonia 823, Tel. 920001. Very good.

Presidente: Av. 18 De Julio 1083, Tel. 920003. A good deal.

Columbia: Reconquista 468, Tel. 960001. Very nice.

America: Rio Negro 1330, Tel. 920392.

Klee: Yaguaron 1365, Tel. 920606.

There are also moderately priced hotels in this area, among them:

Hotel Rex: Av. 18 De Julio 870, Tel. 907806. Very close to Plaza Independencia, with large, clean rooms.

Balfer: Cuaréim 1328, Tel. 920073. Nice and clean.

Many restaurants and hotels may be found in the seaside neighborhoods, particularly the Carrasco quarter, a ten-minute bus ride from downtown. Here we find the famous *Hostería Del Lago* (Tel. 612949), beyond doubt one of the most impressive in the area.

Wining and dining

Restaurants are concentrated along Avenida 18 de Julio and the vicinity, and many are relatively cheap. The pizzerias serve excellent and inexpensive fare. *Confiterias*, a sort of cross between restaurants and cafés, are also found in abundance. They offer simple dishes and sandwiches, and are good places to eat breakfast and lunch.

The evening meal is generally eaten late, after 9pm. The typical Uruguayan supper is to be found, of course, in the restaurants. Most of the dishes are similar to those offered in Argentina (see the "Food" section in the chapter on Argentina), and excel both in quality and quantity.

The *Hotel Victoria Plaza* has a superb restaurant with an elegant atmosphere and excellent service. *Otto's Restaurant* on Rio Negro Street, corner of San José, serves excellent meat dishes at reasonable prices — highly recommended. Chinese restaurants are scattered along the smaller streets crossing and parallel to Avenida 18 de Julio. The few kiosks in Montevideo offer mainly soft drinks and sandwiches.

Typical foods in Montevideo are *churro* — a sausage baked in dough or a roll — and *buseca* — a special and very spicy ox-tail soup with beans and peas. The word "steak" is unknown in Montevideo's restaurants; you have to order a specific cut: *lomo*, the finest and most expensive, or the cheaper *entricot*, which is also superb. The quality of the *asado*, which is grilled beef, and the *parrillada*, mixed grill, depends on the restaurant. Stay away from them in restaurants with poor sanitary conditions since the meat here is usually very fatty and poorly cooked. The array of side dishes is extremely limited in all restaurants, consisting usually of rice with gravy, mashed or fried potatoes, and salad.

The café-concert is a recommended blend of a light supper and music. This is a popular Uruguayan entertainment spot, where people spend an evening in small and pleasant cafés to the sound of a small band, generally made up of guitar, accordion, and singer.

By law, menus must be affixed to restaurant entrances. The

prices displayed include service and taxes. You should also add a tip for the waiter — 5% in restaurants, and 15% in cafés.

Transportation

Public transportation downtown is very convenient. The buses are old and when you want to get off, instead of ringing a bell you say "psst" to the conductor. A mistake will usually infuriate the driver and conductor. Bus stops are marked only by small signs on streetcorners or sometimes on the wall of an adjacent building, marked with the route number. The lines at the stops are not always orderly, but people are always quiet and polite. Fares are very low, since public transportation is subsidized.

Many taxis cruise the city, and are easily obtained even at rush hour. The fare tends to be reasonable, and is indicated on the meter.

Driving a private or a rented vehicle is rather easy but hardly essential, given the proximity of Mondevideo's sites.

Tourist services

The most efficient and convenient Tourist Bureau is located opposite the entrance of the *Onda* bus terminal on Avenida 18 de Julio. Here you can obtain all essential information concerning transportation, orientation, first aid services, special events, and anything else on your mind. The staff will provide you with color maps and a wealth of material on various topics. The Government Tourism Ministry's branch office on Plaza Libertad provides a variety of reading material and maps.

Most airline offices are located around Plaza Entrevero, near Rio Negro and Avenida 18 de Julio.

The large *Exprinter* travel agency has a branch at 700 Sarandi Street; one may also avail oneself of the *Brenner* agency in the Old Quarter.

Tourist sites

Plaza Independencia and **Avenida 18 de Julio** are the main centers of Montevideo. The enormous Plaza, the heart of the city, has an equestrian statue of Artigas in its center, above a small mausoleum. The statue, by the Italian artist Angelo Zanelli, dates from 1923.

A number of magnificent buildings surround the plaza: the monumental **Victoria Plaza Hotel** on its northern side and, opposite it, the **Government Palace** (built in 1870) which, in contrast to the rest of the nearby buildings, is relatively small and modest. The famous **Solís Theater** (opened in 1850) is on

MONTEVIDEO

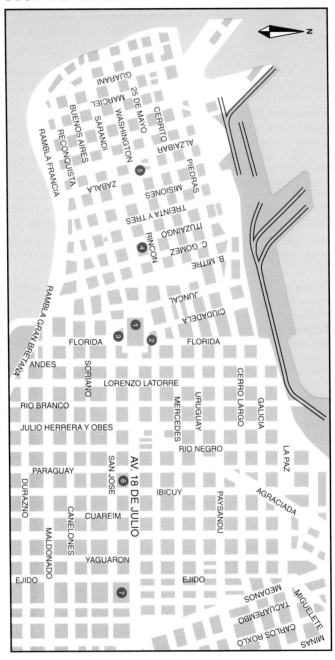

one side of the plaza, to the right of the Government Palace; beside it is an interesting **Museum of History**. On the plaza's eastern side is the **Salvo Palace**, one of the most beautiful and impressive in the city.

The Old Quarter
The Plaza effectively marks the edge of the Old Quarter, which stretches westward to the harbor. A number of old houses remain here, and the quarter still serves as a financial and commercial center.

Rincón Street leads us toward **Plaza de la Constitución**, the oldest of Montevideo's public squares. On its western side is the **Municipal Cathedral**. Continuing down Rincón Street we reach **Plaza Zabala**. In its center is the statue of the city's founder — Zabala — astride his horse.

The monumental **Customs House** is a short walk east of here, close to the **port** which was constructed in 1901 and has been expanded several times since. This port handles 95% of the country's import and export traffic.

At 234 Buenos Aires Street is the grand **Sephardi Jewish Synagogue**, with a number of halls for celebrations and events. On Jewish holidays when travel is forbidden, this building is empty, due to its distance from the residential quarters where Montevideo's Jewish population lives.

Along Avenue 18 de Julio
On the other side of Plaza Independencia stretches Avenida 18 de Julio, a mix of business, light industry, fashion, and restaurants. The section closer to the plaza is given more to entertainment and tourism; here we find restaurants, pizzerias, cafés, cinemas, clubs, hotels, and so on. As we get farther from the plaza and head east towards Plaza Libertad, the Avenue's character changes, its buildings bursting with shops. Salesmen standing in the doorways lure passers-by to enter and are usually polite and graceful. Prices are marked clearly in the shop windows; bargaining is not only unaccepted, but arouses resentment and ridicule.

At the corner of Rio Negro Street we come upon **Plaza del Entrevero**, adorned with trees, lawns, and park benches. Two blocks further on we reach **Plaza Libertad**, with a towering statue of liberty in its center. The *Onda* **bus terminal** is opposite, with the Tourist Bureau located across from its entrance. Four blocks eastward we reach **Plaza Perez**, better known as **Plaza El Gaucho** for its statue of the legendary cowboy. Here we find the new City Hall. Continuing eastward, we pass the University and the adjacent **National Library**, founded in 1816. The library is housed in an interesting and impressive building constructed in 1956; a statue of Dante graces its courtyard. At the intersection of Avenida 18 de Julio and Avenida del Artigas, is an Obelisk erected in 1956 to commemorate the heroes of Uruguayan independence.

The Avenida 18 de Julio extends to the entrance of the beautiful and well-kept **Batlle y Ordonez Park**. The park contains numerous statues and sculptures of which the most famous is *La Carreta* — six oxen pulling a cart, accompanied by a cowboy on horseback. The statue, the work of the Uruguayan artist José Belloni, was cast in 1934. Within the park is a 70,000-seat **soccer stadium**, built in 1930 for the World Cup. Near by are tracks for both runners and bicycles.

The **Zoological Gardens** are also not far from here, and present a variety of flora and a charming zoo. Next to the Gardens is the large **Municipal Planetarium**. The Gardens can be reached from Plaza Independencia and Avenida 18 de Julio on foot, or by buses 141, 142, and 144 — a five-minute trip.

Other Sites
The **Congress Palace**, dedicated in 1925, is certainly one of the largest and most impressive public buildings in Montevideo. The palatial marble structure is located in the center of a large plaza at the top of Lavalleja Avenue, north of Avenida 18 de Julio.

Several miles down Lavalleja Avenue is **El Prado Park**. This park — one of Montevideo's most beautiful — is home to the municipal **Art Museum** and **Historical Museum**.

The **National Museum of Fine Arts**, opened in 1911, is located in **Rodó Park**. The city's largest park is located behind Ramirez Beach, and has a large artificial lake used for boating. During the summer this park is packed with local residents and visitors. In the evening, thousands flock to the amphitheater for concerts or other performances.

Montevideo (literally translated "I see the mountain"), takes its name from a hill at the western tip of the Rio de la Plata, which rises to 139 m above sea level. A small **fortress** on the top of this hill was built in 1724 to defend against the Portuguese, who had settled in Colonia. Today, the fortress serves as a **military museum**. Beside it is an old (1804) **lighthouse**. The hill affords a superb view of the city and La Plata shore.

Montevideo is surrounded by the sea on three sides; **beaches** are found everywhere. Though the beaches are sandy, wide, and fairly clean, they lack facilities such as showers. Navy personnel serve as lifeguards, and must be obeyed strictly. Ball games of any sort are absolutely forbidden, which makes life easier for the thousands of bathers, who populate the beaches chiefly during the peak months of December and January. Nevertheless, a driving rain on a sizzling summer's day, scattering bathers in all directions, is a rather common occurrence. **Ramirez Beach** and **Pocitos Beach** — the latter with a handsome promenade bordered by nine-story buildings — are the most pleasant and popular in Montevideo.

Nightlife
Unlike Buenos Aires, its neighbor across the Rio de la Plata, Montevideo is not noted for its cultural life, art, and dazzling entertainment. Yet the Solís Theater (in Plaza Independencia) does present concerts, opera, and plays. Foreign artists also perform here.

Nightclubs, discotheques and folklore clubs are found downtown, along the streets adjacent to Avenida 18 de Julio, and in the neighborhoods parallel to the tourist beaches.

Cinema is popular, and American and European films with Spanish subtitles are shown at the numerous theaters throughtout Montevideo. On Avenida 18 de Julio and the nearby streets are an ample selection from which to choose. Posters for adult movies are marked with green stripes: the more stripes, the more pornography.

You can spend a typical and enjoyable Uruguayan evening in a café-concert, a special institution that combines a show with a light meal and something to drink. Performances begin late (10pm or later), and are packed on weekends.

Gambling (and, for that matter, prostitution) is legal here and most casinos are Government-owned. The famous hotels — especially the Casino Carrasco — feature gambling halls that operate into the early morning hours.

General Information
Banks and currency exchange
A number of **Casas de Cambio** — currency exchanges — are located downtown where dollars can be changed into pesos or other currencies. Travel agencies are generally willing to exchange currency at the going rate, unlike hotels, where the rates are lower. The exchange rate varies according to the pace of inflation.

Because there is no black market, and foreign currency may be purchased without restriction, travelers' cheques can be cashed or purchased and bank transfers can be carried out freely. *American Express* and *Diners Club* also maintain branch offices here.

Postal and telephone services
It is best to mail letters from a post office, where they are postmarked and sent without stamps. Speed of delivery depends on the country of destination. It takes a week to ten days for a letter to reach the United States or Western Europe. Telephone service is convenient and fast. The central post office is located in Treinta y Tres 1418.

Shopping
In this sphere, too, Avenida 18 de Julio is the leader, principally along its eastern stretch (further away from Plaza Independencia). The abundant shops offer items of all kinds, with prices posted in the display windows. The streets crossing and parallel to 18 de Julio also offer a wide selection, mainly in galleries and shops. The best buys are leather goods, sports jackets, skirts, belts, purses, wallets, and woolen goods — sweaters, gloves, and the like. All are of excellent quality and reasonable price. Fashions do not always tend to be the latest so it's best to stick to classic styles. The prices of jewelry containing gems mined in Uruguay — especially topaz — are relatively low.

An exciting flea market is held every Sunday 8am-1pm on Narvaja Street, across from the University; the street is filled with goods of all kinds, from rusty nails to porcelain, crystal to antique furniture. Highly recommended.

Important addresses and phone numbers
Police: Tel. 999
Lost and Found Objects: Tel. 297187
First Aid: Tel. 411111
Firemen: Tel. 401141
Mobile Coronary Unit: Tel. 800000
Automóvil Club del Uruguay: Tel. 982020
Telegrams: Tel. 125
Pluna: Colonia 1021, Tel. 980606
Uruguay Auto Club: 1532 Libertador General Lavalleja.

American Embassy: 1776 Calle Lauro Muller (Tel: 409-050).
British Embassy: 1073 Marfo Bruto (Tel: 78165; 991-033).

Punta del Este
Traveling 135 km east of Montevideo we reach Punta del Este, Uruguay's most famous resort. Each summer, tens of thousands

of Uruguayans and tourists — mainly from Argentina and Brazil — stream here to spend their vacations.

British forces landed in Punta del Este in 1808 on their way to conquer nearby Maldonado. Tradition claims that the little peninsula was frequented by vacationers even in Indian days. Today the city is a resort for the affluent, brimming with everything needed to make a vacation prestigious and enjoyable. The city is situated between ocean and river, and at times you can distinguish between the color of water to the east — the ocean — and that to the west, the Rio de la Plata.

Punta del Este resembles Miami Beach: a long, narrow, heavily built-up strip of land caught between the gulf and the ocean. Downtown has high-rise residential buildings; the streets are straight and clean, and the sea air is strong. Punta del Este, though, is nothing like Miami Beach. Its pace of life is far slower and the manner of vacationing much simpler. The sense of tranquility and security is relaxing and pleasurable.

The peninsula is crowded with hotels and restaurants. Despite the variety, prices are generally high. Summer visitors are best advised to make reservations, otherwise they will have little chance of finding accommodation. The area on the west side, near the yacht harbor at Mansa Beach, is quieter than the other side, Playa Brava (Stormy Beach), and the wind is not as strong.

Vacationers spend most of the day at the beach, enjoying the soft white sand and the caressing sun. Most of them engage in water sports such as boating, fishing and water-skiing, as well as a wide variety of "landlubber" sports such as golf, tennis, horseback riding, and more. Evenings are spent in the excellent seafood restaurants, in nightclubs, discotheques, and casinos. All this notwithstanding, Punta del Este remains a relatively quiet city, with no particular "touristy" aura.

Slow trains, and rapid and frequent *Onda* and *Cot* buses link Punta del Este with Montevideo. The bus trip takes about two hours, passing along the way many residential quarters constructed on all sides of Punta del Este in recent years. The bus terminal at 27 Gorlero Street houses a small information bureau that can provide details of special events and ways to spend your time.

Visit the **Isla de Lobos**, where a giant lighthouse directs ocean traffic to the Rio de la Plata. The island, a nature reserve, is home to a large colony of sea lions. Boats set out for the island each morning from the marina and it is advisable to buy tickets in advance.

U *RUGUAY*

There are direct flights between Punta del Este and Buenos Aires.

Vocabulary

English	Spanish	English	Spanish
good morning	*buenos días*	train	*tren*
hello/good bye	*hola, adiós*	subway/ underground	*metro*
good evening	*buenas tardes*	railway station	*estación de tren*
good night	*buenas noches*	ticket	*billete*
please	*por favor*	taxi	*taxi*
thank you	*gracias*	car	*coche*
pardon, excuse	*perdón*	plane	*avión*
yes	*sí*	airport	*aeropuerto*
no	*no*	boat/ship	*barco*
what...?	*qué...?*	port/quay/ wharf	*puerto/muelle*
when...?	*cuándo?*		
where...?	*dónde?*	slow	*despacio*
there is...	*hay*	fast	*rapido*
there is not...	*no hay*	gas	*gasolina*
What is the time?	*Qué hora es?*	gas station	*surtidor de gasolina*
How are you?	*Cómo estás?*		
far	*lejos*	hotel	*hotel*
near	*cerca*	hostel	*albergue*
big/large	*grande*	room	*habitación*
small	*pequeño*	toilets	*servicios*
new	*nuevo*	bath/shower	*baño/ducha*
old	*antiguo/viejo*	restaurant	*restaurante*
left	*izquierda*	café	*café/bar*
right	*derecha*	table	*mesa*
first	*primero*	chair	*silla*
last	*último*		
open	*abierto*		
closed	*cerrado*	waiter	*camarero*
entrance	*entrada*	breakfast	*desayuno*
exit	*salida*	lunch	*almuerzo*
		dinner	*cena*
		water	*agua*
bus	*autobus/ omnibus/ colectivo*	drink	*bebida*
		wine	*vino*
		beer	*cerveza*

English	Spanish	English	Spanish
juice	*jugo*	road, highway	*carretera, autopista*
milk	*leche*		
butter	*manteca*	street	*calle*
jam	*dulce*	avenue	*avenida*
cheese	*queso*	square	*plaza*
eggs	*huevos*	alley	*callejuela*
bread	*pan*	esplanade	*paseo*
salt	*sal*	bridge	*puente*
pepper	*pimienta*	monument	*monumento*
sugar	*azucar*	fountain	*fuente*
gravy	*salsa*	church	*iglesia*
soup	*sopa*	palace	*palacio*
salad	*ensalada*	fort/castle	*castillo*
fish	*pescado*	town/city	*ciudad*
meat	*carne*	village	*pueblo*
chicken	*pollo*	museum	*museo*
steak	*bife/churrasco*	park	*jardin público*
grilled meat	*asado*		
mixed grill	*parrillada*		
chips/fries	*papas fritas*	east	*este*
dessert	*postre*	north	*norte*
cake	*torta*	west	*oeste*
fruit	*frutas*	south	*sur*
ice cream	*helado*	valley	*valle*
bread	*pan*	mountain	*montaña*
menu	*menú*	range	*cordillera*
hot	*caliente*	hill	*colina*
cold	*frio*	forest	*bosque*
bill	*cuenta*	river	*rio*
receipt	*recibo*	falls	*cascadas*
		lake	*lago*
cinema	*cine*		
theatre	*teatro*		
pharmacy	*farmacia*	Sunday	*Domingo*
shop, store	*tienda*	Monday	*Lunes*
post office	*correos*	Tuesday	*Martes*
hospital	*hospital*	Wednesday	*Miércoles*
police	*policia*	Thursday	*Jueves*
embassy	*embajada*	Friday	*Viernes*
		Saturday	*Sábado*
market, bazaar	*mercado*		
how much does it cost?	*cuánto cuesta?*	January	*Enero*
		February	*Febrero*
expensive	*caro*	March	*Marzo*
cheap	*barato*		

English	Spanish	English	Spanish
April	*Abril*	17	*diecisiete*
May	*Mayo*	18	*dieciocho*
June	*Junio*	19	*diecinueve*
July	*Julio*	20	*veinte*
August	*Agosto*	21	*veintiuno*
September	*Septiembre*	30	*trenta*
October	*Octubre*	31	*trentiuno*
November	*Noviembre*	40	*cuarenta*
December	*Diciembre*	50	*cincuenta*
		60	*sesenta*
		70	*setenta*
1	*uno/una*	80	*ochenta*
2	*dos*	90	*noventa*
3	*tres*	100	*cien*
4	*cuatro*	101	*ciento uno*
5	*cinco*	110	*ciento diez*
6	*seis*	200	*doscientos/as*
7	*siete*	300	*trescientos*
8	*ocho*	400	*quatrocientos*
9	*nueve*	500	*quinientos*
10	*diez*	600	*seiscientos*
11	*once*	700	*setecientos*
12	*doce*	800	*ochocientos*
13	*trece*	900	*nuevecientos*
14	*catorce*	1000	*mil*
15	*quince*	2000	*dos mil*
16	*dieciseis*	million	*un millón*

The Spanish language

Spaniards stress that they have very much in common with Latin Americans. Those reply that in fact, they share almost everything, but the language...

The grammatical rules are the same for all Spanish speakers, and people with a basic knowledge will find the way to manage out, but the pronunciation can differ a lot from one region to the other, and so can many words. For instance the same bus rolling the streets is called "*omnibus*" in Uruguay, "*colectivo*" in Buenos Aires, "*micro*" (masculine) in northern Argentina, "*micro*" (feminine) in Chile, "*bus*" in Peru.

As for the pronunciation, in Buenos Aires and Montevideo the "*y*" and the "*ll*" have a very hard sound (like the French j). The word *calle* (street) is pronounced "*caye*", while in these places it is pronounced "*caje*" (as the French j). In Ecuador and northern

Peru, the "*ge*" and the "*gi*" sound like the "*gue*" and the "*gui*" in Venezuela, and so on.

j is pronounced *ch* (as in Scotish *loch*)
h is always silent
ñ is pronounced as *ni* in *union*
ai is pronounced as *i* in *hike*
oi is pronounced as *oy* in *boy*
au is pronounced as *ou* in *loud*

Nevertheless, this should not deterre you from trying to contact the people in their language, as this is the best way to get to know the continent.

I<u>*NDEX*</u>

*I*NDEX

INDEX

*I*NDEX

1421

Gavin Menzies

the year China

discovered the world

NOTES

NOTES

NOTES

NOTES

NOTES

NOTES

NOTES